Advance praise for Rod Haynes' *Unauthorized Disclosures*

— — —

"Haynes recalls his service in the U.S. Navy in the 1980s in this memoir....

"Despite his rocky past, Haynes joined tens of thousands of other '90-day wonders' who raced through Naval Officer Candidate School to join a revitalized Navy. ... Haynes, a gifted storyteller..., paints an engaging and nuanced picture of naval life during the '80s. ...

"An often astute account of military life during the Reagan years."
– *Kirkus Reviews*

"Rod Haynes's memoir ... portrays military life without filter, transcending glamorous and heroic images to explore the daily struggles, leadership challenges, emotional battles, and personal growth during his decade of military service. ...

"It's an honest story of life that transcends the honor of uniforms and medals, capturing the inner pain, growth, and resilience of the human spirit."

5 Stars! ★ ★ ★ ★ ★
– *Chanticleer Book Reviews & Media*

"I just finished reading the galley proof you gave me of *Unauthorized Disclosures*.

"I was completely taken with it. I had two books that I was reading simultaneously, and I put them both aside because I couldn't put yours down. I loved the dialog. I loved the insight into life in the Navy. And the simple authenticity of the narrative and, more importantly, the authentic unpretentious humanness of the whole book gave me a connection that I don't usually get from nonfiction.

"It was a real gift."
– *Leslie DeBrock, author of* The Frog-Eyed Gospel

Military & Front Line Service to Others – 1st Place – Best in Category
– *Chanticleer International Book Awards*

Unauthorized Disclosures
A Navy Memoir of the 1980s

BY ROD HAYNES

Bywater Press
Bellingham, Washington

Copyright ©2025 Roderick S. Haynes

All rights reserved. No part of this book may be reproduced or used in any manner without the prior written permission of the copyright owner, except for theuse of brief quotations in a book review.
To request permissions, contact the author at limerocker1@yahoo.com.

PaperbackISBN: 978-1-7330675-8-4
EbookISBN: 978-1-7330675-9-1
Library of Congress Number: 2025-902466

First paperback and ebook editions, June 2025

Edited by Kevin Stewart
Cover art by Chuck Harbaugh
Cover author photo by Phillip Terry
Design by Jeffrey Copeland
Published by Bywater Press, Bellingham, Washington, www.bywaterpress.com
Printed in the USA by Village Books
2025-06-12

Contents

Author Notes	1
Prologue	4
Under a Bridge in Seattle	13
Facing Reality	17
Leap of Faith	24
Homeward Bound	31
Welcome Aboard	40
Senior Chief Sherman	49
Sleet March	53
OCS Routine	58
Drill Instructor Duty	63
Ellen Kincaid	66
Met Café	71
Chicken City	79
Commissioning Day	86
Temporary Duty in Philadelphia	90
Philly Brig	95
The Army–Navy Game	100
Imagine	104
Leaving Philadelphia	109
Lighthouse Tavern Newport	113
Brooklyn Navy Shipyard	118
James Lee	125
Learning the Ropes	129
Gay Pride Parades and Blanket Parties	134
KKK	140
Adventures in GITMO	147
The Ghosts of Wallabout Bay	167
Extortion Letter	171
Detective Work	177
Dad Comes to Brooklyn	186
Underway At Last	192
Navy JAG Visit	196

Charleston Naval Station	199
Chief Petty Officer's Initiation	203
Old Slave Market	209
General Quarters	215
GITMO Revisited	222
Tragedy at Cable Beach	227
Stormy Weather	233
Bermuda Liberty	238
A Navy Chief Weeps	242
New Job	245
Thanksgiving, 1982	248
Med Cruise 1983	251
Straits of Gibraltar	255
Beirut	258
Party Beneath the Streets	264
Left Behind	268
Mail Buoy Watch	276
Beirut International Airport	279
Fatherhood	282
Shore Duty	286
Boston University	289
Reunion	292
Frozen Fenway	294
Surface Warfare Department Head School	298
Captain Simmons	306
DFC	310
Home at Last	314
Mayport Family Service Center	318
Old Friend	320
Navy Adventure Ends	327
Epilogue	331
Acknowledgments	335
About the Author	337

Author Notes

In the years following America's exit from the Vietnam War in 1975, crew shortages aboard aging warships crippled the United States Navy. Thanks to OPEC-initiated oil shortages, people in cars waited hours to refuel at gas stations before heading home to watch America's favorite newscaster, Walter Cronkite, remind his viewers about the spiraling cost of groceries. On the movie screen, a different type of newscaster – an actor in the film *Network* – instructed his viewers to throw open their windows and shout, "I'm mad as hell and I'm not gonna take it anymore!"

The U.S. embassy in Tehran was overrun in November 1979 by so-called "radical students," who seized 52 hostages. Several months later, two U.S. helicopters on a mission to rescue the hostages collided in a sandstorm outside Tehran, killing eight servicemen. Americans felt something was seriously amiss at home while the world questioned their country's leadership ability. President Carter was consequently voted out of office after one term in November 1980. Promising a return to American exceptionalism at home and abroad, Ronald Reagan won an impressive 489 electoral votes, earning only 50.7% of the popular vote.

The Iranian hostages were released moments after President Reagan took office, a deliberate slight against now-former President Jimmy Carter by Iran's Ayatollah Khomeini. The Republican President quickly allocated trillions of tax dollars to upgrade the American military. Naval Officer Candidate School (OCS) provided an essential pipeline of naval reserve officers required to serve four years of active duty after completing four months of accelerated training in Newport, Rhode Island. (See "The Maritime Strategy," U.S. Naval Institute *Proceedings* magazine, January 1986.)

In 1980, there were 62,000 commissioned naval officers on active duty. That figure grew to 88,000 officers when Reagan left office in 1988. More female officers joined the Fleet in the Age of Reagan than ever, driven partly by the military's critical shortage of junior officers. The enlisted ranks also grew exponentially, with a new upbeat Commander-in-Chief in the White House, helping the country move beyond the after-effects of the Vietnam War. I reported to Officer Candidate School

(OCS) without realizing that many regular naval officers from Annapolis or Navy ROTC looked down on "90-day wonders," like myself. Critics of OCS believed that the four-month training program diluted the value of the Navy ROTC and the more rigorous, four-year path to commissioning offered by the Naval Academy.

Hollywood's portrayal of the Vietnam War's impact on American culture has changed significantly over time. Films like *The Deer Hunter* highlighted the war's devastating effects on families and friendships. Other introspective movies from that era include *Apocalypse Now*, *Full Metal Jacket*, and *Born on the Fourth of July*. In the 1980s, the film industry shifted focus, supporting Navy recruitment efforts with movies such as *An Officer and a Gentleman* and *Top Gun*. These films sharply contrasted with the somber post-Vietnam War narratives of the late 1970s. The release of these pro-military films aligned well with President Reagan's goal of expanding the Navy to 600 ships. Public support for the armed forces became the norm during Ronald Reagan's time in office, as those in power capitalized on popular sentiment to reaffirm the United States military presence, which had faced challenges in the preceding decades.

Modern history attributes the fall of the Berlin Wall in 1989 to Reagan, as democratic countries worldwide watched with approval. Two years later, after spending over a decade in uniform, my time in the Navy ended, leaving me with life experiences that I hoped to share with others someday.

I am now 69 years old, taking inventory of life. When I tell new friends I was once a commissioned naval officer, disbelief or laughter is a common reaction to the news. Nevertheless, I tell them it's true. On the brink of homelessness in early 1980, I took a solemn oath to commence training at the Naval Officer Candidate School at the Newport, Rhode Island Navy base. This book chronicles what followed.

The Navy and I got along well during my first five or six years on active duty. To be sure, I had a few minor scrapes with authority, making the occasional misstep as new officers of the line sometimes do. Luckily, in those early days, the Navy forgave my sins of omission and commission as learning experiences that were not egregious enough to warrant ending my career. It helped that the Navy chiefs I worked with – and sometimes for – assured my superiors I had sufficient potential to warrant keeping me around for a while.

Eventually, my natural dislike of authority in most forms surfaced, leading to severe consequences for both me and my family – details I will share later. My decision to "Go Navy!" might seem ill-considered to some, but, like many aspects of life, my situation was not simply black or white, good or bad. After my promotion to lieutenant, my career trajectory changed significantly. As the department head responsible for three separate divisions on the ship, my previous behavioral quirks were no longer tolerated as they had been when I was a division officer. I was now expected to enforce rules rather than find ways to evade them; conformity was expected from everyone under my command. Despite this expectation, I did not strictly enforce all the rules and protocols imposed by the system that governed my life.

A decade after returning to civilian life, I turned to writing to help make sense of my experiences. Writing allows me to separate coherence from chaos and gives me a sense of purpose – even legitimacy – as an ultra-Type A person. I find that writing is healthier than binge drinking. It is cathartic and, ultimately, emotionally satisfying. Reading and writing literature serve as constructive outlets for self-expression, much like my interest in photography. Engaging in reading, writing, and photography is far less taxing on my body and soul than the troubling paths I pursued in my younger days. Many of us come to these profound realizations too late, but the hard lessons I've learned can be shared with others for their benefit. That is my intent, anyhow.

This memoir is a comprehensive distillation of a collection that spans fifteen years of diaries, journals, letters, and personal memories I have gathered in cardboard boxes in my office. It took me fifteen more years to transform these writings into something I believe is worthy of sharing. I hope my story entertains and inspires my readers.

During my years of active duty, I learned valuable lessons. Sailors often expressed their frustration and humor, saying, "You can't make this shit up." See whether you agree with this traditional sentiment veteran sailors are known to express.

Happy reading!

Prologue

My friends and I were having the time of our young lives navigating the wreckage that was America in the 1970s – from a distance. We indulged in endless beer binges and hazy bong parties fueled by mediocre weed scored from the hard streets of Providence, Rhode Island. In 1973 millions of transfixed viewers watched Congress confront the power of the Oval Office on TV, armed with critical rulings by the United States Supreme Court that limited the executive branch's power.

President Richard Nixon's humiliating exit led to a significant decline in public confidence in American politics. President Gerald Ford unexpectedly pardoned his predecessor two weeks later during my first week of college in rural Wisconsin. The country, believing Nixon had struck a backroom deal with his Vice President before resigning, erupted in anger and disbelief. Whether Ford's action helped the country, as he had hoped, move past Watergate is still debated today. The pardon was probably the least harmful course of action, although many people vigorously opposed it at the time. I still question the merits of the pardon myself.

In the spring of 1975, the Vietnam War was in its final death throes after the Paris Peace Accords of 1973 ended America's direct involvement in the fighting. Again, looking on from the comfort of their living rooms, Americans watched broadcasts of North Vietnamese nationals overrun the U.S. Embassy in Saigon. Terrified South Vietnamese parents shoved their babies at crewmembers as U.S. helicopters lifted off from rooftops within the compound, leaving the unfortunate left-behinds to endure years of "political reeducation" by their Communist captors, or worse. The choppers flew east, shuttling the traumatized passengers to the aircraft carriers waiting offshore in the South China Sea. North Vietnamese and Viet Cong insurgents meanwhile overwhelmed South Vietnam's capital city. Back at sea, aircraft carrier crews hastily shoved working helicopters overboard to make space for their refugee guests.

Ho Chi Minh's Communist regime – Ho had died in 1969 – emerged from the war badly battered but politically intact. Both sides suffered horrifically, the conflict leaving at least one million Vietnamese and nearly 58,000 Americans dead and thousands more (on both sides) wounded

Prologue

Disposing of Helicopters off the flight decks of U.S. aircraft carriers, South China Sea, April 1975.

and/or psychologically damaged for the balance of their lives. Americans could not comprehend what the prolonged conflict meant. Why did it happen? How did the country lose? The war in Southeast Asia caused massive human suffering at a high financial cost to all participants. The damage was not limited to diminished treasure and enormous disruption of lives. American foreign policy was severely tarnished by the war's end, leaving internal divisions and human suffering that still afflict this country today. Over the years following the war, and the subsequent brutal violence by the Khmer Rouge in Cambodia, massive numbers of refugees fled Southeast Asia by boat and aircraft, many losing their lives in the process.

I turned 18 on November 10, 1973, ten months after the military draft ended. I was lucky. In the late 1960s, I'd watched young men from Lincoln, Rhode Island, join thousands of other draftees sent to war. Some came back physically or psychologically maimed. Others, including a sizeable number of volunteers, died for a cause political leaders could not articulate. Too many vets died *after* coming home, shattered by what they saw and did. One popular young man in our neighborhood was killed when his Corvette struck a tree at a speed of 100 MPH less than a month after he returned from Vietnam. War survivors were cursed at and spat on, upon returning to the States. Many of these enraged protesters had used college deferments or conscientious-objector status to avoid going to war, actions justified, they claimed, by their country's instigating an immoral war in Southeast Asia.

In 1976, the nation commemorated its bicentennial with grand parades and a spectacular fireworks display at the Statue of Liberty in New York Harbor. The Tall Ships event showcased exotic sailing vessels from around the world, evoking a fleeting sense of national pride. The euphoria quickly faded, reverting to persistent despair and anger. As the 1970s wore on, I hunkered down in my college dorm, drinking beer and smoking pot to shut out the real world and its destructive turbulence. Times seemed hard out there, but I had my priorities to pursue. My friends and I felt it better to let the rest of the planet fend for itself.

President Carter Road Race

A newspaper photo of President Carter collapsing near the finish line of a road race in 1979 sparked a national PR uproar. As a long-distance runner, I had experienced similar indignities in races before, so the picture didn't faze me. Many Americans, however, instead saw Jimmy Carter – and, by extension, America – in freefall in the picture. Pundits later suggested the incident seriously damaged Carter's reelection chances.

The Iranian hostage crisis in November 1979 was, ironically, a perfect capstone to a throwaway decade for Americans. The people I gravitated to were mainly oblivious to the country's struggles, preoccupied as we were with our own unremarkable lives. We never knew physical deprivation of any kind. The ready availability of nutritious food, clean clothes, our families, and decent shelter was a given. I went to college, as did my friends. The people I ran with had legally avoided the military draft by a whisker, though others weren't so fortunate. We were the proverbial "entitled white middle-class young males," blissfully unaware of our privileged existence until I finally got a clue years later.

Waiting an hour in Mikey's Rambler at the Sunoco gas station on Smithfield Avenue was the most significant inconvenience in our otherwise monotonous lives in the 1970s. We watched world events and domestic politics unfold with detached interest. Back in 1968, my family had suffered the traumatic loss of my older fourteen-year-old sister Jen to Cystic Fibrosis. I loved and admired Jen for the pure joy and creativity she brought to our family and friends. Eight years earlier, nine-month-old baby Meg had also fallen victim to CF. Adolescence came next for me. Four years later, I graduated from a New England boarding school as a glass-half-empty guy. My friends said I was overly cynical and sensitive. Who was I to argue?

Jack Nicholson's film *Five Easy Pieces* changed my life when I was sixteen. Set in the San Juan Islands north of Seattle, the movie ended with Nicholson's character back where he was at the start of the film: running away from accountability. In the final scene, Nicholson's character abandoned his wallet, car, and pregnant girlfriend at a rural truck stop, hopping into a logging truck bound for Alaska. I naively chose to ignore *Five Easy Pieces'* life lesson about facing your demons instead of running from them, stubbornly admiring Nicholson's contempt for American culture in the 1970s. He was unrestrained, honest, acidic, and, yes, cynical. I was Jack Nicholson. He was me. But unlike my hero Nicholson, no logging truck magically appeared in Lincoln, Rhode Island to take me someplace else to start again. I decided to do something unconventional, something radical, consequences be damned.

Five Easy Pieces convinced me of the importance of seeing Puget Sound. And so I postponed enrolling in college in September 1973, landing work at a specialty food order-filling factory in South Providence, an enterprise infested with local mobsters. I worked that blue-collar job to raise money for a trip across America the following spring. Experiencing America was the escape I felt I needed. I could find myself traveling, I assured myself. But was I running away from something or smartly moving toward a more promising future? I didn't know, but that did not stop me from doing it.

Prologue

Author, Age 15

In April 1974, I bid a fond farewell to my coworkers at the warehouse after receiving a harsh yet valuable education from blue-collar America. What I believed to be a wondrous adventure now beckoned me. My best friend Joey and I boarded a bus in downtown Providence on a foggy morning. I carried a large Kelty-brand backpack as I visited every state in the continental U.S. over the next two months. Our first stop was New York City. Stepping off the bus, I immediately handed five dollars to a group of Hare Krishna dancers in pajamas, who were shaking tambourines at the entrance to the bus station. I didn't know better.

Joey and I made our way south to Florida, stopping by Disney World to apply for jobs at the amusement park. Roaming its pristine grounds dressed as Goofy in a stoned state held a certain allure for me, but not having a permanent address was a deal-breaker, so we moved on. On Easter morning, we woke up hungover in an abandoned building in Little Havana, Miami, unsure of how we had gotten there. We were on a beach near Fort Lauderdale the night before, watching a drunk kid vomit into the ocean at midnight. To our left stood a band of young adults Joey and I dismissively referred to as "Jesus Freaks." They baptized born-again disciples in the same water where the unfortunate inebriant had just

Prologue

April 1974, age 18, Greyhound Bus trip begins

unwittingly deposited the contents of his stomach. The incident only affirmed my deep-seated skepticism about most things; I still consider the scene a raunchy metaphor for the state of the world at that moment.

A week later, by chance, we attended an eclectic rock and roll performance by sixties icon Dion, followed by headliner Frank Zappa, at the University of Wisconsin Eau Claire. The pairing seemed odd, but we didn't care. Later that night, we curled up in sleeping bags under a nearby bridge in the pouring rain, undetected by campus security. A major spat in Carlsbad, New Mexico, led to Joey and me traveling alone for the remaining four weeks. Joey wound up broke and depressed in Las Vegas, investing the rest of his money in a colorful, somewhat amateurish tattoo of a radiant sun permanently engraved on his left shoulder. As for me, without my friend around to corral my impulsiveness, I quickly fell into various stages of trouble, somehow surviving and moving on, only to repeat the cycle at the next destination. Later that summer, back home in Rhode Island, Joey and I reconciled. We remain close friends today.

My solo journey ultimately landed me in Vancouver, British Columbia. Experiencing the region firsthand, from its mountains and sea to its evergreen, pragmatic culture, exceeded all my expectations. Someday, I'd live in the Pacific Northwest for good. Being physically separated from family and friends by an entire continent was probably one reason I liked the region, but I never admitted as much. Two weeks later, amid a long, torturous bus ride across the country toward home, a rural hospital outside Pittsburgh diagnosed me with acute appendicitis, abruptly ending my bus adventures. Back home in Limerock, my parents, no doubt weary of me ricocheting around the North American continent, were relieved my wanderlust was over. President Nixon resigned in early August 1974, six weeks after I returned to Rhode Island. I started my freshman year of college in early September 1974, contemplating what I had seen and done in my travels. I'd taken on the country on its terms at the tender age of 18, emerging, for the most part, intact. I continued struggling with self-esteem, though I felt better than before I left home. While I proved I could go to Vancouver, BC and back, and live to talk about it, I hadn't permanently shed old torments; doubt and anger ate at me still. I was still my harshest critic.

At college, I eventually fell head over heels for a girl – Megan West from Maine – while skiing through Wisconsin cornfields one frosty night under a bright, white moon. We found ourselves far from civilization, negotiating a desolate midwestern prairie. I hoped it was a start to something that would last. It didn't. I visited Megan West at her home in Maine on Christmas Day 1977, exchanging pleasantries with her family. I failed to make a good impression on Megan's dad – affectionately known as FD or "Father Dear" by his daughter – when he interviewed me to determine my fitness for Megan. FD immediately warned Megan that he'd cut off her college funds if she returned to Wisconsin to complete her sophomore year in January. He was inconsiderate, putting it diplomatically, but I lacked the confidence to confront FD and sustain his daughter's affection for me at age twenty-two. He saw my weaknesses – self-doubt being the main feature – which gave him an opening to act with a cruel finality that destroyed my relationship with his daughter.

In my younger years, this simple fact about love eluded me: if you don't know and accept yourself, expecting love from someone else is unrealistic. I did not understand a healthy relationship starts with some measure of self-awareness and respect for, or a genuine acceptance of, the complex individual each of us is becoming. True wisdom is the product of repeated successes and failures in life. I needed more of each to find out who the hell I was. With luck, I might come to like that person. Immersing my disjointed self into Megan West's young life – she was also mired in the state of "becoming" – was not the answer. I needed more seasoning but went forth blissfully unaware of this key truth. The whole thing hurt severely. It was a necessary rite of passage for a young lover to experience. We parted ways in early 1978, which brought me great sadness. Our relationship had lasted for about eight months. It became one of the most painful experiences in my young adult life. I was beyond heartbroken when Megan and I went our separate ways. I never understood her father's over-the-top intervention. I've always wondered if more sinister motives drove his actions, but in the end it did not and does not matter. Megan and I were officially done.

Fairytale endings are not a given in life, particularly in the fantasy world of college. Emotionally a wreck, I graduated from college in May 1978 after spending my final semester in rural Wisconsin plotting silly, vindictive acts of revenge against FD that went nowhere. I returned to Providence to watch the final, unhappy acts of my parents' marriage unfold while taking a job as a copy editor at the *Providence Journal*. Losing two children to terminal illness inescapably strains the bonds of any partnership, my folks bitterly discovered. In the end, they divorced following years of drunken acrimony. One year later, I quit my job at the *Journal* and packed my trunk again. Amtrak carried me west to Seattle, my excitement building as the East Coast receded and the West Coast beckoned. Lacking a workable fallback plan did not concern me at the start. Being deliberately planful wasn't a priority at a time when it was called for. Fate would provide, I naively believed.

Jack Kerouac famously wrote in *On the Road*, "I had nothing to offer anyone except my own confusion." Kerouac reveals more self-knowledge in his celebrated work than his wry comment suggests. Though flawed, his writing uniquely captures a young man's journey to find America and, in the process, hopefully find himself. Kerouac's defiant work stands out because the literary market of the 1950s had never seen anything like *On the Road* before. His radical testament inspired some people while angering others. George Clooney once said, "The Fifties happened in black and white," which mirrors my way of thinking about the sheltered post-war society that forged my young life.

On the Road was, in the end, a jarring rejection of contemporary American culture, deliberate in its anti-establishment message targeting complacent mainstream Americans living routine lives. Kerouac was one of the original beatniks, an emerging "anti-status quo" subset of artists challenging the numbingly conventional suburban post-World War II culture, everyone sought after America saved the world for democracy. I was a product of that dull, traditional existence, what the television rock group The Monkees mocked in their popular song, "A Pleasant Valley Sunday," in the late 1960s: "here in status-symbol land."

On the threshold of adulthood, I lacked perspective, which Kerouac had, to some degree, despite his damaging life choices. In the end, of course, substance abuse killed Jack Kerouac, along with countless other writers, artists, rock stars, and athletic heroes, past and present. More than a few non-celebrity Americans still make similarly tragic choices. While his literary skills are indisputable, Kerouac's apparent affinity for self-destruction had the final say. Perhaps the self that Kerouac knew himself to be was someone he did not fundamentally embrace. Or was it, instead, the culture he confronted that Kerouac disdained? Kerouac comes off as an authentic, unabashed character, revealing ugly truths about America and some of her citizens who sought something other than what conventional living offered them. I admire that uncompromising brashness in people, too often emulating the behavior to my detriment.

Boeing aircraft dominated the local economy in the Puget Sound area in the 1970s. The cyclical nature of the business killed off many industry-dependent businesses when Boeing faltered early in that decade, causing widespread economic malaise. The Pacific Northwest was slowly emerging from an extended economic gloom when I arrived. Microsoft and other software companies, including Amazon, later provided vital economic stability to the area, yet during the winter of 1979–1980, people were departing the region in droves. The economy hit its nadir – rock bottom – in the first half of that decade. No one knew that things were now turning around until later. Airplane mechanics continued washing dishes in restaurants to make mortgage payments. Where did a twenty-four-year-old man with a year and a half of work history and a warped sense of adventure fit in?

Under a Bridge in Seattle

Space Case and I crossed paths for the first time at the Seattle YMCA on Pike Street. Like much of America in 1979, I struggled to find direction, purpose, perhaps normalcy – whatever the hell that meant. Being lost and hoping to be found was not a workable strategy; that was becoming clear. I took little comfort in knowing people around the country were in similar straits. That's when Space Case presented himself to me in the lobby of the YMCA.

He asked me to lend him a few bucks – any amount would do. I declined, but Space Case went on talking. I could not grasp whatever point he believed he was making. The weird thing was that, right away, I decided I liked the guy, which sometimes happens when I meet strangers, especially the bizarre ones I seem to attract, like fly paper.

Space Case quickly affirmed how unburdened he was by life. His singular concern was scoring his next high, and he wanted me to join him. I was skeptical, knowing friends who became hopelessly addicted to drugs, discovering too late they'd made dreadful choices. I opted instead for the reprieve from everyday living that smoking good weed offered. Hard drugs were a different story. I was wary of even dabbling in them. Street drugs were too expensive, and I was unsure of what was in them, anyway. I needed to *earn* money, not spend the little I had to pursue temporary bliss. The problem was that getting a job now was proving to be so goddamn elusive. My looming homelessness was nobody's fault but my own. I had a secure job in Providence recently, but I felt it necessary to chase after one more adventure, requiring me to jettison my secure employment.

During my first night at the Y, someone mentioned seeing a highway billboard in South Seattle from a few years before, the one that became part of the city's 1970s lore. In big, bold lettering, the sign read, "Will the last one out of town please turn out the lights?" The Puget Sound corridor was an economic wasteland in the mid-1970s. The region was regaining its footing somewhat, but progress was slow. No one felt anything happening regarding local hiring, at least not yet.

###

A dreary, gray curtain of fog and frozen sleet encircled Space Case and me where we sat huddled beneath the Alaskan Way Viaduct. The Viaduct was a rickety elevated causeway bordering Pioneer Square that ran parallel to Elliott Bay until its recent demise. Car traffic roared overhead, throwing icy sheets of water onto us. "Why don't we go someplace else?" I grumbled. "Maybe a supermarket?"

Space Case waved his hand. "Nah. Street people like us," he said, "hafta deal with shitty weather. It's like this in winter. You get used to it. You'll see."

"Listen, I spent four winters in central Wisconsin. Try sitting through a Green Bay Packer game in a blizzard with a strong wind blowing," I snapped. Then, shivering badly, I added, "But man, I'm *cold*."

Space Case replied, "Uh, the Packers are a football team, right?"

I rolled my eyes. "No, they play roller derby. Of course, the Packers are a fucking football team, you idiot," I answered, instantly regretting my nastiness. Being mean to Space Case was not correct. I then tried convincing him that spending his last twenty dollars on a warm bed at the YMCA for a few days was smart. Space Case had other plans. He handed his cash to a coke dealer that materialized from fog, like something from a Charles Dickens novel. That explained Space Case's stubborn refusal to leave Pioneer Square. Seller and buyer shared a few words to consummate the exchange of cash and drugs. Then, the ghost-dope dealer faded away into the mist.

We were alone again. Space Case broke the silence. "This guy's shit's pretty good most of the time," he said, carefully unrolling the baggie of white powder on his knee. Space Case thrust the coke at me. His lack of selfishness impressed me. Whatever Space Case possessed, he considered community property. His brand of generosity was something you rarely encountered on the streets. Maybe I sensed that goodness when I took to him so quickly after we met.

"Thanks, I'll pass. Better look out. If that powder gets wet, you'll be the proud owner of a soggy $20 bag of Elmers' glue." It was 9:30 am. A cocaine binge was not on my to-do list that day. Space Case carefully pinched a fat line of white powder along his left wrist beneath his upraised jacket, protecting the powder from the elements. He leaned forward, pinched a nostril, and turning his head to one side, carefully ingested the coke with a long, obnoxious snort. Back home, my buddies and I occasionally dabbled in coke, but it wasn't our primary choice of drug. Possession of cocaine got you in a bunch more trouble than if you only got busted carrying a half-ounce bag of weed. Plus, Coke was pricey. It wasn't worth – we told each other – the money we usually pooled together to make a purchase. The drug was for addicts and rich people, not us. It wasn't worth the hassle, and we never saw the point, anyway.

"This shit works so much better than the weed at the Y did last night," Space Case said to himself in between two sharp coughs. He turned towards me, saying, "It was cool. Dave only charged us $5 for the two joints, but you can't beat good coke." He carefully licked the residue off his wrist before pulling his shirt sleeve back into place. Space Case faced me directly, one eye focusing slightly upward, the other looking down; his face was flushed red. He was enjoying whatever he had just put up his nose. I didn't care – my shivering was worsening.

"Oh, I don't know. That pot was good enough," I responded. "It was better than most Rhode Island weed. Coke's too expensive and… never mind." I didn't verbalize my concerns about getting hooked on it. I stood up from where I was leaning against a girder. "Okay, hot shot. You're broke again. What now?" I stamped my feet. The damp chill of Puget Sound in winter was getting to me. Even native Washingtonians found wintertime a weary grind month after tedious month, everyone grimly hanging on until late May when a Seattle watercraft holiday known as Opening Day signaled the end of the region's winter hibernation. In the Pacific Northwest, people were afflicted with Seasonal Affective Disorder (SAD), a mental health condition brought on by day after day of grey, weepy skies and little or no sun. Preferred remedies included sitting under bright lamps or going south to Tucson or Hawaii for a month to break up the monotony. I hadn't heard of SAD before arriving in Seattle, but many people in the Pacific NW struggled with the phenomenon.

It was Space Case's turn to lean against the girder, eyes shut. A Cheshire Cat grin creeping across his face slowly revealed the gap between his two front teeth. "I'll make more money today," Space Case mumbled in his devil-may-care way, again directing his words at an imaginary friend, I guessed. "My competition isn't around today, and people feel sorry for you in bad weather."

"Listen, Jerry—"

Space Case stood up as his eyes snapped open. "Hey, Rob, only call me 'Space Case.' That's my name, 'Space Case.' Period." He quickly went back to his semi-comatose pose, his agitation gone. "I ain't no cartoon mouse," he whispered.

I sighed. "I gotta find a job. I'm in a serious financial mess." I looked around, wanting to walk somewhere, anywhere, to find whatever it was I was looking for. Panic was setting in.

"Join the fucking club," he answered dreamily. "Just relax. It will work out. Look at me. I got life by the balls. Take things like they come."

"No, man. Listen, I'm circling the toilet. My checking account is low. I don't know what to do."

He sighed. "I already told you, but you don't listen. Live on the streets with me. I'll show you around. This is my third year here. I'm surviving. It's like that beatnik Ker-wak wrote back in the fifties, 'bout being free and livin' on the road: no obligations, no schedules, no nothing. You'll love it. Look at me."

"His name was 'Jack Kerouac'," I said. "And he wound up dead before he was fifty. See, I'm not ready yet to ask for money from strangers. I got to go check into something today and see where the chips fall."

"Hey, loan me $10 before you go?" He glanced at me somewhat quizzically, one eye slightly open.

I hesitated before reaching for my wallet. "God damn it, here's five bucks. Take it *only* if you promise to buy food. No drugs. Promise me or I keep it." I held the bill just out of my new friend's grasp. I wasn't in any position to give cash away.

"Yeah. Yeah. I'm already set for today anyhow," he mumbled as he reached out, snatched the bill, and stuffed it in his coat pocket. "I'll buy hot dogs and a Sprite. So, this is goodbye, huh? Well, so long." Space Case turned towards me and, opening an eye, he winked once.

"Good luck. Remember, that fin I just gave you is for food *only*."

"Yeah, yeah. See ya, Rob. You know where I'll be. Just look me up." He closed his eyes again.

Taking one last look around, I pulled my jacket collar close, wet snow still plopping down on Pioneer Square. Space Case was still nailed by splotches of muddy snow tossed from the cars zipping along on the Viaduct high above him. He didn't care. I began the long slog uptown towards Pike Place Market. A block later, I turned around and peered back through the falling snow. Space Case was where I'd left him. I told myself to keep moving.

Facing Reality

I never saw Space Case again. Leaving Pioneer Square, my first order of business was finding a pay phone on First Avenue. The extracted soil used as city waterfront fill to extend the shoreline outward came from the hills surrounding Elliott Bay, making the downtown area less hilly than before the early pioneers' arrival, but not entirely. Negotiating the streets in treacherous conditions was challenging, but I had little choice. Today, downtown Seattle's street configurations confound unfamiliar drivers with steep inclines and unexpected dead ends. Locals relish telling visitors the urban legend about the city layout being planned by drunks. It seemed entirely plausible to me.

Walking north on First Avenue meant climbing steadily uphill towards Pike Place Market, taking me directly through one of the town's two most notorious red-light districts. This section in the city rivaled Aurora Avenue North, a dangerous place any time, day or night. I passed by TRIPLE XXX movie houses, sex-toy shops, drinking dives, and assorted fast-food outlets jammed together, their cheap dancing lights and curling, tawdry pictures of strippers viewable through dirty display windows. For navy ships and commercial container vessels making port calls in Seattle, this part of First Avenue was a must-go destination for sailors, civilians, and military alike. I was nearing the Market now, noticing crowds of fast-moving people disrupting the traffic on First Avenue. You had a good chance of getting smacked by a car driven by a tourist, unaware of this unpredictable mob scene obscured by bad weather.

Crowds of homeless people hung out at Pike Place Market, playing music, dancing, or preaching. Others held crude cardboard signs, primarily seeking cash handouts. Was I about to become one more nameless occupant of an overcrowded rock bottom? The possibility seemed too real.

In summer, the Market competed with the Space Needle at Seattle Center and the commercial piers down on Elliott Bay for tourist dollars, drawing panhandlers. Even in wintertime, a sizeable crowd of panhandlers was out and about. I saw two indigents in stupor sprawled on separate sidewalks, one with his left hand partially submerged in ice water. I pressed on. Streetwalkers brazenly swigged unwrapped bottles of cheap whiskey or wine in the open. No cops were in sight. Three people hit me up for money, but I just shook my head, pushing past them. In the past month, I'd run into these folks around Seattle, in the University District, Capitol Hill, Queen Anne, Beacon Hill, the International District, and other places. These were desperate, defeated people shuffling along in trances like some scary zombie movie. It was dismal.

Across the street stood a phone booth with its lower plastic panels kicked out. It stood next to Lucy's Tavern, a raunchy dive bar reeking of beer-soaked tables and an overpowering odor of wet dog drifting out the front door as I walked by. A large "Olympia" beer fluorescent light at the entrance had a jagged hole in its center, the work of some boozehound's misplaced anger. It was only mid-morning. Loud, gusty laughter reverberated from Lucy's, mixed with the recurring, rhythmic crack of pool tables in action. Several weeks earlier, during a phone call home, I agreed to call Dad collect at his office once I had news to share. None of my family or friends understood my fixation on the Pacific Northwest. It was now 12:45 pm on the East Coast. Knowing Dad enjoyed eating lunch at his desk as he perused his draftsman's architectural schematics or flipping through color-plated art books, I asked the operator to connect me to Irving B. Haynes & Associates in Providence, Rhode Island.

Clutching the phone, I said, "Please tell the office secretary that Irv Haynes' son Rod is calling." The operator put the call through, and I waited, feeling unsettled.

"Irving," Dad's secretary Janice called, her hand partially covering the phone mouthpiece. "It's Rod calling collect from Seattle. Are you available?" A slight pause.

There was a brief, muffled series of noises before a familiar voice came online.

"Rod, that you?" The old man sounded cheerful. It was a decent start.

"Hi, Dad. Greetings from snowy Seattle. How're you?"

"Wait, just a second. Let me put this sandwich down...so how are ya? Got some news?"

"Wish I had something good to share," I said. "The printing office manager hasn't returned my calls about the job listed in the paper. So, I'm going back to check it out in person. Nothing's happening. I'm fried. Did you get the contract award for the Nightingale renovation project?" Dad was a prominent restoration architect in Providence. He submitted a bid to renovate an East Side brick building formerly owned by Colonel Joseph Nightingale, a Revolutionary War officer. A slew of Providence architects submitted contract bids. The project would be a significant coup for the lucky firm selected to lead it. Dad's reputation in a town known for political corruption was solid because he played straight. One month later, the project was awarded to his firm.

"No news yet, but I feel good about it. Listen, Rod, two Navy recruiters were sniffing around here yesterday. They said they had something for you to sign. I told them you moved to the west coast in October. They looked mighty unhappy when I said that."

"Tough bananas. It's been three months. Why don't they leave me alone?"

"You told them you were considering enlisting. Or did I miss something?"

"The Navy is interested in anyone under forty with two working arms, two legs, and a faint pulse. How's Mom doing?"

A long, uncomfortable pause. "Your mother is fine. Do you need money?"

"No," I lied. "Still got a decent reserve. What I need is a job. The economy is bad out here. But I got some leads." I didn't want to sound desperate.

"How's the apartment? Has your ex called you or written to you?"

"I'm living at the 'Y' downtown. It's cheaper – no word from Megan. Honestly, I'm glad. She's just a headache. I'm finally getting over her."

"I doubt that. Love is cruel, they say, especially lost love. I wonder if the 'going west' idea is still a good one. I didn't understand why…"

It was the question I asked myself every day since leaving Rhode Island. "I sometimes think I didn't have a choice."

"Whaddya mean?"

"This isn't the time to wax poetic about my life. Or yours, Dad. The fear of looking back thirty years later, knowing I didn't take a chance, motivated me to act. If not now, when could I do this stupid thing of running away to the West Coast? But it's getting ugly. And yes, I'm mad at myself for creating this mess."

"You're just adventurous. *Extremely* adventurous. You had security at the *Journal*, which many people look for nowadays. You walked away from it to take a shot at the great unknown. That takes guts."

"I don't understand me, Pop. A secure job just isn't enough. Coming home after college wasn't the smartest move."

"Maybe. Maybe not. I'm not able to answer that for you. But you have time, and you're a smart guy. Do what you gotta do, Rod."

"Right. You know, Dad, I'm not expecting you to answer for my decisions, but it's good we got to talk. I'll call you in a few weeks. Sorry 'bout calling collect, but money's a tad tight."

"Rod, I get it. Keep in touch. We're thinking of you. I'm going to finish my sandwich. Okay, son? You take care of yourself."

"Thanks, Dad. I will. Bye." I hung up, then, holding the phone in its cradle, I weighed our discussion, noting certain things that weren't verbalized. It was like always, I thought, another vague, inconsequential exchange between us. I was always reaching for something I couldn't articulate. Neither could the old man, so we said our pleasant goodbyes and hung up the phone, leaving things as they always were. Floating around aimlessly. I sometimes wondered if the old man had similar feelings.

The snowfall was intensifying, which was unusual. Seattle typically experiences rain or heavy mist at this time of year. What little snow fell quickly disappeared. Stepping from the phone booth, I walked north to the Market. A minute later, on the other side of First Avenue, my eye caught a World War I recruiting poster in a window: *Young men wanted for U.S. Navy.* A young sailor in a blue uniform stood proudly, even defiantly, in the foreground of an old battleship belching black smoke. Ugh. I was again hovering outside a recruiting office, debating my next move. I quickly moved on.

At the Market, I avoided the tacky booths of jewelry trinkets, wood-carved bracelets, t-shirts, dried flowers, and homemade jams. I made a beeline to the fish market to watch the fishmongers throwing fresh salmon back and forth to attract buyers. The men in long, white aprons smeared with fish innards yelled like football quarterbacks barking signals in a big game. Tourist traffic had trickled to a virtual halt because it was January in Seattle, and the economy was flat. Still, those fish-throwing guys always had locals and the few tourists around flocking to watch them perform. They were fun, a temporary distraction.

After catching the bus to the Queen Anne neighborhood, I sat on my haunches in a terraced garden on a steep hill overlooking Seattle Center, the site of the 1962 World's Fair and the Space Needle. Even today, most tourists pointedly visit the Space Needle – offering a revolving restaurant at the top – as part of their Seattle vacation plans. A fun way to get to Seattle Center was to ride the monorail from Westlake

Center, which took approximately two minutes. The train ran on a single elevated concrete center rail high above city streets. Back then, there was a reasonable possibility of being caught in one of the numerous breakdowns plaguing the aging monorail for those who risked a ride on it. Passengers were stranded a hundred feet in the air inside the railcars, sometimes for hours, while technicians worked frantically to get the train moving again. Seattleites were accustomed to the inconvenience. They embraced the quirkiness of the local culture, taking pride in its uniqueness. That appealed to whatever small sense of humor I still retained.

The previous afternoon, I found a job opening for a printing press cleaner at a business in Lower Queen Anne. It was a full-time position, paying the newly revised minimum wage of $3.10. I called the number in the ad and left a vague message since I had no phone or apartment. The business occupied the first floor of a three-story warehouse. Finding the entrance, I stepped inside the front office. A young lady at a desk looked up from her magazine. "Can I help you?" she asked, quite bored. She was around twenty years old, appearing stunning with her short auburn hair and sparkling blue eyes. I had had no social life over the previous six months. It was a pleasure being in the same space with her. She did not feel the same way about me.

"Hi. I'm Rod Haynes. I saw the job announcement in the *Seattle P-I* last night," I said, pushing my hair aside. The *Seattle Post-Intelligencer*, commonly referred to as "the P-I," was one of two major newspapers in Seattle, the other being the *Seattle Times*. "Can I please grab an application from you? I'll fill it out right away."

"Well, twenty people submitted theirs today. We're not accepting any more. Sorry."

My heart sank. "You just advertised last night—"

"Uh-huh. Sorry. Just doing my job." She turned back to thumbing through her magazine.

"Thank you," I muttered, my hopes flattened again. She didn't look up as I made my way out. *Fuck*, I sighed.

Another Seattle landmark – a local favorite anyway – was the *Seattle P-I* Globe, the neon edifice on the roof of the newspaper building glowing brightly in the snow and frozen rain. Here was another excellent photo opportunity, though I wasn't carrying my camera. Why did it matter? I couldn't afford to process the film. More to the point, there wasn't any apartment where I could hang my pics. But I liked photography, probably part of the DNA the old man passed down to me. He was a magician with his Nikon camera.

Hold on. I had a flash of brilliance. Did the P-I classified ad department have an opening for a seasoned classified ad editor? The problem was that if the P-I contacted the *Providence Journal* for a reference, it would undoubtedly torpedo my application. I'd quit my job after working there for only twelve months. The quality of my work at the *Journal* was never an issue, though the idea that I was the perfect employee was laughable. Maybe the P-I would take my word that I would be an asset to them and not bother confirming my work record with Pro-Jo. Why not give the P-I a shot? I entered the lobby. A uniformed guard at a round desk with a half-dozen telephones within easy reach looked up, asking in a level voice, "Can I help you?" He put down the bag of corn chips he was working on.

"Yes, I was hoping I could visit the classified ad—"

"Placing an ad?"

"No. I worked in the classified ad department at the *Journal*, and I was thinking..."

"Looking for a job?" He demanded, emotionless.

"Matter of fact, yes, I am."

"Sorry," the guard said firmly, finally. "The P-I's not accepting applications."

"Couldn't I just—"

"Nope." He stood up. "Look, kid, I got more than two dozen people daily coming through those doors lookin' for work. The paper's got three or five filing cabinets full of applications. They don't need no more, they don't want no more. They're firing folks, not hiring. Sorry. That's the story here; that's the story around town." The guard pointed directly at the illuminated EXIT sign. "Ya gotta go. Sorry."

I sighed. "Thank you."

"Yup. Good luck." The guard sat back down and resumed munching his corn chips.

"Right," I mumbled to myself. Walking from Queen Anne back to Pike Place Market took me twenty-five minutes. I was not just broke. I was *broken*, out of ideas, and out of time. My stomach was churning faster now. Should I accept Space Case as my new mentor and learn the intricate art of panhandling? Was it time to crawl back to Rhode Island as a failed adventure-seeker? Could I catch a trawler to Shanghai, working as a deckhand, and take my chances in the exotic Far East? I shook my head. I'd seen this film before. Going to China would be one more impulsive decision, leading me to another dead end – ten thousand miles from home. Were young Americans like me even welcome there? I felt like a flattened Coke can on the freeway of life. Was I worried, or was I angry, or was I sad? How much of each? I knew one thing: as Kerouac wrote about, I had plenty of confusion to offer any interested takers. There weren't any in this town.

I went into an electronics shop on 2nd Avenue, standing before a small portable TV, pretending to be a buyer, fingering the knobs and plastic exterior. It was almost 3:30 pm. There were two other customers nearby. Flipping through the TV channels, I saw regular programs interrupted by updates about the Iranian hostage crisis. The whole country had been following this high-risk fiasco for weeks. The TV reported that there were no new developments. America's prestige was at stake. Her citizens wondered if the Persians would ever release the hostages. It seemed like the Ayatollah and his crazy minions had President Carter over a barrel. Any attempt at rescuing the hostages would get them killed. A solitary figure from across the way slowly approached me, looking at me, then glancing away. Was she a store detective? She veered off down an aisle towards the back. It was time to split.

A Navy recruiting commercial flashed across the TV screen: *Join the Navy and See the World*. Mom's father, Captain Edwin T. Day, immediately came to mind. Grandfather designed battleship hulls in the Quincy, Massachusetts, naval shipyard during World War II. Pictures of him in his uniform had graced Mom's dresser and the desk in our living room throughout my childhood. There was also Uncle Bob, Mom's brother-in-law, a lieutenant commander in the Navy Reserve. Our family tree has many sailors represented across its branches over the past few generations.

Stop this. Enough with the good old days, I scolded myself. *Frolicking in the past was a waste of time. Gotta head back to the Y for some shut-eye.* A gnawing, dreadful emptiness stifled a faint inclination to be more optimistic about life. My supply of brilliant schemes was exhausted, my spirit dead. What was there to be cheerful about?

Leap of Faith

At 7:10 am the following day I rushed down to the coffee room in the basement to beat the crowd. The space was a gathering spot where Y lodgers congregated, smoked cigarettes, and drank free coffee as they swapped information, legal and otherwise. Some of the back-and-forth banter could be useful, I guessed. Grabbing a cup of joe – it was bitterly rancid – I sat on a tattered couch to eavesdrop on two guys at a nearby table, deep in conversation. Thumbing through an old newspaper, I held it high enough to shield my prying eyes and ears. One had recently been let go from the Boeing plant in Renton, a town ten miles south of Seattle.

"Sixteen fuckin' years, and I get an indefinite furlough. Not enough seniority," the guy spat. "Gave up my apartment in Astoria, came here to save money. I ain't stayin' in this dump, that's for sure."

His friend asked, "D'ja go down to the union hall?"

"Yup, on Monday. I get four months of benefits, sixty percent of my base pay, plus medical. I didn't understand all they said. I was supposed to file the paperwork and then wait. We got the union pullin' for us, anyhow."

"What you gonna do now?"

"Going to my folks' house in Reno 'til it gets better here. It takes time to turn things around. Any way you look at it, it's bad."

The two men drained their coffees, lit a cigarette, and walked towards the elevator. I slid in beside them. I was in the lobby a minute later, looking for a phone book. The front desk clerk reached below the counter and, snaring a ratty, three-year-old book, tossed it across the counter towards me. I searched for the Navy recruiting office phone number and walked to the pay phone on the far wall. Taking a few deep breaths, I called to say I might be stopping by this morning, but I wasn't sure. They said appointments weren't required; I was welcome anytime. I quickly hung up.

Twenty minutes later, I was back on First Avenue near the Market, glancing through the recruiting office window. The Army, Navy, and Air Force recruiters shared office space inside. Nervously chewing my lip, my stomach in knots, I slowly turned the doorknob, pushed the stuck door open with my right foot, and entered the office. A young black man sitting at a metal desk against a wall stood up and identified himself as Quartermaster Second Class Randy Jefferson. His jet-black uniform had four rows of colorful ribbons and silver devices on his left breast pocket. His shoes were shiny black.

The guy looked sharp, I admitted to myself. Jefferson grabbed my hand and, shaking it vigorously, said, "You the dude who called earlier this morning? Yeah? It's great you came in." Jefferson continued, "Want some coffee? No? Water? Grab a seat. No, over there. Yeah, that's good." His manufactured enthusiasm turned me off.

I sat down, eyeing him warily, then glanced around the office. We were alone. I told Jefferson about my adventures with the two Navy recruiters back home. I wondered if I was already locked into a military contract. Did I need to return to Providence to report in?

Jefferson asked, "You sign any papers?"

"They tried to get me to sign, but I left town first. I didn't sign a thing."

"Did you raise your hand and swear to support your country and the Constitution?"

"No. I remember taking an entrance test, though."

"Was it the ASVAAB?"

"Yeah, that's the name."

"Nothing else?"

"That's it. Nothing more," I replied uneasily. "I don't even know the results." I didn't tell him I failed the OCS test.

"Cool. You don't owe them two nothin'. You and me, we starting new right here."

I asked about becoming a Navy photographer or maybe a journalist. Jefferson ignored my question while handing me a questionnaire. I raised the pen briefly, then put it down, reiterating my interest in becoming a Navy journalist.

Jefferson waved away my question. "Nah, you don't want that. I'll explain in a minute. Let's fill in those spaces from there to right there, okay? Answer best you can."

I worked on the questionnaire for a minute. Deliberately testing his patience, I looked around the office, focusing on everything except Jefferson and my paperwork. A minute went by.

"Hey, man, you hearin' me? Pay attention." Jefferson demanded, snapping his fingers twice. "This is important. Do this stuff right now, or we can't do nothin' else. You dig?"

I exhaled. "I hear you," I said, looking at him. *What the fuck was I thinking, anyway?*

"So, where were we anyway? Oh, yeah. Drugs," Jefferson continued, tight-lipped. His eyes darted left and right as if divulging a top-secret nuclear weapons code. Jefferson leaned closer and whispered, "Just say, 'I tried pot once, but it made me sick, so I never did it again.'"

I stifled a laugh. *Seriously?* Jefferson leaned back in his chair, his eyes shooting lightning bolts at me. The situation turned weird fast. I flashed him a what-did-I-do-wrong look of innocence. No sale.

The outer door to the office swung open. Two officers entered, making a beeline for their workplace, located further back in the building. Noticing Jefferson and me, they turned on a dime and walked towards us. The officer casually picked up my questionnaire, reading it like Petty Officer Jefferson wasn't present. The officer extended his right hand to me; his attention focused on the paperwork he held in his left hand. I shook it.

"Hello. I'm Lieutenant Jack LaRouche," he said. "Meet Lieutenant Ed Fitzsimmons. Would you join us in our office for a minute? Petty Officer Jefferson will stay here." Fitzsimmons shook my hand. Lieutenant LaRouche nodded at the door to his office. "We can talk turkey in here."

"I guess so," I replied, glancing sideways at Jefferson, whose mood had instantly changed. He was now royally pissed; his exuberance vanished.

Once inside the space, Lt. LaRouche pointed to a chair. "Grab a seat. So, you finished up at Ripon College in June 1978. Where's that at? What's your degree? Take any engineering courses?"

"Ripon's a hundred miles northwest of Milwaukee. I got my BA in History and English. No engineering courses, but I was in Army ROTC sophomore year before dropping it. After graduation, I took a job at the *Providence Journal*. I moved out here last fall."

"Why'd you drop ROTC?"

"My grandfather was career Navy, and I'm proud of that. The army just wasn't a good fit. I think going to sea beats rolling around in mud any day." The officers nodded approvingly. I went on. "Growing up in Rhode Island, my family would sometimes visit the officers' club at the

Navy base for Sunday brunch with my Uncle Bob. He's a reserve naval officer."

"What rank?"

"Lieutenant Commander. I like how the Navy operates." I didn't know anything about how the Navy operated. Two officers were hanging on every word I said. I suddenly felt patriotic. My Grandfather Day served in WWII and the Korean conflict as a naval architect for twenty-six years. Because he was not an unrestricted line officer, Grandfather could never command a warship or submarine at sea. Mom was always proud of her father's lead role in designing the hull of USS *Massachusetts*, now permanently anchored in Battleship Cove, Fall River. Grandfather designed several other warships during World War II, including the cruiser USS *Providence*.

"So, what makes you think you'd make a good naval officer?" Lt. LaRouche's voice interrupted my introspection. "I mean, why should we consider you for OCS?"

I paused before responding, thinking about the question. "Well, I'm told I'm a good leader who embraces challenges. I'm not brilliant, but I'm smart enough. I've traveled extensively around America in recent years on my own, so I believe I'm self-reliant. After seeing this country for myself, I love it even more. I mentioned that I come from a naval family, so tradition is important." I cleared my throat. Having uniformed officers listening to me made me feel good. "Now, I know this sounds hokey, but I've always admired ships at sea. I wonder how they operate, where they're headed, how the sailors work on them, and how they engage in battles at sea. I have an adventurous streak inside me and always have. One last thing: the thing that's going on in Iran right now pisses me off. I want to serve my country. Something's got to be done."

I didn't say I had only thirty dollars to my name, and I desperately needed a job. I didn't think the two lieutenants cared about my broken heart – how I needed to get far away from a girl in Maine. They didn't care about my parents' marital problems, so I didn't bother going there.

There was something else I only discovered later. At the time, I didn't realize that a uniform could allow me to be someone else while being part of a group. The uniform projected a love of country, professional competence, loyalty, and courage, even if the person wearing it lacked those attributes. The story a sharp uniform told viewers was not necessarily an authentic portrayal of its wearer. Later, I let people see me in uniform and let them draw their own conclusions, whatever they might be. I tried to appear rugged and knowledgeable, hoping those checking me out would be impressed. This strategy often worked well. I was suddenly less concerned about what people thought about me. The uniform was my shield, my costume, and my cloak.

There was a long silence. Had I said too much? The two interviewers exchanged a glance. One had his eyebrows raised. I looked down again in submission. I told myself to keep still and allow someone else to speak.

Lt. Fitzsimmons finally broke the silence. "That's fine, I suppose. What about illegal drugs? You ever take any?"

I paused. My stomach suddenly tightened. I heard myself slowly say, "Well, to be honest, I tried pot in college once. It made me so dizzy I never tried it again." *What a fucking crock!* I tried looking directly into their eyes, managing only intermittent contact.

"Right. So, you're telling us you'd pass a urinalysis screening if you took it Thursday morning?" Both officers looked at me intently.

God damn it! The blood drained from my face. Forcing a weak smile, I gulped twice, searching for the right words, answering in a barely audible voice. "No problem." I cursed myself for sharing that fat joint with Space Case a few days before. Well, goodbye, OCS. Now what? The elation from a few moments earlier had imploded like the old 1930s movie clip of the *Hindenburg* collapsing into a flaming wreck at a New Jersey airfield.

"Great. No problem, we can knock out that whiz quiz. We'll do it this week," Lt. Fitzsimmons chirped. "We'll call the doctor and schedule you. The results happen fast."

"Ever taken the written test for Officer Candidate School?" Lt. LaRouche asked.

I hesitated one last time. "Well, yes," I stammered. I told them about taking the OCS screening test eight months before in Rhode Island but that I missed qualifying. My interviewers exchanged glances again.

Lt. Fitzsimmons spoke up. "Are you aware you can retake the OCS test after six months?"

I shook my head, no, I hadn't heard that. "But I wouldn't be signing anything immediately, so what's the rush?" I wondered out loud, knowing time was of the essence. Something in my life had to give. Right now.

"Why not take the test right now?" Lt. LaRouche asked.

"You're already here. Might as well…" Lt. Fitzsimmons added.

"Uh, well, I don't know. Give me a minute." Despite the fear of the test results, I had not completely given up on becoming a naval officer.

Looking at the Navy enlisted community was, maybe, my fallback plan. Starting from the bottom rank at boot camp and working my way up was not very tempting. I'd rather be an officer than wear the silly white Dixie-cup sailor cap and get stuck with an ordinary navy job without any real prestige. The whole navy would be issuing orders I had to follow without comment. Everyone dumping on the swabbie was a bad image to fight off.

Then there was Grandfather Day. Mom would be proud to have a son wearing the same uniform as her father. Steady paycheck. Travel. I reminded myself there were no other job prospects. The recruiter's silky words tempted me to let the Navy take control of my career and life decisions. I thought of one other potential bonus if I joined the Navy, a big one. Megan, my ex-girlfriend from college, would think I'd finally grown up when she saw me in uniform. Maybe she'd swoon over me, demand I take her back. I could then tell her it was too late for all that. I had no time for her now. I was going off to see the world and fight the Soviet Union. Maybe I'd catch her some other time. She'd cry, and I would shrug and walk away like Humphrey Bogart in *Casablanca*. She'd think twice about not responding to my letters, then. I smiled thinly while pondering the possibilities.

The hell with it. I agreed to take the OCS test on the condition that if I passed, I'd have a few days to think things over before signing anything (this was precisely what I did back in Providence with the recruiters there, but why bring that up now?) The piss test results would most likely eliminate my eligibility for OCS. What would all this accomplish anyhow? But the lack of a Plan B to fall back on convinced me to go for it.

Moments later, after assuring me they weren't interested in twisting anybody's arm, Lt. LaRouche said, "Let's go do it right now." He brought me into a small back room containing two desks, produced a sealed booklet, sliced open with a letter opener, handed me a black pen, and patted me on my shoulder, wishing me good luck.

Diving into the test, I immediately realized the questions were familiar if not exactly the ones I had read back in Providence. I stumbled over the same math and fundamental mechanical engineering problems that tied me in knots the previous time. The OCS test was more comprehensive than the enlisted battery of tests, which assessed technical interests and abilities, basic writing, and general knowledge. Besides covering advanced technical subjects, the OCS test included naval history, advanced writing skills, and leadership and management questions. In Rhode Island, I waited in a hallway for an hour while they graded my test. In Seattle, the officers emerged smiling from their office in twenty minutes.

They said in unison, "Good news. You passed." Right away, I experienced a mixed feeling of relief and anxiety. Then, I felt cornered. I wanted to get out of there fast, with no more discussions about anything. I shook both recruiters' hands a final time, assuring them I would let them know by week's end. They reminded me I still had to complete my physical, a prerequisite for reporting to OCS. While leaving, I looked for Jefferson. He had cleared out. It was only midday. Exiting the building, I pondered the OCS test that had just been completed: the outcome was puzzling and odd. I told myself just to let it go.

The Navy offered to fly me from Seattle to Providence, but I chose a one-way Greyhound bus ticket home instead. I needed time to think. And I was in no rush to return to Rhode Island and witness my parents drink to excess in an atmosphere of stony silence and resentment. My decision to become a naval officer stemmed from a combination of family tradition, a steady paycheck, the chance to travel, and a way to curb my impulsive wanderlust. Was it desperation? In some ways, yes. I had journeyed across North America four months earlier to start anew, but the Pacific Northwest felt unwelcoming to someone uncertain about his identity and future. Many young men faced similar struggles. The military offered a break from these uncertainties; I would receive orders and follow them without much say in how to live my life, including being told what to wear, what to do, and when to do it. The downside was not liking someone else calling the shots. I didn't know how I would react to the strict oversight I was now confronting.

Walking back to the YMCA that afternoon, I thought long and hard about my day at the recruiting office. I was handing my young life to the United States government. If, better put, *when* there was war, I would have to comply with wherever they sent me and whatever job they ordered me to do, no questions asked. That included killing human beings. Worse, if, during an emergency at sea, a lieutenant had told me to go three decks below and close the hatch behind me to save the rest of the ship, I would have had to do it. The question was, *could* I do it?

Homeward Bound

I left Seattle on a cold, drizzly January night armed with two sandwiches, three candy bars, and two cans of Coke. I had eight dollars in my pocket, and my SeaFirst bank account was closed, with the Navy covering the cost of shipping my bags home to Rhode Island. The Navy offered to fly me home, but I needed time alone to think. The recruiters did not understand my desire to travel across the country by bus in the dead of winter. Reminded of my bus travels nearly six years earlier, I motored through eastern Washington's rolling, frozen hills overnight. The following day, I woke up in central Idaho. The winter was noticeably crueler, more threatening than the typical snow flurries in Seattle. The isolation of the northwestern portion of the old Oregon Trail hit me hard. I had no sense of safety.

You could quickly lose your life out here on the high plains if your vehicle broke down without carrying survival gear and food of some kind in the trunk. I contemplated the pioneers from the Old West and their struggles with hostile natives, poor soil, burning summers, and freezing winters. Some – like the Donner Party – famously resorted to cannibalism. Thousands perished from cholera, exposure to the elements, or malnourishment. The indigenous people living in these lands had decidedly mixed feelings about hordes of newcomers intruding in their lives, scattering wildlife and claiming land the locals relied on for survival. The newcomers brought measles and smallpox, decimating the local people. Some natives resorted to violence, causing blue-coated soldiers to destroy entire villages as punishment for their misdeeds. As hostilities worsened, many travelers gave up and returned east. This land was unforgiving.

The bus driver drove through white-out conditions from Boise to Minneapolis, with high winds pushing snow drifts in all directions. We saw many abandoned vehicles off to the side. The winds haphazardly *whammed* against the side of the bus, relented momentarily, and then struck again with renewed fury. It went on for hours. How could anyone navigate a bus through these elements? And were there any food supplies onboard in case we got stuck in a snowdrift? Passengers seemed a little nervous.

I sat thinking about what lay ahead. The irony of returning one more time to Rhode Island did not escape me. Would I ever finally leave Little Rhody behind? My recent anxieties resurfaced as I pondered my immediate future. What the hell had I just done? Would the Navy and I get along? What if the answer was no? I was joining the military; sometimes, military people get killed serving their country, accidentally or on purpose. You could fall over the ship's side at night, and that would be that. Once again, I put myself between stations in life. I had enough of feeling ambivalent.

On the final segment of my bus journey, I spent my last dime on a Milky Way candy bar in Philadelphia. Six hours later, the bus arrived in downtown Providence. There was Dad in his car reading a *New Yorker* magazine. Exiting the vehicle, he gripped my shoulders, exclaiming, "Hey!"

We drove north on Route 146 towards Limerock. Beyond asking Dad the standard questions about his business and his reply that times were very slow, and he might have to lay off a drafting technician or two to make payroll, we said little to each other as we approached the house. From the driveway, we saw Mom peeping out of the kitchen window. The door opened, and she hurried up the hill in her rubber boots through several inches of muddy snow to where I stood clutching my backpack.

Her first words were, "Oh, I don't know, Rod. Do you honestly want to enlist in the Navy? Whew!" Mom continued, holding her nose, "Even outside, you stink! When did you last shower? Get cleaned up. I'll put some food on the table." I headed down to the house. Setting my bags down on the living room floor, I headed to grab some clean clothes. I couldn't remember taking a more satisfying shower.

Aside from avoiding discussing the failed expedition to the Pacific Northwest, I had little to say as we sat down to eat. My parents avoided talking to each other, instead focusing on me. Both had bourbon and water in hand. The big chill between my parents had not warmed up. It was noticeably worse than before I left Rhode Island. A moment later, Joey's clunky blue station wagon crunched the driveway stones, and Darrell and Mike stepped out and walked down the front yard, chatting and laughing. I walked outside to greet my friends.

Unexpectedly, Darrell snatched me by my shirt collar, leaving our chins inches apart. "Are you fucking crazy, Haynes?" he said.

Joey and Mike burst out laughing. They all reeked of pot. I told Mikey he smelt like he had bathed in beer that night. No, he replied.

He spilled half a bottle of Schlitz on his shirt when Joey hit a pothole on Wilbur Road Hill.

I wrested myself away from Darrell, debating inviting them inside. Joey moved right past me. From the foyer, he greeted Mom and Dad, who had repaired from the dining table to sit on opposite ends of the dining room's sectional couch before a roaring fire, each caressing their watered-down bourbons. For whatever reason, Joey always liked talking to Dad. He considered himself an amateur painter with talent, so he always invited Dad's thoughts about art. Dad, never offering faint praise, considered Joey's talent promising. Dad inevitably steered the conversation towards his latest piece sitting on the easel in his studio. Mom and Dad got a kick from Joey's brash attitude and lack of reserve. Mike meekly waved hello and stood back silently. Darrell mumbled a few words and hung behind Mike, gesturing with his thumb towards the door. "Right now," he mouthed to me.

"We're heading out," I announced, reaching for my jacket.

"Well, there's a surprise," my father chuckled nervously. My mother mentioned one more time I looked tired and hungry. She'd prepared a pot roast dinner for me. Couldn't my friends wait for me to finish eating? I said no, thanks, I'd eat it for lunch and dinner tomorrow. The four of us headed out, waving goodbye.

Darrell whispered, "No change with them, huh?"

I said it didn't seem so.

We drove along Great Road for less than a minute when Darrell leaned back from the front seat, thrusting a fat joint in my face. "Rod, light this up. It's quality Jamaican. $30 a lid. Billy has a good connection in Manville."

Before my departure four months before, we were leading uncomplicated lives, fueled by countless bottles of beer, occasional hits of acid, and a steady supply of mediocre marijuana. After returning from four years of college beer and bonging, I grew weary of the same routine, so I split for the West Coast. And yet, here I was. Again.

"Can't," I replied, pushing Darrell's hand away.

My friends hooted. "What have we here? Rod's found religion! Did travel cure his pot addiction?"

"Shut up, you guys. The Navy's gonna make me take a urinalysis in a few weeks. Gotta stay clean. I mean, first, I gotta get clean. I don't have a choice, so don't try to talk me into it. And I thank you for not smoking now. You'll contaminate me even if I don't take a direct toke. I'm holding my breath 'til we stop the car. Beer only for me."

Mike laughed, "Rod, I got an idea. I'll take that piss test for you; I'll go in your place and say it's me; I mean, I'll be you. Or you be me. Or vice versa."

"Thanks, you fucking druggie, you're all heart," I said with a smirk. "Let's go to the Elk."

Darrell said, "Way ahead of you, buddy. That's where we're headed. Like old times."

The Golden Elk Tavern was in Albion, a French-Canadian village three miles away. It consisted of a perfectly square brick building with a stark white exterior. The Elk, a former American Legion Post, shared a property line with the Albion Fire Department next door. Inside, the chairs and barstools had red plastic coverings; the majority were split open, their white cotton stuffing spilling out. The floor covering was brittle, peeling linoleum colored light mustard or yellow. It was hard to tell which. Schlitz, Pabst Blue Ribbon, and Narragansett beer – Rhode Island's so-called "finest lager," made in Cranston, RI – were the three choices on tap. A non-working jukebox collected dust in one corner. The lighting was noticeably subdued. Patrons came to this establishment to drink and exchange insults, not to admire the décor, knowing that drinks were reasonably priced and most of the crowd kept to themselves. I never saw a punch thrown by anybody inside the Elk, but minor scuffles in the parking lot occasionally broke out at closing time. We considered the Elk a slight notch above the offerings of a classic northern Rhode Island dive bar, but only barely. Beer was cheap, close to home, and the place always seemed open for business, thanks to the loyalty of a small number of clientele, all blue-collar locals. It suited our drinking needs. And we *belonged* there, we believed.

Piling out of the station wagon with my buddies, I opened the door and ushered them inside. "Good to be back home again, isn't it?" Darrell asked no one in particular, plopping down on a bar stool. I recalled a special time a dozen years earlier. Darrell, Mike, and I were toiling as caddies at Kirkbrae Country Club. The thirteenth tee on the golf course stood less than seventy-five yards away. Starting at the age of twelve, we bonded as caddies at the nouveau riche golf course many members of the New England mob called home. Developers built the golf course in the 1960s on a fine tract of land, formerly a sizeable family-owned dairy farm overlooking the Blackstone River valley below. This was prime northern Rhode Island real estate.

I smiled, asking, "How did we buy beer here at age twelve?" My thoughts drifted back to simpler times.

"The golfers sent us over. The bartenders knew that. Darrell was only fourteen when he grew that big Afro and sideburns. He never got carded here. They knew Darrell 'cause Mr. Scott was a regular. They didn't give a shit anyways," Mike told Joey. "Remember those nights we would take our beers to the golf course, lay on the slope of the tee box, look up at the moon, and talk things over? Good times, huh, Rod?"

"The best. We started drinking too young, but that's Kirkbrae's fault," I said. "We should sue them for child endangerment." Kirkbrae held golf tournaments throughout the summer, attracting participants from Southern New England. Crusty Al Sullivan, the caddy master at the club, would pick four or five caddies to drive golf carts loaded with beer and ice around the course. The tips were great, and we enjoyed sampling beers while careening down perfectly manicured fairways. Being fourteen years old and driving golf carts while drunk on a private golf course in the summertime was one of the highlights of our youth. It made the lives of the *Brady Bunch* kids on TV look boring.

"Are you out of your mind with this navy shit?" Darrell interrupted my reminiscing. "You're really asking for it. I mean, what the fuck, Rod?"

"It?," I snapped back. "What 'it,' am I asking for? Let's hear it, Einstein."

"Leave him alone, Darrell. I think he's got something here," Joey said, swigging his beer. "Going through that military training could do him good. Just because *you* wouldn't do it doesn't make it bad for him. Any of you guys got life plans yet?"

"Yeah, Darrell, go ahead and tell us what your goals in life are," I said, cradling my beer. "Well?"

Mikey interrupted, looking Darrell in the eye. "You think Rod's nuts for doing this, huh? Well, what's your old man think?" Mr. Scott's opinions counted among us. As a young man, he shipped out to sea – getting no one's permission – and joined the merchant marine at age sixteen. Mr. Scott spent most of World War II in convoys, bringing vital supplies to England through the Nazi wolf pack-infested waters of the North Atlantic. He saw supply ships torpedoed along the U.S. eastern seaboard, and a lot of comrades drowned or burned to death in exploding ships. The subs sometimes used city lights on the American eastern seaboard to find their targets, despite authorities pleading for them to be turned off.

Darrell grunted, "The old man's not against it. He says Rod's gonna hate OCS, but if he can take the bullshit, Rod will make out okay. Oh yeah, he said, remember God gave you two ears to listen and only one mouth to talk. It's your self-control that worries all of us. You're so impulsive."

I respected Mr. Scott's thoughts. After the war, he graduated to piloting tankers and container ships from the open Atlantic Ocean near Newport to Providence, forty miles north. He was licensed to navigate large ships from Newport to Providence through dozens of miles of islands and shoal water. He was a smart guy. He spent too much time yelling at Darrell, though, a lot of it about being late for school or the routine discovery of pot residue in his pants pocket when Darrell's mother washed his clothes.

Mike shared his thoughts. "Darrell, just because you don't like the military doesn't mean Rod has no chance with the Navy. As the commercial says, 'Join the Navy and see the world.' Honestly, what's the downside?"

"The downside? We're talking about the military, man. This isn't a joke, Rod. If you pull that class-clown crap you got famous for in Mrs. Palmer's algebra class in the Navy, and you won't be sent to the principal's office. You'll go to the brig."

"Alright, man, alright. I could have a few challenges here or there," I said.

Joey chuckled suddenly, a wistful look in his eyes. "You remember the party at URI the first time you tripped?"

"What are you babbling about, Joey?" I asked indignantly.

Darrell grabbed my shoulder. "Yeah, you know. Don't pretend like you forgot. You dropped that hit of window pane, and a half hour later, you came into the room and told Mikey you're gonna get laid tonight."

"Oh, no. You're not talking about that stupid recruitment-poster story again. Let it go." We all laughed.

My three friends and I spent much time partying with our University of Rhode Island friends in the Spring of 1974 while Joey and I planned our sixty-day bus trip across the country. One time, Darrell handed me a hit of window pane acid, instructing me to place the tab under my tongue. In my stoned state, I quickly ingested it, not knowing what it was. Less

Old Navy Recruiting Poster

than an hour later, Darrell and Mikey found me trying to convince a girl in a Navy poster to have sex with me.

"It was my first acid trip," I said. "Everyone knows it. Just stop, will you?"

Darrell was defiant. "Nope. You own this one for as long as you live. Now there's even more to the story."

"What do you mean, more?" I asked, staring back at my best friend, more agitated now.

"The recruiting girl got her man. You joined the Navy 'cause she told you it was a good idea. You're doing what she told you to do."

That was enough. "Fuck off, Darrell."

"No, no, he's right," Mikey laughed. "She got you to sign up. And you *still* didn't get lucky with her."

"How's life treating you, Darrell?" I replied defensively. "Everything coming up roses in your world? Let's talk about that."

"This isn't about me, Rod. It's what you have been doing for the past five or six years. I think you're crazy, or at least you act like it." Darrell shot back.

"Hey, Darrell, that's—" Mike interjected before Darrell cut him off.

"Shut up, Mikey. You had your chance. You and me and Joey talked about all this earlier tonight when we did those two doobies at the lime quarry. Now, you're Rod's best buddy. I'm not worried about hurting his feelings. Seriously, Rod, I mean, what the fuck?"

"Why are you so worked up? Nobody's making you, 'Go Navy.' You're acting like I'm supposed to know me and where I'm going. And I still haven't heard your primary plan. Stop pointing fingers, man. You worry about you. Got it?" I looked away, now thoroughly aggravated.

"I don't have a plan yet. But I'll tell you what: none of 'em will involve signing my life away for six years."

"Listen, pal, no offense, but at least I'm trying. Yeah, I've been back and forth, here and there. That's true. I need a challenge that will make me think and apply myself. The Navy'll do it." I thumped my forefinger into the filthy linoleum on the bar for emphasis.

Darrell snorted. "Your 'challenge' is gonna smoke your ass, my friend. I'm not trying to throw water on this, but you better think about this. Seriously, Rod, what makes you think the Navy is gonna be different? You think you can quit the Navy when you find out it isn't the fun time the recruiters promised you?"

"No, you *are* trying to talk me out of it. You know what, Darrell? If you don't like the military, then don't do it. There's no goddamn draft anymore. I don't see you doing wonderful stuff. I admit that working in a camera store is decent, but not for a lifetime. Unless you wanna become a pro photographer."

"I'm not making a career out of it. I like photography. What's the big deal?" Darrell straightened up, staring back at me.

"I didn't say it was. Do you like cameras? Good for you. I like the sea."

"You better. You're gonna be riding around the ocean for a very long time," Darrell said quietly. "And the sea isn't Narragansett Bay. It's the fucking Atlantic Ocean."

Joey tapped Darrell's elbow. "Take it easy, Darrell. Yeah, Rod's got to learn about controlling his temper. As a matter of fact, except for me, I think he's got the most leadership potential of anyone here tonight. Rod, you just gotta put the pot away for good."

"Look, Rod," Darrell said, sighing, "I'm not saying you can't do this like the Navy is too hard. This isn't about your capability. I'm just saying it's *not* for you. You never stay put long enough in any place. You're like Ricochet Rabbit in the cartoons, bouncing around the country. The

Navy will get on your nerves within a month or two and then you'll be sorry, man. I'm not looking to argue with you, man."

"I don't know," I replied after pausing to think. "Here's the thing, you guys, Darrell's right. I've been moving everywhere for the last five or six years. I can't stay put in one spot. But in the Navy, you got no choice. You're always goin' someplace else. It fits me that way. And I know if I decide it's not for me, they'll put me in a stockade til I change my attitude. I know that going in. I'll behave. I'm broke, and I need work. I feel cornered."

"That's exactly my point. You panicked and signed a contract. The military stockade is Fort Leavenworth. It's a federal prison. That's hard time, friend. When they send you there, your adventure will really begin," Darrell said. "And your wanting your momma to fix things ain't gonna happen."

"Will you stop? I never cried for my mother, even when I was five." I glared at my friend. Darrell looked away, biting his lip. "Didn't do it once, man." My best friend suddenly waved both hands to surrender whatever point he was making.

We bought three or four more rounds while I told my buddies about my adventures in Seattle. They got a kick out of hearing about Space Case. Things calmed down. Then, it was time to go home. I was dog-tired and needed to sleep for a day or two.

Welcome Aboard

In the early evening of March 19, 1980, I tossed my duffel bag into the back of Dad's Honda Accord. We drove south to Newport, on the southern tip of Aquidneck Island, where Narragansett Bay meets the Atlantic Ocean. Dad and I agreed to share one last civilian meal before I reported to Officer Candidate School, a ten-minute drive from the restaurant.

Dad and I dined at the Chart House on Bannister Wharf in downtown Newport, an upscale seafood eatery. I didn't know then that two Naval Academy graduates owned the restaurant chain. My father was a veteran of World War II for only a matter of weeks. He was an eighteen-year-old army draftee in boot camp at Fort Sill in Oklahoma in May 1945, preparing to ship overseas. One rumor had Dad's outfit redirected to the Pacific theater, where the Allies were slowly gaining the upper hand. They were taking horrific punishment as the Japanese grudgingly fell back towards the main islands of their country. The island-hopping campaign was taking its toll as the Allies slowly wore down the Imperial Japanese war machine.

"You know," Dad told me as we slurped our drinks, "I still remember the afternoon in Oklahoma when the Fort Sill commandant called the troops together. We didn't know why. He stood up there in front with a big, sappy grin. 'Men,' he said, 'the krauts surrendered earlier today. Anybody caught reporting back to base sober tonight will be put in hack for stupidity.' All of us cheered for each other and America. Boy, did we tie one on that night."

This was Dad's one military tale from World War II, at least the only one he shared with me. I knew he spent time in Germany right after the Nazis surrendered, playing the piano in military pubs. He arrived in Europe less than a month after the shooting stopped. A few months later, President Truman dropped the atomic bombs on Hiroshima and Nagasaki. All Dad's unit had to do in Germany was sift through the rubble of the former Third Reich, give chocolate to starving kids, and drink German beer. True, they guarded prisoners, but the captured Germans were just as happy as the Allies that the war was over for them.

Dad always maintained he was lucky not to have seen combat and that his unit never had to liberate the concentration camps all over the vanquished country. Nobody he trained with was dodging bullets and fighting enemy soldiers up close. I'd heard the Fort Sill tale many times, with no variations. "Good one, Dad," I said to him. "Order another round for us, will you?"

The meals arrived. I barely touched my broiled scallops, picking at the salad, pushing the green beans around my plate, and slamming down as much vodka and wine as I could. We lingered while the wind and sleet intensified out on Narragansett Bay. The wave action directly outside our window where we sat was intense and angry. We both knew I was stalling. I rapidly gulped two mouthfuls of wine, draining my glass.

Dad piped up, "Your Grandfather Day spent many years in the Navy. He'd be proud of what you're doing. Remember that in the tough times ahead." He pointed his fork directly at my nose. "You're ready to do this, right?"

I cracked a small smile. "I guess so. Come to think of it, what am I doing?"

Dad then said something I've never forgotten. "Rod, your best asset is that you like people, and people like you. Don't be ashamed of it. Take care of those around you. But remember, one day, you might have to make life-or-death decisions in a crisis. You can't be friends with the sailors you lead. The sea is not forgiving. You could find yourself in a terrible place, having to order people to sacrifice themselves to save others. That's just a possibility," he quickly added. "The one making the supreme sacrifice could be you. OCS is all about training to go to sea and lead men in a rugged environment."

I nodded, pondering Dad's comment. "Women, too. Not just men." Glancing at my watch, I quickly stood up, unable to further put off the inevitable. In less than an hour, I would be considered UA, Unauthorized Absence, by naval authorities. Not a great start to my career. I gestured towards the door. We declined the server's offer to peruse a dessert menu. We were not a dessert family.

"Yes, time to go," Dad agreed.

Outside, Dad shivered, zipping up his jacket. He pointed out towards Narragansett Bay. "Check out those conditions. You'll be dealing with this kind of nastiness hundreds of miles out to sea before you know it. Hang on tight. Keep your wits. Be ready."

I shifted my feet restlessly, searching for words. I didn't want to think about rough seas and fighting wars just then. We drove north in silence, rattling across the cobblestone streets of old Newport through the wet, inky black night. I had a good buzz going. I caught myself wishing I had avoided drinking at dinner. Too late now. On the outskirts of town, we turned onto West Main Road. I was feeling anxious and more alone than ever before, even with Dad sitting next to me. Neither of us spoke. Three minutes later, we approached Gate One of the Newport Navy base. Leaning back so I wouldn't breathe on him, I handed the guard a thick manila envelope. He extracted my orders, scrutinized them, and, returning the packet, directed us to King Hall, my residence for the next sixteen weeks. We drove off into the night through the center campus of the Naval War College.

Sheets of rain cut across the limited light thrown by the aging streetlamps lining the road. The place looked like a *Twilight Zone* setting; there were no people or moving vehicles. Dad rounded a curve and hit a pothole before stopping directly before a brightly lit entrance to a brick building with raised metal letters reading "King Hall." Neither of us moved. After a long pause, I jumped out and quickly scanned the scene one last time as a free civilian. Dad grabbed my gear from the trunk. The car's wipers swept away the icy droplets from the windshield. I peered inside King Hall and spotted five men in black uniforms with shiny decorations on their collars. All stood rigidly at attention, eyes straight ahead. My clothes were soaking wet now, and my stomach was in knots. Dad stood next to me. I didn't look at him. I knew I had to move, but I didn't want to.

I kept peering at those mannequin-like figures in those uniforms inside that immaculate space, wondering if I could be like them. Did I want to be like them? The eerie clanging of flag lanyards against the flagpole five feet from me sounded unearthly, even scary. My foot caught the edge of the flagpole base. I almost did a faceplant in a mud puddle but regained my footing. I quickly glanced back at those uniformed guys inside King Hall.

"Easy does it, Rod."

"Easy? I don't think so, Dad. You get to drive away. Meanwhile, I get to stay locked up in this prison for the next sixteen weeks. I do not like the setup." I was gnawing on a fingernail, anxious to move but not wanting to go inside.

"No, it won't be easy. I didn't mean it that way. If you want it badly enough, you'll see it through." Dad's eyes bore in at me.

Nodding slightly, I hugged Dad goodbye, adding I'd be home when allowed to leave the base on liberty. "Will you please take care of Mom? She looks so unhappy."

He looked past me, his hands clapping me on both shoulders. I watched my father climb back into his car and drive away, slowly splashing through puddles of frozen water into the night. Show time.

Exhaling deeply, I looked ahead, pushing open the glass entrance doors to King Hall. With a duffel bag over my right shoulder and Navy orders in my pocket, I told myself to look confident. The foyer had a dazzling white tile floor, gleaming brass fixtures, and a sparse but orderly overall appearance. Someone was working very hard at cleaning, waxing, and shining all this stuff. It didn't occur to me that I was about to become one of many hard-working janitors in King Hall for the next four months.

I pushed the inner door open, stumbling into the foyer, eyeballing all five officer candidates standing at attention on the quarterdeck. It replicated those on Navy ships worldwide, whether in repair status in Philly or on a liberty port visit in Hong Kong. The quarterdeck watch team handled all the ship's ceremonial, safety, and security functions when in port. These watchstanders in King Hall meant business, silently standing erect and looking exceptionally professional. They reminded me of the officer recruiting posters at Seattle Navy Recruiting District. This was real. I was finally here – although I wished I wasn't. I approached the front desk and said, "I'm Rod Haynes. I'm supposed to report here by midnight. My orders told me, see, right here? Now, what do I do?" I leaned away, shielding my mouth with my left hand. All eyes bore in at me, the faces unmoved.

The OC (officer candidate) in charge silently recorded my arrival in the official deck log. He sized me up, frowning. Using the tip of his pen, he pointed to a nearby spot. "Good God, you are a mess. Back up. No, don't walk on the mat. Stand right there at attention. Wait 'til your platoon leader gets here. Put your gear down. Keep your mouth shut. Your eyes should be locked straight out towards that flagstaff outside. Do it now."

"Thanks, I need a bathroom—"

"I said, no talking. Park your butt right there. NOW," the OC said in a sharper voice, his pen again pointing towards the spot. "Stand at attention. Look straight ahead. DO NOT SPEAK AGAIN. Go!"

I sullenly stood where directed, tasting that last vodka gimlet, now wishing I'd slammed one more drink down before leaving the restaurant.

Puddles of rainwater were collecting around my shoes. I tried covering them, but the liquid pools slowly expanded. The OC picked up the phone and spoke a few words in a low voice before quickly placing the phone down and resuming his rigid position. The mechanized human robots from Woody Allen's movie *Sleeper* came to mind. I almost chuckled but didn't. Reverting to my old high school class clown antics would not find favor among these sullen mannequins.

Five excruciating minutes passed. A female OC dressed in a black uniform with white leggings suddenly appeared on the second level of the stairs. Staring down at me with an exaggerated sneer, she stomped down the steps and, standing directly before me, looked me up and down once, twice. Her eye and eyebrows were narrow slits, her lips clenched. It was like she was inspecting a piece of furniture or a vase for cleanliness. Her cap was pulled down over her eyebrows in a menacing way. She was escorted by a male who was also in a sharp-looking uniform. He stood back, to her left, appearing just as unhappy as his female partner.

She said, "Follow me. Keep your mouth shut. Move!" We hurried up two floors and entered the double-glass doors, nearly colliding with two people on their knees, intensely focused on the step by the door sill. They were holding toothbrushes, repeatedly thrusting them in a bucket of soapy water standing between them. They ignored us as they kept scrubbing. The female OC said quickly, "We call 'bathrooms,' 'heads,' and 'passageways,' 'p-ways.' Get rid of your sand-crab talk, or you'll be in trouble. Got that?" I nodded, pretending to understand whatever she had just said.

Balancing my gear on my shoulder made it hard to keep up with my escorts. I kept switching it between my two shoulders. Echoes of directions and threats filled King Hall, followed by loud, unified responses from officer candidates standing in multiple passageways.

We passed by two more p-ways, descending two sets of stairs – my escorts called them "ladders" – snaking our way towards my company quarters. It was now time to meet Yankee Company, Class 8002. The male OC stopped suddenly and turned to the left, facing a closed door. Following close behind, I stumbled into him, almost dropping my seabag on his perfectly polished shoes. He hissed, "God damn it, back off!"

Later that week, I learned that the guy escorting me was in the middle of his first day as a D.I. – a drill instructor – and that he was trying his best to put on a tough act. I bought every bit of it.

He growled, "Here's your home for the next four months. Get used to it. Stand by for heavy rolls." Heavy rolls. Another new phrase to ponder.

The drill instructor announced his presence in the room we were facing by pounding twice on the closed door. Shoving it open, he stepped inside, gesturing for me to stow my gear in an empty locker. The drill instructors disappeared as I looked up and locked eyes with my new roommate standing at attention. He was overweight and sported a jagged crew cut and a crooked smile. He suddenly thrust his hand at me. "Hello, my name is Marvin Schwartz. I will be your roommate for the next four months. Where are you from?" It was like he was speaking through his nose. This was odd.

I shook Marvin's hand, sharing my name with him.

Schwartz quickly launched into a long, irritating speech about his wonderful college, New Jersey "the Garden State," his 1972 Mercury Cougar roadster, his adoring mother, a wicked ex-girlfriend, the weather outside, corns on his feet, study habits, and his secret ambition to become an admiral. Somewhere in there, he insisted Iran should be nuked for messing with America. I melted into myself, my mood plummeting. I was now really concerned, recalling *Cybil*, the woman with 16 personalities, the one Sally Field portrayed in a movie. At least this guy was only channeling three people. He was built like John Candy, the affable, overweight Canadian comedian in the film *Uncle Buck*. His voice mimicked Dan Ackroyd's annoying Conehead character on *Saturday Night Live*. Lastly, his personality recalled the guy playing the ukulele on television's *Laugh-In* when I was young, Tiny Tim. I rapidly took stock of my situation. Things were grim. I randomly drew a confirmed weenie as my roommate to help me navigate the next four months of training hell. Then, out of nowhere, Mom's favorite lecture when I was nine years old silently presented itself: "Rod, I want you to be nice." *Sorry, Mom*, my mind answered back. How about this: *Mr. Marvin from New Jersey, will you please just shut the fuck up?* But I said nothing. Maybe Marvin came with an on-off switch. Nope.

I opened my seabag, pouring its contents onto my bed – which I later learned was called a "rack" – to transfer them into a small bureau. I pulled off my soaking wet sweatshirt, rummaging in my bag for a towel, stumbling back as I lost my balance. My new roommate stared at me wide-eyed. Schwartz realized I was drunk. I steadied myself by leaning on a footlocker, looking down at my feet, thinking this was all wrong. I reverted to panicking. Disgust followed. My morale crumbled like a dry saltine cracker in a clenched fist.

I'd known this guy for, what, all of three minutes. I was already prepared to duct-tape his mouth shut and shove Marvin right into his locker and lock it. I contemplated running back to the front of the building and grabbing the phone from the Gestapo guy in charge, explaining I needed to place an urgent call. I would demand Joey DeConstanza come and pick me up at the Broken Keel dive bar in Newport in thirty minutes. I'd wake up in the morning in my bed, pretending nothing was wrong, thinking of how I'd manufactured one more insipid mistake in my disheveled life. Maybe moving to Arkansas was what I should do next. Nobody would look for me there. All these jumbled thoughts raced through my mind as I hurriedly finished dressing. Still, Marvin would not be quiet, not for a minute. We were rudely – I was secretly relieved – interrupted by the slam of a door being kicked open at the far end of our p-way. My head was pounding just then. Two D.I.'s – one of them I recognized as my female escort from earlier – came striding in, yelling for everyone to, "Get the hell on the line. Move! Move! Move!" I pulled a dry sweatshirt over my damp head, jamming my feet into my soaking-wet loafers.

Schwartz and I bolted outside, throwing ourselves up against the bulkhead outside our room, one on each side of the door. Thirty or forty officer candidates joined Marvin and me, with three sets of female roommates not separated from the men. I later learned two sets of women roommates, all four reasonably attractive, lived a few doors down the hall.

The booze was wearing off. I badly needed to take a leak right away. Arriving in King Hall was shocking enough. Schwartz's non-stop gibberish compounded my headache exponentially. The female D.I. yammered about regulations, uniforms, timelines, restroom visits, exams, books, and urine tests. The sound level of her voice was slightly below screeching, firing a series of agonizing lightning bolts straight through my head. I was bewildered, confused, upset. This was a bad idea.

A pudgy man with slick black hair and a tall cowlick like Alfalfa from the old *Our Gang* television series stood at attention directly across from my spot. He stared straight at me, smiling ever so slightly. The two leaders were hollering non-stop at the far end of the hall when he whispered and nodded toward Schwartz, "I see you just met your boy, Schwartz. Great shipmate there." He sniffed the air and stared into my eyes as I looked away, trying to be inconspicuous. "Say, son, tell us how many drinks you had tonight. Your eyes look cock-eyed. Are you shit-faced right now?

Uh-oh, you know that ain't good. Don't let these dicks find out you're four sheets to the wind."

Feigning surprise, I whispered back, "Sorry, what do you mean?"

From the corner of my eye came the flash of a uniform. One of the two DIs was directly in my face, yelling, "You there, the drowned rat we picked up ten minutes ago. Who said you could talk?"

"Uh, nobody did, sir? Sorry," I whispered. I wish he'd back off; he was crowding me.

He said, "Shut your pie hole." He immediately spun around and marched down the hallway, issuing another long, rambling set of instructions. Most of it I heard, but none of it made sense.

The two D.I.s ordered us back to our rooms. Not five minutes later, they again instructed us to get out on the line, only to dismiss us quickly, within thirty seconds. We stood inside our rooms awaiting an encore. It came shortly. These two overexcited jokers were getting on my nerves.

"Yankee Company, Class 8002, get on the line. NOW! NOW! NOW!" Back we went to the p-way, where we absorbed five more minutes of information issued at warp speed. This drill of exiting and entering our spaces went on and on for maybe six or eight more times that first night. We all kept yelling, "Yes, Ma'am. Yankee Company Class 8-0-0-2," repeatedly. I'd had enough. There was no purpose to this. I wanted to piss and then sleep. That, and for Schwartz to volunteer to go back to New Jersey. Right now. I'd buy his goddamn bus ticket myself.

Our tormentors gave us seven minutes to "shit, shower, and shave." As I brushed my teeth, Alfalfa approached me, grinning. "Hey, Bud. Name's D.J. Conklin, from Paducah, Kentucky."

I frowned. "Rod Haynes," I answered warily. "Forgive me if I don't thank you for helping make my life suck tonight. You don't play nice."

"Now listen, Bud, *you're* the one who showed up here wasted. That ain't on me." D.J. grinned. "Welcome to Hell Week. Do exactly what they tell you, and yell at the top of your lungs. You can't do nothin' right no matter what you say or do. All of us are in for a week of abuse; there's no escapin' it. Pretty soon, it'll calm down, like it did for us at Great Lakes boot camp. Those D.I.s got to get themselves through OCS, too, you know. They'll get bored yelling at you."

"What makes you so smart?" I should have been furious with the guy, but something about him made me smile inside despite my wanting to punch his lights out. He was jolly, like Santa Claus. And extremely confident.

D.J. laughed. "I'm enlisted, a Second-Class Gunners Mate who got my own nasty case of the stupids and decided to become a naval officer. But I'll be tacking on my butter bars in mid-July right alongside you. We'll be fine, you'll see." He laughed again. Butter bars were the single gold bar insignia ensigns wore on their collars as brand-new naval officers.

"You know, it weren't too smart showing up here after drinkin', 'specially the first night. Gotta admit it's something I would done, too, if I had the chance, but my wife came to Newport with me, and I can't be doing that, at least not yet. First impression of you is good, which is a plus you'll appreciate later. Wait 'til we get some liberty, then we'll do some serious steaming: navy talk for going out and raisin' hell. For now, just keep your head low, watch what I do, and do it. And for God's sake keep that trap of yours shut. Get moving..."

"All right already, all right. I'm trying to decide whether I like you. I'm leaning toward I don't want you within fifty feet of me for the next four months." As I spoke, I stood back from his face, doing my best to scowl.

"That's your loss, Bud, 'cause I can help you if you let me. You got to toughen up. Act smart. Stay low. One last thing, Rod. Your boy Schwartz already pissed off his shipmates, and he's only been here six hours. He's slow and he can't march good, and he won't shut his yapper for nobody. We *all* got ourselves a project on our hands with Schwartz. He'll be a real burden on you, not having a good roommate to help you get you through this. But I will help if you let me. If not, that's okay, too."

I made an ugly face. "Wanna trade roommates?"

"Not on your sorry-ass life, not on his, neither." D.J. laughed a deep belly laugh. I decided I liked him after all.

At 0200 hours, we were told to turn in and be ready to rise in the morning. I collapsed face down into my rack, with Schwartz already loudly snoring ten feet away. He sounded like a walrus with a head cold. I closed my eyes and immediately conked out.

Senior Chief Sherman

The frenetic pace of Hell Week eased five days later. The daily routine would remain highly stressful throughout the four-month course, but now the emphasis was on learning to be a naval officer. Classroom sessions, practical training, and military drills replaced the endless stream of verbal abuse. The shock-treatment phase was history. The senior class of Yankee Company became our helpful mentors; those who tormented us the most that first week became our closest advocates. Darren, who yelled at me the first night after D.J. Conklin set me up, was a decent human. He said I was hilarious. I shrugged.

Yankee Company lived on the first deck of King Hall in the p-way closest to the water. The view outside my window was of the lower Narragansett Bay, just north of where the bay met the Atlantic Ocean. Each day, I looked outside. In 1944, Jack Kennedy graduated from Harvard and was stationed at Melville weapons testing grounds near King Hall. My room overlooked the body of water where he and his colleagues practiced operating Patrol Torpedo Boats before shipping overseas. JFK and the crew of PT-109 fought the Japanese Imperial Navy. He won multiple U.S. Navy awards for his exemplary leadership.

The next evening, at dinner, an officer candidate wearing his service dress blue uniform strode into the center of the hall. "Officer Candidate Roderick Haynes, Yankee Company," he said. "Front and center!"

I was with the rest of Yankee Company at the far end of the hall, eating a meal of meatloaf and noodles. My mind was rapidly compiling to-do checklists and memorizing nautical terms, oblivious to the OC's announcement.

D.J. Conklin nudged my elbow, murmuring with his head down, "Hey, that boy's lookin' for you, Bud. Git moving."

"What now?" I asked wearily before it suddenly came to me. "Oh, shit. I'm late for watch!"

The bulletin board in our p-way contained everyone's watch schedule. There were no reminders. We were to report to the quarterdeck fifteen minutes early to assume the watch, attired in the uniform of the day – all-black uniforms like what they wore the night I arrived at King Hall.

Slowly raising my hand, I stood up and sighed, "Yes, I'm Haynes." All four hundred pairs of eyes in the mess hall turned towards me. I whispered to D.J., "Stow my tray for me. I'm screwed. See you in a month."

The OC stalked over towards me, looking at me with contempt. He shouted, "You're in deep trouble, pal. You're thirty minutes late for your first watch. They got three of us out looking for you. Get moving." His thumb jabbed towards the exit.

We double-timed it out of Ney Hall amidst nervous laughter and excited chatter. Officer candidates took sadistic pleasure in seeing their shipmates catch hell, even if the targeted OC was from their own company. It temporarily took the heat off the group. The next morning, I was ordered to report to the chief petty officer in charge of Yankee Company, Tommy Sherman. His office was on the fourth floor of King Hall.

"Officer Candidate Haynes, Class 8002, reporting as ordered, Senior Chief. Request permission to come aboard," I yelled, slapping twice on the hatch from the outside, my hand stinging. His office door was wide open. I stood at attention, trembling, eyes straight ahead.

"Get your ass in here, front and center, you whale carcass," the senior chief bellowed. He sat in a swivel chair, his back to me, staring at the parade grounds four floors below. I glanced at his reflection in the window, watching as he stroked his chin. "Now, let's see," he said evenly. "I want to know why you were late for watch yesterday."

Ships plaques, framed commendations, and a sizeable crossed-cutlass emblem covered the back wall. Senior Chief Sherman was an enlisted surface warfare specialist. D.J. Conklin had mentioned his Navy campaign ribbons, and warfare badges a few days before.

I realized I'd been asked a question. "No excuse, Senior Chief, I just made a minor mistake, and it won't—"

The senior chief's voice exploded, echoing down the hall. "First God damn watch in the United States Navy, and you decide eating God damn meatloaf and noodles is more important than being at your appointed place of duty on time! You're just a fine piece of work, ain't you? Mighty fine, I say. You know what we do with shit-birds like you?"

I remained at attention, nervously watching the senior chief. He spun around in his chair and began rolling a pencil back and forth on his desktop. He looked up at me, his eyes flashing. Lowering his voice, he said, "Cage them eyeballs, Officer Candidate Haynes. You are at attention. Lock 'em straight ahead. Taking time off 'cause you forgot something, don't want to come to work, or whatever excuses you got, don't cut it aboard a Navy warship in my fleet. You get me, mister?"

Senior Chief Sherman leaned forward on his knuckles, his face twelve inches from my chin.

"Yes, Senior Chief," I said, wishing he would stop shouting. Why couldn't he—

"I don't believe you *do* understand, Officer Candidate Haynes. I have something that may teach you not to be so stupid. Or maybe it won't. Get over here. See that parking lot down there? Look familiar?"

I walked over to the window and glanced outside. The senior chief was pointing to where we had been practicing our marching maneuvers for the entire week. I returned to my original position, standing at attention. "Affirmative, Senior Chief."

"You will report there at 1300 hours on Saturday afternoon. Bring your piece with you. After you march, both your room and your uniform get inspected. Your roommate does too, so you tell him I said that. The uniform of the day is the service dress blue uniform. Remember: you and your room get inspected – not just you!" The senior chief nodded towards the window. "Remember that white line in the parking lot? You were walking on it yesterday."

"Yes, Senior Chief."

"You will march back and forth on that line 'til I say otherwise. Then you will shine all them toilets in the head while your shipmates are downtown drinking beer on liberty."

I wanted out of OCS. Who needed this chickenshit nonsense? This loudmouth son of a bitch wasn't about —

"I ain't gonna send some boot ensign who can't even make it to his first watch on time out to my Navy until I straighten that officer candidate out before he gets there. And I do love problem children needing fixin'." Senior Chief Sherman raised three fingers, showing that three unfortunate officer candidates were required to complete the program twice in two years. "I'm lookin' for someone new to go through the program twice these days. I love retreads. You want to be my latest retread? I need a new project. I'm bored."

"Uh, no, Senior Chief. I don't want to. No, definitely not."

"I'll say this one more time. *I own your ass* 'til July 10. If I hear any more bad reports about you, if it's classroom grades, drilling, or leadership screw-ups, you and I will talk again. If you fart too loud or keep flunking them room inspections, or I hear you were goofing off during drill, I guaran-damn-tee you, this talk today will seem like picking daisies in a cow pasture. Do you get my drift, son?" His breath was foul, reeking of cigarettes and strong coffee, and he had at least three cavities in his back teeth.

"Yes, Senior Chief."

"Well, I don't believe you do, not one bit. Get out. You just pissed me off and now my morning coffee tastes shitty. Get outta here!"

He took a swig from his mug, his eyes locked on me. I did an abrupt about-face and marched out of his office, feeling shattered and humiliated. I felt like leaving Newport, yet I knew there was no running this time.

Sleet March

The blustery, full-force nor'easter hovering over King Hall my first ten days at OCS was still there on Saturday afternoon. I stood in the parking lot, stiffly cradling the butt of my drill rifle in my right hand, pointing the barrel straight up. My "piece," was issued two days after I arrived at OCS. It was not a functional weapon but strictly intended for drills only. Senior Chief Sherman ordered me to begin marching at precisely 1300 hours, pending further instructions. Cupping their chilled hands, two sailors laughed and smoked cigarettes while pointing at me, their car parked along Narragansett Bay. As I stepped off, I coughed twice. I felt like hell. The past week was physically and mentally the worst one so far. Hell Week ended a few days before. Was I already at my breaking point? Oh, how I loathed that bastard Senior Chief Sherman.

The cold and wet conditions at OCS caused the "Newport Crud," a lung infection every officer candidate contracted at least once in non-summer months. They warned us the night of my arrival that the constant exposure to the outdoors added to the stress, made us all susceptible to the Crud. We traveled in close quarters, twelve to fourteen hours daily, making the illness easy to spread. As luck would have it, Schwartz was the first in Yankee Company to contract the Crud. He duly passed it around to the rest of his shipmates.

I woke up one morning with a hacking cough, a runny nose, and a raging fever. I stopped by the infirmary. The corpsman confirmed my suspicions: "Yup, no question, Officer Candidate Haynes. The Crud's gonna get worse for you and your shipmates. A lot worse. Welcome to Newport in March. Take these pills and follow the instructions on the label exactly. Give it three to five days. Maybe you'll get it twice." Gobbling them down, I quickly rejoined Yankee Company, marching outside in a chilly, misty morning. My fever broke several days later. The Crud cycled among us four or five times at OCS.

As I marched alone that day, a group of aggressive seagulls stood in a military formation around the area, hoping for a snack. I detested their scavenging attitudes. Fucking birds. I seriously considered lowering my rifle and charging them with a banzai yell, but then I felt a pair of eyes scrutinizing me from on high. I told myself to keep moving or risk facing Senior Chief Sherman again on Monday morning. My weekends would consist of marching around the parking lot until commissioning day if I didn't straighten up. I felt sorry for myself. I was being singled out, and it wasn't fair.

An hour passed. The wind subsided, the sleet momentarily tapered off. A bright white sun peeked through the heavy gray clouds for twenty minutes. I went on marching without rest. The blisters on my feet popped and bled. I heard a low whistle from a line of small trees against Ney Hall. Swinging around to start another sequence on the white line, I glanced off to one side without moving my head. D.J. Conklin stood in the trees in civilian clothing, smoking a cigarette cupped in his left hand. He was smiling broadly.

I could barely hear his voice over the wind. "Hey, Bud, how you holdin' out?" D.J. called out. "That piece of yours gettin' heavy?"

I shot D.J. a thumbs up as I cradled the gun, winking as I spun around and continued marching down the white line.

"Chin up. Think 'bout something else, you know, keep your mind off your troubles. We'll get some brews next weekend at the O-Club. Don't stop, don't give Senior Chief Sherman the pleasure of counseling you again on Monday. 'Bye now."

My wet, cold clothing caused me to shake violently. My face and hair were flecked with melting sleet and frigid to the touch. My hat, known as a cover in navy jargon, had a crust of ice ringing it. My shoes were soaked through, my bloody blisters barking pain. "The O-Club" was the Newport Naval Officers' Club, a familiar boyhood haunt. What fond memories I had about that place.

The Club was a boxy, white building perched precariously on a crag overlooking Narragansett Bay, close to the Naval War College. In summer, visitors enjoyed panoramic views of the bay from the club's dining room windows on three sides, including a close view of the massive Newport Bridge. I watched its three-year construction, from 1966 to 1969. Then, right after it was done, Richard Nixon sent all the warships home-ported in Newport to other home ports. Southern Rhode Island lore had Nixon acting to exact revenge on New England for choosing JFK over him in 1960. His vindictiveness destroyed the local economy, leaving vacant houses with peeling paint and overgrown grass, resembling a post-nuclear war American landscape, with deserted streets, ruined buildings, and no people anywhere.

When I was a kid, we went to the O-Club for brunch on Sundays, guests of my Uncle Bob. The buffet always featured shrimp, Yorkshire pudding, and thick slabs of roast beef. It was almost like we were royalty.

Ships of all shapes and sizes moved in and out of the narrow opening to the Atlantic Ocean. I observed ship traffic from the comfort of the O-Club. My cousin Jimmy was an accomplished small sailboat racer in all four New England seasons. He loved the "frostbite sailing" club he first joined as a young boy. This area was perfect for honing your sailor skills unless large tankers or container ships appeared without warning, creating treacherous wakes as they lumbered their way northward through Narragansett Bay to Providence. Darrell's father piloted these vessels for a living here and in Portland, Maine.

In the foyer entrance area of the Club, oversized oil paintings of past American naval war heroes greeted visitors. I inspected their dress uniforms with gold epaulets, long sashes, carved swords, and arranged medals. The cuffs had gold braid signifying their rank. Warships sat in the harbor, flags waving, their crews dressed in white and blue uniforms, all busy with tasks. Where were those ships headed next? To battle? To the South Pacific? Was there rough weather ahead? Mom regularly mentioned – though I did not need reminding – that navy blood flowed in our family's veins. For as long as I could remember, she proudly displayed pictures of her father wearing his military dress uniform in prominent places around our house.

Sleet woke me from my dream state. I wasn't a kid anymore – trudging through a flooded parking lot at a naval base in March. A deep-seated gloom permeated my thoughts. I resisted it, concentrating on where I was and why I'd taken on this OCS challenge. The mental tug of war I'd foreseen in Seattle was in full force now. The next four months promised to be an extremely tough go. Like D.J. told me, I had to stay sharp and rely on my shipmates. I vowed to see this through, no matter what. At 1600 hours, a junior enlisted sailor stepped out of King Hall, slowly approaching me through the pounding sleet in the gloomy twilight. Could I finally go inside? Three freaking hours marching in a parking lot in a sleet storm in Newport, Rhode Island, was too much.

"Officer Candidate Haynes," he said. "Senior Chief Sherman directs your return to the barracks for inspection in thirty minutes. He said put on your service dress blues. He ordered you to clean the head on the second deck tonight after the inspections. I recommend you be on time, Officer Candidate Haynes."

The young man ran back through the frozen rain into King Hall. My sleet march in the company of seagulls was almost over. It had been a hellish three-hour ordeal. Twenty minutes later, Schwartz passed his inspection. Our room looked great, thanks to him, but I could not get out of my wet uniform because my body was convulsing. My rain-soaked shoes were ruined. Senior Chief Sherman shouted that I was a disgrace and flung the mattresses and bedding around the room. He spun around and stomped down the passageway, muttering threats. I had the urge to hit him in the back of his head with a leadership manual I had hidden under my pillow just before marching that afternoon. Senior Chief Sherman was now my sworn enemy. I was seething and exhausted.

Later that evening, after cleaning the head, I was sulking in my room alone. Schwartz left in a huff right after Senior Chief Sherman trashed our racks. I almost felt sorry for bringing these miseries on Schwartz, who was entirely innocent here. Then, D.J. Conklin stuck his head inside the door, leaning against the entrance frame. "Hey, Hay-ness, what's your major malfunction?" He reeked of bourbon.

"Hey, D.J., how many did you have tonight? Why aren't you at home with your wife?"

More than a few prior enlisted personnel brought their families to temporary housing either on base or in town while at OCS. They saw them on weekends when everyone else went on liberty.

"Had a big ol' fight with her. She threw me out this afternoon, so I came by to see you march out there. You need to work on your cadence, son. This is what six tumblers of Old Grand Dad and a few draft beers will do for you." He slumped further down against the door frame.

"Right now, you're the one looking trashed. Seriously, man, thanks for being out there today, D.J. You could get your ass in a sling pulling stunts like that."

D.J. waved off my comment. "Nah. I'm prior enlisted. I got this handled real good. Bye-bye, now." He stumbled into his room, quietly shutting the door behind him.

I continued shining my belt buckle and shoes, preparing for another inspection in the morning. Given all that happened in those early days at OCS, I should have felt awful. But I got through that miserable day I marched in the sleet. I decided I needed to take each day at OCS on its terms. That's how I would survive this training crucible, day by day. I wasn't about to let that blowhard Senior Chief Sherman get the satisfaction of making me start OCS all over again. I could make it on the first try. I knew I could despite that flaming asshole Senior Chief Sherman.

OCS Routine

I quickly became close friends with D.J. Conklin and Peter McIntyre from Holyoke, Massachusetts. Like D.J., Pete had a great sense of humor, filling my critical need in otherwise bleak surroundings. Peter and I got along so well because we barely cut the mustard in class. Marvin Schwartz was the top student, drawing even more wrath from his shipmates. Everyone acknowledged his brilliance, but his incessant jabbering quickly became too much for Yankee Company. I was seriously concerned about how Schwartz would fare in the Fleet. His weird habit of never shutting up was genuinely worrisome. D.J. believed Schwartz was not fit to be a naval officer. His hostile take on Schwartz poisoned the minds of the rest of Yankee Company. I requested permission to move to a new room three weeks after arriving. I told myself that a change of venue might help me get a leg up. Everyone knew I sought distance from Schwartz. I didn't care what he thought about me or anyone or anything else. I was no longer speaking to him. Schwartz spent the balance of OCS living alone in his room. I did similarly, far down the p-way, where I didn't have to see him every waking moment of the day.

My classmates were all exceptional individuals – academically astute, highly motivated overachievers, and extremely competitive. More than a few were valedictorians in their college graduating classes. The group included a cowboy from Arizona, a political aide from DC, an MBA from Michigan, an Iowa farmer's son, a police officer from Miami, and a Cajun pre-law student from New Orleans.

I couldn't resist comparing myself to the rest of the Company. I was at rock bottom if academics were the sole barometer of success. I told myself everyone had shortcomings, though I saw few flaws in D.J. Conklin beyond his apparent love affair with alcohol. I observed my shipmates tackling the challenges before every officer candidate, things like marching the company to class or directing them in close-order drills. I showcased my leadership skills any time I could, on the athletic field or Narragansett Bay, conducting formation drills underway or running the physical exercise routines that were part of daily life. I was as talented a runner as anyone else in Yankee Company, but I was never top-shelf material – just an above-average runner. Leading came naturally to me. D.J. Conklin grudgingly acknowledged, "You did pretty good today, Rod, but your grades still stink. You gotta pick it up, son." That comment from the guy I respected most at OCS cut me, but I knew it was true, and D.J. rarely pulled punches. Whenever test results were posted, I wanted to hide in my room in King Hall. I felt inadequate, and out of place.

As the weeks passed, some officer candidates became romantically involved. At least two marriages in Yankee Company were threatened when commissioning day rolled around. Perhaps they had marital problems before coming to OCS. I knew of one marriage resulting from our four months of training. I couldn't understand how those couples gauged their suitability for each other inside the high-stress bubble of OCS. The close monitoring of actions and thoughts caused me to believe the relationships at OCS were a way of unwinding. Marching around the Newport Navy base wasn't a reliable test of a lasting relationship. Running off to a hotel near the base on weekends was an escape valve from the relentless pressure we were all up against.

On the weekends, King Hall was like college, with couples taking over the rooms and the roommate having to find another place to sleep. This was long before OCS got a lot stricter about socializing on weekends. These days, U.S. Marine drill instructors control every aspect of officer candidates' lives. The intensity of socializing, fraternization, and interaction between the sexes was off the charts in 1980. It is no longer the case today. I was as guilty as the rest. Two favorite ways for us to blow off steam were drinking or having sex, or, with luck, one after the other.

We practiced helm and speed-control orders on diesel-powered YP – Yard Patrol – boats in Narragansett Bay. Training included sending and receiving flag and flashing light signals, radio communication, and maneuvering solutions. We adjusted to the movement of the ship, including the seasickness. On a day when the seas were incredibly rough, D.J. brought canned smoked mussels and cigars aboard the boat, eating the food right in our faces. Then D.J. lit his green stogie. Ten minutes after leaving the piers, ten or twelve OCs turned various shades of green and heaved their guts over the side. I was not one of them. I felt queasy, but Uncle Bob had taken us out on Narragansett Bay on his small motorboat every summer when I was a kid. I knew how rough the conditions could become on Narragansett Bay, with little or no warning. I was ready for D.J.'s hijinks.

Yard Patrol Training, Narragansett Bay

    The OCS band played songs from movies like *Patton* and *Exodus*, John Phillip Sousa military marches, and other traditional military tunes. OCS had a talented group of officer candidates who excelled musically and academically. They had a large brass instrument and percussion section, perfect for our Pass-In-Reviews. The band's songs inspired us, even in our less-than-perfect marching method. Executing military formations was much easier when accompanied by live music, offering cadence and rhythm to our efforts.

    Marvin Schwartz was often placed out front as the company "guide on," the individual carrying the Yankee Company pennant. We adjusted our marching steps to Schwartz, who kept shuffling along a half-step out of sync, reminiscent of Curley's antics of *Three Stooges* fame. Schwartz once dropped the pennant in the middle of a sharp wheel to the right. D.J. Conklin sputtered curses at Schwartz beneath his breath while we turned before a large crowd gathering. Within the ranks, we bit our lips, shaking with laughter. Later that afternoon, Yankee Company was called out for making "a disgraceful mockery of the Pass-in-Review." Senior Chief Sherman called us "a pathetic, out-of-control clusterfucked group of losers." D.J. agreed. That aside, I was proud to be marching in the company of my shipmates, wearing my country's uniform. I knew my shipmates felt the same way.

D.J. Conklin always did well in class. He was brilliant and had five years of fleet experience under his belt. Schwartz excelled by memorizing textbooks, front cover to back. In some ways, D.J. came off as a *Deliverance*-like backwoods character from the famous movie, but that was misleading. He had the upbeat attitude of a high school cheerleader, though he despised early morning hours. His uniform appearance, grades, and leadership ability placed him at the top of the class. He had confidence, and he knew his Navy routine cold. I was envious when I wasn't admiring him.

My grades at OCS were mediocre at best; the same was true in the advanced officer training schools that followed later. OCS leadership always posted individual test scores in the p-way for public viewing. I typically finished in the bottom third; I failed the test a few times and had to retake it. One of the practices was having fellow shipmates evaluate our fitness for a Naval Officer role. Leadership, athleticism, likeability, and loyalty were all considered, among other traits. My peer evaluations usually put me in the top ten of the thirty-five officer candidates in Yankee Company. Schwartz inevitably brought up the rear. D.J. Conklin finished first, second, or third every time evaluations happened.

One of the best classes at OCS, in terms of pure fun, was ship handling. We underwent training in a Quonset hut containing a shallow cement swimming pool. Officer candidates drove plastic Navy ship models around the pool with remote-control devices. It helped us understand how ships responded to rudder orders at different speeds when approaching piers. Negotiating a tight channel with an offsetting wind was challenging. Those plastic models were barely different in appearance from those I played with in the bathtub when I was three years old. The significant difference was that these Navy models cost much money to build and maintain.

D.J. challenged me to a race between his destroyer and my frigate. We lined up our ships and slammed our remote-control speed sticks into "FULL SPEED AHEAD" mode. The corner was too sharp, and I didn't turn the rudder enough, causing the ship to crash into the pool's edge. The accident caused a superficial crack in the gray-colored plastic freeboard on its starboard side. Seconds later, I felt a fist grabbing my left arm. "Officer Candidate Haynes, you and your clown friend seem to like practicing collisions at sea. Ever been in one?"

"No, Chief. Sorry. I didn't mean any harm."

"This is not a bathtub. I ain't your mommy. You two dickweeds just caused serious injuries to sixty sailors on that ship who got no warning it was going to hit the pier at five knots. So, you wanna play like children, huh?"

"I'm sorry, Chief. It was foolish." *Good God, if Senior Chief Sherman got wind of this ... .*

The Chief turned and barked at the class: "'Sorry' don't cut it here. These models are expensive ship-handling training tools. They are not toys. Officer Candidate Haynes and Officer Candidate Conklin, you two jokers will report here Saturday afternoon. You will both learn how to repair ship models. Plan on spending four hours here. Got me?"

"Aye-aye, Chief," we muttered together. We spent Saturday repairing the model while the chief observed. D.J. was more familiar with the materials, so I stayed quiet and let him take charge. D.J. and the chief bantered back and forth while the chief ran a heat gun and paint over the crack, with D.J. handing him tools. No other repairs were necessary. The Chief's real intent was robbing us of a few hours of free time during the weekend. The two appeared to be buddies working on a Cub Scout project. I detected a relaxed familiarity between them, a rapport I never experienced with any chief at OCS. I was sometimes jealous of D.J., but I maintained a respectful silence at that moment.

Drill Instructor Duty

Every Saturday morning, there were athletic competitions between the companies, including track, swimming, and basketball. The "Olympics" would be held indoors if the weather outside did not permit racing or other outdoor competitions. Like everything else at OCS, they tabulated scores to determine winners and losers. At the halfway point, I gained respect from my shipmates when a new junior class was scheduled to arrive a few days later. We were battling Oscar Company that Saturday morning. Near the end of the competition, the organizers announced the relay race would determine the winner that day, the last event. The perimeter around the parade field before King Hall was approximately a third of a mile. Three males and one female ran on each company's relay team; each member was required to run a lap. I volunteered to run the anchor lap for Yankee Company.

We quickly fell behind on the first lap, then further behind after the second and third runners completed their legs. When I was handed the baton, I was sixty yards behind the lead runner, the situation seemingly hopeless. I grabbed the baton and got a jackrabbit start, closing fast on my opponent. I caught the runner in the last turn, blowing past him in the last twenty-five yards of the race, beating him going away. All of Yankee Company witnessed the "miracle finish." They hoisted me on their shoulders, carrying me off the field. It was my *Chariots of Fire* moment, a snapshot from my OCS life I would never forget. Something changed at that moment; I felt better about myself, even though it was just a foot race. The Company celebrated liberty in a downtown drinking establishment that night, with D.J. leading the charge. We felt much closer from that moment through commissioning day. Three days after the race, Yankee Company (the senior class) nominated six members as drill instructors for the incoming junior class. My name was on the list. I did not understand why I was among the chosen few.

Senior Chief Sherman summoned me to his office when he heard the news. "Well, now, Officer Candidate Haynes, the word is your shipmates think you should be a drill instructor. How the hell did that happen?"

"Senior Chief, I just heard about it. I don't know what to say. It feels great, something positive for a change."

"Maybe you done good for yourself since your march with them seagulls. I like to think you learned something. So, you got a boost from your shipmates. I heard the race on Saturday was close, and Yankee Company pulled it out. But I'm wondering if you can keep up with your books and be a drill instructor both at once. Being a D.I. is no excuse for screwing up in class. You're not doing good with your books, all the way along I been watching you. What do you think? Can you keep up? Don't blow smoke up my butt. Be honest."

"Senior Chief, everyone knows I'm not one of the smart ones at OCS. I rank in the bottom half with those tests. *Please* let me try this. It would be good for me. I want to practice being a military leader before I hit the Fleet. I need this. Please. Don't make get on my knees and beg you here."

Senior Chief was skeptical. "I don't know, Officer Candidate Haynes. You won't make it to the Fleet if your grades worsen. You don't have too much leeway right now, anyways. You made a little academic progress this month, but not a lot. Don't piss it away so you can yell at the new ones coming in. You still got six weeks to go. Most of that is in the classroom."

"I know, Senior Chief. I've got some expert help around here. They won't let that happen. And you can just fire me if I can't hack being a D.I."

Senior Chief Sherman looked me squarely in the eye. "Officer Candidate Haynes, remember this: it ain't up to D.J. Conklin whether or not you make it through here. You can't take him with you out to the Fleet. He's got his own business to take care of. You got to stand up and move forward on your own. Stop leaning on your shipmates to get you through. You either got what it takes, or you don't. By yourself."

"How did—"

Senior Chief Sherman laughed out loud. "You think I don't know about Conklin and you hanging together? I seen him talking to you that day you was marching in the sleet out there. I know about that. The enlisted guys keep me posted. Maybe I heard a few good things about you, but your grades always need improvement. Classwork is important here, but books aren't the only measure of leadership potential. Conklin says you'll probably be a decent leader of the bluejackets in the Fleet, so you got one positive thing in your corner. *Don't you get cocky.* I mean it.

I'll knock you down so fast—" Bluejackets were another name for enlisted personnel.

"No, I won't, Senior Chief. I promise. Please let me try. I can do it. You'll see how good a leader I can be."

Sherman leaned back in his chair, stroking his chin, his eyes narrowing. "Hmmm. I'm not sure you *can* keep your grades up and be a decent D.I. If I see you beginning to slip, even just an inch, I'm pulling you off D.I. duties. Got it? No whining, no excuses. No joke. You're slidin' on a razor's edge. And I don't give a shit that Conklin got picked along with you to do this D.I. stuff, too. Don't lean on him to get you through this."

"Yes, sir, Senior Chief."

"Don't give me that 'sir' crap. I ain't no officer. How many times I told you I work for a living?"

"Yes, Senior Chief. I understand."

"No, I'm not sure you do, leastways not yet. Dismissed. Get out of my space."

"Thank you, Senior Chief." I turned to leave, just stepping through the door.

"Oh, one last thing, Officer Candidate Haynes."

I stepped back inside his office and stood at attention. "Senior Chief?"

"You give 'em hell. And don't be a nice guy with the new chickadees. You ain't their friend. You're their leader. Remember I said that. Be a leader. Being liked don't matter, people can get killed if their leaders make mistakes. You get my drift or do I gotta spell it out for you?"

"Yes, Senior Chief. No need to explain, I got it loud and clear. Thank you." For the first time since my arrival at OCS, the senior chief wore what appeared to be a thin smile.

Ellen Kincaid

Halfway through OCS, I became what I had hated most. I was a drill instructor on the fourth floor, inflicting all the fear and abuse I could muster on many brand-new officer candidates in Yankee Company.

D.J. Conklin and I worked the first shift. He was running the show. I hoped to be like him someday if only a little. D.J. spewed volumes of information the new candidates needed at OCS and stuff they didn't need. Everyone was riveted by each word D.J. said. I stood watching the show, mesmerized. His shoes were impeccably polished, mine passably so. He perched his cover perfectly on his head, and he had starched his uniform impeccably, complete with rows of new ribbons. He scrutinized the candidates, his lips pursed, eyes narrowed. All had problems only D.J. could fix. D.J. wasn't shrill, he was never out of control. He had a presence that oozed professionalism. He was authority made flesh. I could not keep up with him. I stood in awe of my friend. He did most of it without screaming but was incredibly stern and nimble with his Navy knowledge.

What impressed me most was D.J.'s ability to shift in and out of his Drill Instructor character. One evening, just before we left the dining hall, D.J. said that effective leaders are excellent actors because that's their job, at the heart of what they do.

"Here's what I mean, Rod. Do you remember the movie *Patton*, where one of the staff officers pulled the General aside and made remarks they couldn't tell when he was acting and when he was not? Patton instantly replies, 'It isn't for them, or you, to know it. It's only important that I know.' See, that's the key, right there. Don't take things too seriously; you must know and trust yourself. You got the con. You are driving that ship. You show you don't know, you will lose their your subordinates; I promise you that. It happens quickly, then they don't respect you anymore." I nodded my understanding.

Two women did not respond to "Get on the line right now" instructions on the second day. I banged on the door and announced that a male was entering the space. Inside, I saw a beautiful blonde officer candidate sitting on the edge of her bunk, looking troubled, her roommate standing behind her. I walked up and growled, "You two ladies got a problem? Get your butts out on that line."

"Yes, uh, sir. We understand," the blonde replied.

I read her nametag. "So, what's your malfunction then, Miss Kincaid?" I stood over her with my arms crossed, trying to be intimidating.

"Well, uh, the thing is..." she stuttered. "I can't... you see..."

Her roommate quietly shut the door and grabbed my arm. "Look, Mr. Haynes, here's the deal. Ellen has her period. She needs to go to the head now 'cause she doesn't have any supplies. Get it?"

I stammered, then looked away. I could feel myself blushing. "You two stay right here. Nobody moves. That's an order." I ran out, grabbed D.J.'s arm, and dragged him to one side away from the group on the line. "Listen, D.J.," I whispered, "one of those ladies there has her period. What the hell do I do?"

D.J. paused. "Well, shit. Okay, Linda's in the office down the p-way. Go tell her." Linda Rios was one of our shipmates from Yankee Company. A female drill instructor was always on the floor whenever a male D.I. was in mixed company. Linda was all business and one of the best officer candidates in Yankee Company. I respected her immensely.

"Linda, I got a situation down the P-way with the two ladies in room 417."

"What's up, Rod?"

"Yeah, right." I shuffled my feet and pulled at my collar. "Uh, well, Ellen Kincaid has her... period. And I don't... what the hell do I do?"

"Start by taking a slow breath, Rod. It's under control. I got it." Linda left the room with her purse. Five minutes later, Ellen and her roommate were both standing on the line outside their room, taking the day's ration of abuse from Linda, D.J., and me.

The role of drill instructor was a fearsome responsibility. I wanted to feed the new officer candidates as much information as they could handle and more. I wanted them to learn the routine and how to get by, and I wanted to not do it by abusing them. I did not feel power hungry as a D.I., not that I was aware of.

Three weeks passed. On a late Saturday afternoon, I was alone drinking beer in the Brick Alley pub on historic Thames Street in downtown Newport. I felt a tap on my left shoulder and turned around. Ellen Kincaid was standing there, smiling. I'd seen Ellen from a distance maybe twice since Hell Week. She was easily the most attractive female at OCS, a slim and trim blonde with bright blue eyes. In all ways a stunningly beautiful woman.

"Hey, Mr. Haynes. Just wanted to say thanks for all you did. We made it through Hell Week."

"You're welcome, but we normally don't thank our D.I.'s until we're commissioned. I didn't say squat to mine. I'm glad that Hell Week is over. Grab a chair, have a beer." The only chair available was right next to me. Ellen sat down.

"Thanks. So, what part of the world do you come from, Mr. Haynes?"

"Ellen, my name is Rod. We're shipmates now. I grew up in a village called Limerock, fifty minutes north of here. How about you? Where do you call home?"

"Southern California." Ellen smiled her gorgeous smile as the bartender served up her beer. *My god,* I thought, *she is cute.*

"Yes, thank God Hell Week is over," she said.

I nodded. We clinked our glasses together.

"I saw you the other day at inspection when Alexander called you out front and spoke to you in front of the entire Battalion. You looked sharp, as always."

Thomas Alexander was the highest-ranking officer candidate at OCS. He was up front and center when our companies assembled on the parade field or in one of the indoor marching gymnasiums.

"Don't even mention that pig," she said, rolling her eyes.

"I'm sorry?"

"Alexander called me out front last Tuesday and I thought I was in trouble for flunking my uniform inspection. I was shaking when I marched up in front of two hundred people."

"What happened?"

"He says, 'Hey, what are you doing this weekend?'"

"No way. Are you serious?" I almost knocked my beer over, reaching for it.

"Can you believe it?" Our happy back-and-forth talk screeched to a halt.

I shook my head. "That's sexual harassment, period. Call him on it. Put the son of a bitch on report. You don't have to take that."

She grimaced. "Right. Third week at OCS and I'm putting the battalion commander on report."

"Have you heard about the female midshipman—"

Ellen interrupted, "The one who got chained to the urinal at Annapolis by her male shipmates?"

"Yeah, a few years back. More females are trying to become officers, so they go against two centuries of tradition. It's going to be tough for women for a long time. I wouldn't want to be going through that."

"All the women in the new class got a briefing on what's happening with women in the Navy. It's scary, some of the stuff they said. Let's talk about something else. Why are you here?"

"I already told you. I like to drink beer at the Brick Alley Pub. This place is one of my regular watering holes in Rhode Island."

Brick Alley Pub, Thames St, Newport RI

"Oh, stop it. You know I'm talking about OCS. Why did you come here?"

"Oh, who knows? Family tradition, love gone wrong, no money in the bank, overseas travel. Pick one. I'm not the first to come here for those reasons. The Navy just seemed to be a good choice. I don't regret it," I said. "So far, anyhow. Even with the bumps along the way. And I've hit a few – bumps, I mean. Tomorrow, you'll get a fresh set of answers out of me. I'm consistently inconsistent."

"I'm in it for the adventure," she said, laughing loudly.

"Sounds like you're getting some adventure already. And not the kind you want."

We talked for another hour, sharing information and having a relaxing evening together. I had found a girlfriend for the last six weeks at

OCS. Our chemistry was genuine, but we had very little time to develop a relationship at OCS. We both understood that any thought of permanence was unrealistic. We were both headed in very different directions. On weekends, I showed Ellen New England, an area she had never seen. We enjoyed each other's company. Aside from my relationship with her, I had my mind on a very special day coming up fast.

In time, orders to our first duty station finally arrived. Everyone in Yankee Company's senior class was eager as they came together in the auditorium and waited for their assignments to be projected. The Navy assigned me to the USS *Joseph Hewes*. I would be the Combat Information Officer on *Hewes*, a Knox-class frigate homeported in Charleston, South Carolina. I had no idea what a Knox-class frigate was. Still, D.J., assigned to a guided missile destroyer out of Norfolk, said that ship – a small antisubmarine warfare frigate – was an excellent place for a JO (junior officer) to cut his teeth at sea. The 1200 psi steam cycle used at the Newport Navy Base was modeled on the Knox-class propulsion plants. It was an engineering mockup for training engineering officers slated to serve on surface combatants. With only twenty-two officers on each of those frigates, I expected to gain a wealth of practical experience, unlike a cruiser or an aircraft carrier where there are many ensigns. I was thrilled. I couldn't wait to tell my family and friends about my final duty station assignment.

Met Café

The Met Café was a crumbling, hole-in-the-wall bar on Pine Street near downtown Providence's elevated junction of I-195 and I-95. Rowdy live music, loud conversations, and cheap drinks were the main staples at the Met. But it was the eclectic clientele that gave the place its one-of-a-kind reputation. Vintage Rhode Islanders loved the place to the point of making it a lousy fire trap due to overcrowding. The Met attracted diehard alcoholics gawked at by wide-eyed college students. Every day, characters like my buddies and I converged on the Met from all parts of the Ocean State, looking to party without breaking our budgets. The fact that it was centrally located in the tiniest state in the Union helped draw everyone in. I loved the place.

The floor in the Met was a mix of red and pink peeling linoleum, clashing with the green-colored bar. It gave off a cozy vibe. Deer heads and a marlin fish with a long spike on its nose hung precariously from the back wall. Random rows of old, crumbly dollar bills decorated the ceiling, tacked there years earlier. To my amazement, no one ever reached up and snatched those dollars. Everything behind the bar was covered in six inches of filthy dust, most noticeably the three long rows of antique booze bottles. The last time the deer or fish had dust cloths applied was probably before World War II.

The Met Café, Providence, RI., c.1976

Met Café

The Met hosted a weekly schedule of local rock bands, with mediocre talent making them ideal spectacles for the crowd to applaud. Our standards were low. On Wednesdays, there was no live music. Instead, we filled the jukebox with quarters to hear Rolling Stones and other rhythm and blues artists. NRBQ was a beloved rock band from Rhode Island who had recently moved up to a bigger venue at Lupo's Heartbreak Hotel, a short walk away. NRBQ had two or three of their singles in the Met's jukebox. The Jaguars were a hit at the Met Cafe, dressed in rags and playing and doing Chuck Berry's duck walk down the center of the bar, kicking over beers to the delight of patrons.

Conversation was next to impossible inside the confined interior of the Met while live music was playing. That was true even if you tried screeching into your buddy's ear. The two restrooms at the Met were tiny and disgustingly dirty, like everything else. You'd be stuck to it if you sat on a chair or placed your elbow on one table on the edge of the tiny dance floor. You almost had to ask a friend to bring a glass of water to free yourself from the grimy alcohol residue layering everything. We jokingly reminded each other to keep our vaccination records current before frequenting the Met.

Two weeks after meeting Ellen, she asked me to take her to Providence for the weekend. My parents had recently split, and my mother had moved to an apartment on the East Side of Providence.

I shared my plans for the following weekend with Ellen. "I want to show you where I hung out for six or seven years. You could call the place my training ground for going Navy."

"Is it a dance club? A bar?"

"Uh, yes and yes, I guess you could say that. Some think of the Met Café as a dance club or a bar. But it's more like a filthy dive in a rough part of South Providence where alcoholics get together and live bands march up and down the bar, kicking over beers. The booze is cheap, plus, they delouse the boys' and girls' toilets every six months, whether they need it. I can't describe the Met."

"You just did. And *this* is where you take your girlfriend to impress her?"

"Yeah. You'll never forget it."

"Great. Should I wear armor and bring bear-attack repellant?"

"Not necessary. The Navy gave you all your shots so if you go to Africa or the Amazon River basin, you're all set. I doubt you'll catch anything more deadly than smallpox at the Met, but it's possible. Wear a scuba mask. Oh, forgot to mention we're going there in our summer whites."

"No. We are *not* going there in our uniforms."

"Yeah, we are. Joey, Mikey, and Darrell bet I wouldn't attend the Met in my summer whites. We drink free if we walk in looking spiffy. You wear yours; I'll wear mine."

"You're welcome to do it. I'm out, no way."

"Oh, for God's sake. Give me a break. It'll be cool. The regulars will think it's some military raid or something. I'm doing it, that's final. I'm asking you kindly to join the fun."

"What are you trying to prove, Rod?"

"I want to go in there and blow some minds." I wasn't looking Ellen in her eyes.

"You just want to show off your naval uniform in a dive bar in South Providence." Ellen sighed, "My god. Okay, Mr. Big Shot, I'll think about it. But I'm out of there the first time someone grabs me anywhere. I mean it. I won't put up with some drunken slob pawing me when I'm in uniform. I don't accept any wandering hands on me when I'm in a bathing suit, either."

"They wouldn't dare grab the ass of a naval officer candidate. We'll leave if you get assaulted. And I'll punch the guy on the way out. Agreed?"

Ellen looked thoughtful, and then she agreed. "Alright. I'll see what the fuss is about. I've experienced enough dives to last a lifetime. I don't need to see one more, but I'll go for your sake. We can't embarrass the naval service."

Liberty came down at 1500 hours Saturday afternoon. We were off the base ten minutes later, heading north to Providence. Mom was grilling hamburgers and hot dogs on the balcony. A fresh garden salad sat in a bowl in the center of the dining room table, which was nicely set for dinner. My mother had the role of party hostess reduced to a fine art.

"Thank you for having us, Mrs. Haynes," Ellen said.

"Please call me Helen. You're more than welcome. I would think you want to sit back and relax for a bit. Aren't you two exhausted from all you've been put through?"

"I am tired, yes. Rod told me about your separation from your husband. I wanted to say I'm sorry; I know it's sensitive."

"Thank you. It's hard. I'm adjusting. Would you like a beer? Rod, can you...?"

"Sure, I'll get the drinks."

"Ellen, tell me about OCS," Mom said.

"I like it much better now. I'm doing pretty well with everything they toss at us. The first two weeks were hard. Did Rod tell you how we met?"

"No."

"He was my D.I., my drill instructor, the whole company's drill instructor, for the first week. He ran up and down the passageway, screeching threats, waving his arms around, issuing orders and directions with his buddies. We were all scared. Those guys were hyped up."

"That doesn't sound pleasant. Why did you yell at Ellen, Rod?"

"Mom, OCS isn't supposed to be fun. I wasn't yelling *at* Ellen specifically. I didn't know her then. I was yelling at everyone in sight. Every single one of us goes through Hell Week at the start. It's required."

"They picked you to drill the new candidates?"

"Yes. For whatever reason, Yankee Company thought I'd be a good leader with the new officer candidates arriving at King Hall. By the way, I haven't told you yet, but I got my orders this week."

"Oh?"

"Yeah, when you're halfway through the program, they tell you your final duty station. I'm going to be the CIC officer – that's the Combat Information Center – on USS *Joseph Hewes*. She's an anti-submarine frigate out of Charleston"

"So, you're going to Charleston to join a ship there?"

"No, not exactly. It's complicated. Before I go to *Hewes*, I must spend eight months on USS *John King* in the Philadelphia Navy Yard. She's homeported in Norfolk but got overhaul orders to go to Philly to get her repair work done."

"I don't understand why you're going to Philadelphia if you receive orders to a ship from Charleston."

"The Navy's got a ton of officers being commissioned right now, from the Academy, from Navy ROTC, and OCS. I'll leave Newport and go to Philly 'til next March, when a slot at Surface Warfare Officer School opens for me. I go back to Newport for six months. Then I report to *Joseph Hewes*, but she'll be in overhaul in Brooklyn by then."

Mom frowned. "So, you're going to Philadelphia, Newport, Brooklyn, and Charleston? How do you keep this all straight?"

"I write it down. All that traveling is specified in my orders. The cool thing is, I'm doing the same stuff I did in civilian life, ping-ponging all over. Only this time I get paid to do it. I'm worried I'll get behind my peers because they'll be at sea while I'm hanging around shipyards for the first year and a half."

"Can't you change your orders?"

"No. It's too complicated. My buddy D.J. Conklin told me I hit the jackpot getting assigned to *Hewes* while she is in overhaul in Brooklyn, anyway. Not sure what that means."

"I would like to visit Charleston," Mom said. "The last time I was there was when Daddy and Mother lived in town just before World War II. Bet it's changed."

"I'm pretty sure it's not what it was when you were a little girl. I'll give you a tour when you come, Mom."

Ellen and I drove to South Providence two hours later to check out the Met. It was downtown, ten minutes from Mom's apartment on the Upper East Side of Providence. I knew downtown streets quite well.

"Oh, I don't like this. Why do you want to go into this place dressed to the hilt?" Ellen asked as we drove into the parking lot. "We'll be filthy in three minutes."

"Watch and learn. My buddies said they'd meet us inside." We walked towards the entrance.

"Here goes nothing. Lead the way." I motioned her to go first, swinging the door open. The Met was packed, and it wasn't even 9:00 pm yet. I saw Joey, Darrell, and Mike leaning over their beers at the far end of the bar. I felt hundreds of eyes boring in on the two of us, though the crowd size was only 40 or 50 patrons. We pushed through the bedlam towards my friends, their jaws wide open as we drew close.

"Oh my God! Check this guy out!" Joey DeConstanza gushed, pounding me on my back. "Who are you and what did you do with my buddy Rod?" he shouted above the din. The jukebox blared The Kinks' *Lola*.

"Joey, Mike, Darrell, this is Ellen. She's at OCS with me," I shouted.

Mike stood behind her silently, pointing at her and mouthing, "Wow!"

I frowned, waving him off, saying, "Ellen, say hello."

"Hi everybody. It's like I know you all. Rod's told me all about you." Ellen replied.

"Anything of it good?" Darrell laughed.

"Of course. All of it, he says you three are the best," Ellen said.

"Did I say that? I musta been drunk." I interjected.

Joey handed Mike a ten-dollar bill. "Here, Mike. Get us five cold Heines. This round's on me. These two Navy recruiting posters are drinking free tonight. I can't believe this guy here is Rod. What about that piss test, by the way? Did you pass?"

"I guess so," I shouted. "They didn't say anything. What did you expect? What do you think I've been doing since March, Joey? You're the one who said OCS could be good for me. Remember that night at the Elk?"

"Yeah, yeah, I said it. I'm in shock. I was right, but I didn't think so when I said it. Look at these goddamn white shoes. It looks like you're selling ice cream from a truck. Or a mobster golfing at Kirkbrae Country Club."

"I know. The shoes are the *worst* part of this outfit. They get trashed five seconds after you put 'em on." A hand from behind reached over and snatched my cover off my head. "Hey, you! Goddamn it, give that back!" I hollered at a tattooed young lady who scampered off to the dance floor with my cover cocked sideways on her head. The crowd pointed and smiled their approval. I was immediately cut off from grabbing my cover back.

Darrell laughed. "I was waiting for that. Only two minutes and it's gone. Not bad."

I wasn't happy. "Go get the thing back, will you, Darrell? I'm out of uniform. She'll ruin it with beer stains. That cost me $37."

"In a minute. What did you expect, comin' in here dressed like this? Let it go. Somebody else woulda grabbed it, anyhow. Listen, I'll keep my eye on her. Lilly's not going anywhere soon."

"You know her?" I asked. "For sure?"

"*You* know her, Rod. Lilly's served you beer for the past three years. Don't you remember?"

"No. But it's okay if you say it is. Darrell, I can't leave without my cover."

"Just stop. Like I said, she's alright. Your hat's safe." My friend waved away my worry.

"It's not a 'hat,' Darrell. It's my cover."

"Hat, cover, whatever the hell it is, just calm down," he said. "Have another cold one. Ellen, what do you think of this place so far?"

"Never seen anything like it," Ellen replied. "Never."

"It kinda grows on you, like Providence grows on you, not unlike a jungle fungus. We like it. Ever been to Providence?"

"First time. Luckily, I got me a cute tour guide to show me around." Ellen patted me on the cheek affectionately.

"Providence's great. So is the *Met*," Darrell said. "Okay, so the town needs a facelift. It's still home for us." My buddies and I nodded our agreement.

"I told you guys we weren't scared of showing up like this," I said, wagging my finger.

"You made a statement, that's for sure," Mike interrupted.

"What statement did we make?" I asked.

"Not sure. But everybody's looking at you, so you musta made some kinda statement." Mike replied. Joey motioned me to follow him towards the exit sign.

"Ellen, I'll be right back. Joey wants to talk to me."

"Don't you go far. I *mean* it, Rod."

"Stay with Mikey and Darrell. You'll be alright," I replied, pointing at my friends. "I won't be long. Promise."

I followed Joey outside. No one cared if anyone drank in the parking lot. We each had fresh Heinekens. "What's going on, Joey?"

"You are."

"What do you mean?" I said. "You drunk?"

"No, no. C'mere, look at yourself." One side of the bar had a window that was painted black. No one could see inside or out. A nearby streetlamp reflected my image in the window. "I can't believe this is you." Joey pointed at my reflection.

"What are you talking about, man? Don't make fun of this uniform. I worked hard for it." I stood tall with my hands on my hips.

"Nobody's laughing at you. Holy shit. You went to OCS. You're about to get your commission. That's wild. Don't you think so?"

"Uh, yeah, it's cool." I looked across the parking lot. "Can I go in and dance with Ellen now?"

"That's the other thing," Joey said. "My god, Ellen's a knockout."

"Thanks for your approval. I'm flattered. You're wondering how I wound up with her, aren't you? Tell the truth, man."

"I didn't say that. I just said she's a beauty. But how did she fall for you anyway?"

"Half of Newport sees me with her, and they think, 'What did that guy do to get a looker like her?' I refuse to treat her like a Christmas tree ornament. She's a great person. We click physically and all other ways.

It's pretty good right in the middle of the nasty world of OCS. I'm lucky. She's a sweetheart."

"All I wanted to tell you was we think you did a good job at OCS," Joey slapped me on the back. "We think you're alright."

"I didn't do a 'good job.' I survived that hellhole, just barely. It's almost over. I'm glad to be moving on, away from Newport. Three weeks more."

"You look good."

"You don't look so bad yourself, but I'm already taken, sorry."

Joey laughed. We walked back inside. We were among the last to leave the Met that night. I got my cover back at closing time.

For years, the Met Café was our home away from home. Not long after we stopped going there, Johnson & Wales Culinary College bought the bar and surrounding tarmac to expand the school's parking. The old cinderblock building was demolished, and the lot was leveled. Finally, they marked the parking slots on the fresh layer of asphalt. The demise of the iconic Met Café was a traumatic moment. We grieved when the Met was no more.

Chicken City

I would never have made it through OCS without my mentor and best friend. D.J. Conklin made a vast difference for Yankee Company, Class 8002. Ten days before commissioning day, when D.J.'s life hit a rough patch, I tried returning the favor. We went to the trendy area of Newport and had beers at Pendergasts.

My friend hung his head low, tears trickling down his cheeks. He took his time wiping his eyes with his shirt sleeve, ignoring the gazes of bar patrons. "She threw me out," D.J. said. "Damn it. Can you believe that?"

"What is with you two? You've been married a year, and you're acting like it's been a decade," I replied, trying to get him to smile.

"Fuck it. Debbie's a hick from Kentucky coal country. I knew her sister in high school. I met Debbie when I was home at Christmas and knocked her up after one week. It was a shotgun wedding. A couple of my buddies back home went through the same thing. Happened to more than a few squids I know."

"It'll get better. It's hard to judge things right now. Remember the first day I met you, when you said making life decisions at OCS wasn't a smart thing to do? You were right, D.J. We're about to cross the finish line," I said. "Hang on, man."

D.J. shook his head, slowly collecting himself. "Bud, I worked so hard to get my college degree, then my commission. You got no idea. Debbie and I have zero in common, 'cept where we're both from. And the sex is pretty good. Problem is she wants us back in Kentucky with her family and me digging in a fucking coal mine, coming home every night to seven kids." He shook his head and looked wistful for a moment. Eventually, he looked at me again. "So, get this. Sunday night, we're putting the baby down after coming back from the PX. I grab the remote to turn on *Sixty Minutes*, my favorite show. Debbie comes into the room and snaps, 'You know I don't like that crap. Put on *Hee-Haw*.' I sat there thinking, what the *hell* am I doing here? Now, do you think she's gonna wait at home while I go sailin' over the horizon and come back six months later?" He laughed, but it lacked the gusto that D.J. typically displayed.

I smiled. "Give her time. She only sees you on weekends. Think about it. She's alone with a two-year-old baby in a tiny apartment for weeks. Give her a break."

"No. Debbie's homesick. I'm scheduled to go overseas shortly after gunnery school in November. She'll be gone when I return to Norfolk from the North Atlantic cruise. Seen it a dozen times. Typical sailor story."

"You're a good man, D.J. You'll be a fantastic officer. Everyone in Yankee Company knows it. Your men will follow you anywhere."

"OCS isn't Navy fleet operations, Rod. Don't go by what you see here. Leaders at OCS are losers in the fleet more times than you think. Mark my words. I said that before, too."

"But you know what it takes to make things go in the Fleet."

"I never said this before, and I'll deny it if you tell somebody I said it, but most Navy captains are either drunks or divorced, or both. Making it in this business requires you to sacrifice everything outside the Navy. Don't get me wrong. Most of 'em are good skippers, excellent ship drivers, but their personal lives are screwed up."

"What's that to do with what we're talking about?"

"Everything. This business is unforgiving. When you go out to sea, you can be gone for months. Early in your career, you must make a choice: it's either the sea or your family. Only one can take priority. Remember that, my friend."

"Well, if you must be a drunk to be a good CO, I'm well on my way."

"You won't be laughing about that someday. It's true. Hell, let's order some beers." D.J. slapped the bar lightly. "Hey, barkeep, two more of these, huh?"

Twenty minutes later, D.J. slipped out the back without saying anything to me. At midnight, I ran into two shipmates from Yankee Company at the Lighthouse Tavern on the hill overlooking the navy base and destroyer piers below. They'd come from Chicken City, a fast-food restaurant located down the road at the junction of the two main streets running down the western and eastern shorelines of Aquidneck Island. Chicken City was a fixture in Newport, its gaudy, bright yellow marquee lights blazing away in the dark evening hours after midnight. It was Newport's version of Colonel Sanders, but the Chicken City chicken was

Chicken City, Middletown, RI, c.1975

more slimy and undercooked. I went there once every six months and always regretted it the morning after.

One of the officer candidates, Phil Entwhistle, mentioned an OC had gotten into a fistfight with some locals at Chicken City. The Shore Patrol wagon had been called a few minutes before.

"Dave and I got out of there just in time. He's probably in cuffs by now."

"Anyone we know?" I asked.

"Yeah, D.J. Conklin. He was rolling around the parking lot with some drunk townie. Two or three townies were watching. D.J. smacked the guy hard. We split just when the trouble started—"

"Unbelievable. You never leave a shipmate on liberty in trouble. What's wrong with you two assholes?" I pushed past them, hustling towards the exit. In the parking lot, a cab pulled up with two passengers inside.

Opening the back door, I frantically waved the passengers to get out, assuring the driver I'd pay their fare. Jumping inside, I told the cabbie there was an emergency at Chicken City I needed to get there fast. Rocks and dirt flew as we headed off to the restaurant. We made it in three minutes. I fished a ten-dollar bill out of my wallet and thrust it at the cabbie. "This should cover it all and a good tip, right?" He nodded.

A Shore Patrol wagon siren wailed in the distance as I stepped from the cab.

Beyond the glaring lights of Chicken City, a heavy-set civilian was on the ground. Two men, a trickle of blood oozing from his mouth, propped his head up. D.J. Conklin was close by, held down by two men. I heard the three guys using first names with each other. D.J. had a welt on his right cheek. His nose was bloody. There was that familiar Clint Eastwood smirk on his face, taunting the men holding him to the ground. "You girls had enough?" he said. "Or you want to go another round?"

I hurried over to the group, yelling, "You sons of bitches, let D.J. go!"

The closest one suddenly wheeled around and socked me squarely on the chin as I closed in. I hit the ground flat on my butt, seeing stars. I reached for my mouth immediately, finding no loose teeth. Then I felt heavy work shoes kicking my side again and again. I rolled through the dirt and pebbles of the parking lot, seeking safety. Then I played possum, not moving. A crowd of six or eight onlookers closed in. A Navy van flashing emergency lights with two Shore Patrol military policemen – MPs – inside screeched to a halt next to D.J. Exiting the vehicle holding their clubs high, the MPs ordered the two civilians holding D.J. down to release him, reaching to grab my friend by his left arm. One MP held the crowd back. His partner snatched D.J.'s right arm and pulled it behind his back as they spread-eagled him on the hood of a nearby car. The MPs handcuffed D.J. seconds later, one holding his right arm while the other produced the handcuffs and put them on him. He smirked while being shoved into the back of the Shore Patrol van. At that moment, a Newport police car wheeled into the parking lot, lights flashing. Two police officers stepped out, each holding nightsticks. *Perfect*, I thought, stretched out on the ground off to one side, watching everything unfold. *So long, commissioning. Hello, enlisted life.*

The ambulance arrived. The cop took the emergency responders to the injured person and gathered contact info. The MPs started debating the situation with one police officer. One MP grabbed the chicken bucket while the other continued arguing with the cop.

I silently rose to my feet, creeping towards the MP van on the far side from the police car, moving slowly, catlike. It was like I was invisible; no one looked at me. The injured civilian, D.J., had leveled, was helped to his feet, and, with the assistance of his companions, staggered over to the ambulance's back door. He stepped into the vehicle and wavered momentarily, holding an ice pack to his face. The two officers hand-guided the ambulance out of the parking lot, and it turned south on Route 114.

After a final exchange with the MPs, the two cops backed away and began interviewing the witnesses around the parking lot.

One of the MPs walked around the van and approached me, asking, "You Haynes?"

"Yeah, that's me."

"D.J. mentioned you were nearby. He's in the back of the van. Want a ride? Are you hurt? Did you hit anyone?"

"Hell, no, I didn't hit anyone. I just got sucker punched by that fat-ass townie standing over there. I'll take that ride back to base, thanks."

"Just this once," he gestured towards the van's backdoor.

He unlocked the door, and I stepped inside to see D.J. holding his head. The MP unshackled D.J.'s handcuffs, then said, "I locked you up so those Middletown cops wouldn't run you downtown, you twit." The MP stepped out and closed the door.

"Holy shit," I said to D.J., "You did it this time. You're in big trouble."

The van drove off, took a sharp left at the traffic light, and headed towards Gate One.

"No, Bud, I'm not." D.J. said in a matter-of-fact tone, rubbing his side.

"Yeah, you are," I snapped back. "You're on your way to the brig. What do I tell your wife? How about the navigation final exam tomorrow? Jesus."

"Slow down a minute, will you? I know Terry Jensen, one of those MPs upfront. We went through boot camp together. He was drinking shots of Kentucky bourbon with me last weekend at my house, helping me watch the baby. Terry's moving us inside the gate so those fuckin' sand crab cops can't get at me." D.J. managed a weak smile. "How'd that civilian look? Did I get him good?"

"He's on his way to Newport General. I think you did some damage. His friends still want a piece of you. But the guy you clocked didn't look good. You nailed his ass. Your face looks puffy, and they tore your shirt, man. You hurt?"

"Nah. I'll kick their butts one at one time or together, don't matter to me. I saw you catch one in the mouth, too, Bud. You okay? Any teeth knocked out?"

"Nah, I'm good. My tailbone is a tad sore. I landed on my ass. My uniform is filthy, but I'll be sore for a day or two, then good as new. Probably need a new shirt."

"Those sand crabs are mighty lucky about one thing. If my boys from my last ship were here tonight... every one of those pukes would be on the ground out cold. I ever tell you about that time our ship pulled into Port Everglades—"

"Shut up, D.J., for once, will you? No more war stories. What happened tonight?"

"Well, when those sorry-ass cooks at Chicken City gave me my bucket of chicken, I looked inside, and there weren't but two pieces of meat. The rest of the pile was roasted potatoes. You get six or eight pieces in the bucket, with Jo-Jo's on the side."

"Uh-huh. You're *not* a bluejacket anymore, D.J. If you can avoid getting arrested, you'll be an officer next month. Enlisted days are history for you. Don't screw this up."

The van stopped. We heard feet crunching on gravel, and then the back door opened. We were parked in the middle of the Navy Exchange parking lot, a half-mile from the base gate we had just passed through.

"C'mon D.J. Get your butt out here. We gotta make out this bogus report," Terry said.

"Hey, Terry, loan me ten bucks—"

"Not gonna happen." Terry shook his head. "Not tonight, not never. You owe us now. No more favors, I mean for the rest of the time you're here. None. Next time I see you in a fight on base or off, you go straight to the brig."

"C'mon now. You boys know I was joshin' around, having some fun on liberty, is all." D.J. let out a deep chuckle, winced, and grabbed his rib cage. "Ouch. What's a little boxin' match with the locals, anyhow?"

"We mean it D.J.," the MP said. "This ain't small stuff."

"You'll be saluting me on July 11, a week from this coming Tuesday, boys." D.J. grinned. "Remember that."

"Don't count on it, dickweed," Terry answered right back. "Sorry, *Mister* Dickweed, sir."

"All right fellas, all right. Terry, that's the last time I let you drink my best booze at my house. Next time, it's the cheap stuff from K-Mart for you, fella." D.J. walked over and shook both hands, whispering something with his hand cupped so I couldn't hear him. He chuckled, and then we stepped back to watch the wagon drive off into the night. We headed out for King Hall as the drizzle fell harder and harder.

"Those fellas did me good tonight, Mr. Rod." He was serious.

"I think they meant what they said. Goes for me, too. I'm not going to the brig with you, so if you pull any of this shit again, you're on your own. I'm not joking, even though you're my shipmate and a good buddy, and I owe you a lot. You're my best friend at OCS, you jerk. Ow, my side hurts where those assholes kicked me."

"Lighten up, Bud. We're just two sailors on liberty doing what sailors do. We gotta get you fully trained, right up to Fleet standards. How's your face?"

"I'll live. How's *your* face? Let's go home, D.J. Liberty's over in forty minutes anyway. Damn, look at this big tear on the side here. This shirt is trashed for good." I grabbed him and pointed him towards King Hall. We began trudging along slowly.

"Damn!" D.J. cried, spinning around and pointing towards the van.

"Now, what?"

"Those damn boys in the van stole my chicken. Never mind, the joke's on them. Shit's mostly potatoes, anyway. And it wasn't even cooked right. Let's get back to King Hall prison. Fun's over."

Commissioning Day

The weather in Newport in late June consisted of bright sunshine and cool sea breezes. The sleet and slush and Newport crud illnesses from March were now distant memories. It was a perfect setting for young men and women in a celebratory mood. A few days before commissioning, we held our last off-base gathering at a farm in Middletown, including waterfront property on an inlet leading to the Atlantic Ocean. It was a time for reflection and congratulating each other. I felt sad to be leaving my shipmates behind. We all spent the afternoon diving off a wooden dock and drinking Moosehead beer, trying to process all that had gone on in four short months. Some of us were fast friends now. There were also friendships of convenience, where we tolerated each other towards the mutual goal of surviving until commissioning. I was sorry Marvin Schwartz chose not to appear at our celebrations. We were about to become members of an elite fraternity. I did not know then that I would never see Marvin Schwartz after commissioning day, nor did I hear how his naval career panned out. I hope he fared well.

We were a few hours away from commissioning and then being shipped worldwide to our final duty stations. Some of us only had to walk across the street to Surface Warfare Basic School to begin six more months of training, living in the bachelor officers' quarters on base. Most of us could not attend SWOS – Surface Warfare Officer School – for at least seven or eight months because the training pipeline was crowded with brand-new ensigns.

We naively promised each other to keep in touch, not understanding that our duties would consume our lives; the connections between us would begin fraying almost immediately. Exchanging pleasantries with each other would rarely happen once our naval careers kicked into gear. While I don't recall everyone's name today, I remember their personalities and the misery we shared learning to become naval officers. Today, four months seems only a moment in time. While at OCS in the spring of 1980, it seemed like an eternity.

July 11, 1980, dawned hot and cloudless. The commissioning ceremony was held just before noon in the center of the athletic field outside King Hall. Two hundred-plus metal chairs were lined up in precise military fashion for the graduates and their guests. There was an elevated podium for the speakers and a raised stage for the OCS band. A long line of flags representing all fifty states, the Navy, and the rest of the military services ringed the perimeter of the athletic field. I told Ellen I would be in touch once I set up my apartment in Philadelphia, my temporary duty station while waiting for a slot to open at SWOS Basic. She would receive her commissioning five weeks later, in late August. Her orders were to Naval Air Station Norfolk in some administrative role, which satisfied her. Ellen did well at OCS. I was glad for her. I discovered that our relationship had run its course within a few weeks.

The previous evening, most of Yankee Company gathered for a final farewell downtown, roaming from bar to bar in a pack, joyous that the OCS routine was over. The realization this was our last time together on liberty made it bittersweet. Our gear was packed the following morning, and our rooms were empty and spotless. A new crop of officer candidates would arrive in less than a week. On commissioning day, dressed in our choker white uniforms, we assembled one last time outside King Hall to march to the ceremony with the band blaring our favorite tunes. Yankee Company marched towards the waiting crowd of spectators. The OCS band struck up the theme from *Hogan's Heroes*. I felt exuberant for the first time in years. I had assumed a brand new personality and appearance. It seemed odd but also fitting at the same time.

Inspiring as the live music was on commissioning day, we took a perverse pride in knowing we were the least talented company marching in the final Pass-In-Review ceremonies. We stepped out one last time as Yankee Company, knowing we weren't much better than when we first tried marching in a nearby parking lot in a sleet storm. While thirty-two of us laughed without fear of reprisal, I winced passing by the flagpole outside King Hall, where my OCS odyssey began four long months ago in a drunken daze. Last night D.J. said a brand-new chapter in my life was beginning. I learned some hard lessons at OCS that would serve me well in the Fleet if I applied them. Senior Chief Sherman wasn't around for the ceremony. He was busy harassing officer candidates who weren't even halfway through the program. Plus, knowing he was legally required to salute his former minions in a few minutes, Senior Chief Sherman could not stomach that humiliation. I'd detested the old salt for weeks following my solitary sleet march, but D.J. convinced me it was part of the OCS shitshow for those like me who did not like following rules. I reluctantly

Commissioning Day

conceded that the Senior Chief was doing his job. The guy was a classic senior enlisted leader thoroughly committed to the Navy. My respect for him only grew over the years

Following the opening invocation, we rose and saluted the national ensign as the Star Spangled Banner, played by the newly reconfigured OCS band, invigorated the crowd. Outstanding students and leaders from Class 8002 were recognized before our guest speaker, a two-star admiral from Boston, addressed the gathering. I told D.J. Conklin, sitting next to me, that the admiral seemed to be delivering a canned speech he gave every six weeks or so. The admiral looked bored; he was going through the motions.

The commissioning oath highlighted the gathering. I stood up. Joining my 200 shipmates, we collectively swore to:

> ...support and defend the Constitution of the United States against all enemies, foreign and domestic; that I will bear true faith and allegiance to the same; that I take this obligation freely, without any mental reservation or purpose of evasion; and that I will well and faithfully discharge the duties of the office on which I am about to enter. So help me God.

The band played *Anchors Aweigh*. We tossed one of our old, filthy OCS' covers we had carried to the ceremony for that purpose towards the sky in a traditional display of excitement. We hugged each other and cheered loudly. No one bothered picking up the old covers. I was a different person. Dad had a scheduling conflict and was not at the ceremony, but Mom was in the audience. She seemed proud. I would be ready to leave for Providence after saying farewell to my shipmates. Mixed feelings of relief, pride, apprehension, a sense of taking on significant responsibility, and an aura of longstanding tradition swirled around us. I keep reminding myself that OCS was *over*. I told myself it would take time to grasp precisely what I had just accomplished. Everything else aside, I was thrilled to be leaving Newport, knowing I would return in less than a year for more training.

A few enlisted sailors ran around the crowd of new officers, saluting us, looking to make some quick money. Tradition held that brand-new ensigns must pay enlisted personnel a silver dollar in return for their salute. I had ten single dollar bills in my pocket set aside for the occasion. The money was gone in less than two minutes. I shook the hands of my shipmates, wishing them "Fair winds and following seas," before walking back to King Hall with my mother, where she had parked her car. I asked Mom to take a picture of me standing in an "echo chamber" outside King Hall, where Yankee Company had lined up ten times a day, rain or shine. Our yelling, compounded by other companies doing the same thing in adjacent chambers, crashed around King Hall constantly. Four months of forced marching and drilling, classroom instruction, and room inspections were *over*. The reality that I was a brand-new naval officer was only now sinking in.

'Echo Chamber,' King Hall, Newport Navy Base, July 11, 1980

The night before, I said my goodbyes to D.J. Conklin and Peter McIntyre over beers in a dive bar in downtown Newport. *You guys mean the world to me*, I told them, meaning it. D.J. laughed and clapped me on the back. Peter was more emotional, saying little. Like me, he couldn't believe he made it through. The uncertainty of whatever came next overwhelmed us, though we eagerly looked forward to the next chapter of our lives.

Mom and I loaded my gear in the car. We drove off towards Providence, where I would spend the next ten days in leave status. I felt good.

Temporary Duty in Philadelphia

Before boarding the Amtrak bound for New York City, I'd assured Mom I would write a letter detailing my first impressions of the "real Navy" when I had something to report. Seven hours later, a taxi cab delivered me within a half-block of the Philadelphia Navy Yard. I approached the Marine guard at the gate. He came to attention, snapping off a sharp salute, which I returned in kind. I will never forget that first "real world" military salute. I asked the guard where I could find USS *John King*. Grabbing a map from the guard shack and a red marker pen, the guard drew a thick, squiggly line through the streets on the shipyard map, to the pier where USS *John King* was located. After taking two wrong turns, I stumbled across Echo Pier, the ship's designated berth for her nine-month overhaul period. My shoulder ached from the seabag perched on it. I was sweating profusely. My white shoes were filthy. I felt nervous, also full of pride.

The keel of vintage early-1960s guided missile destroyer *John King* sat securely on a long straight line of wooden blocks inside a drydock, surrounded by the fast-moving Delaware River on two sides. The bulk of the ship's paint had been methodically chipped off by junior enlisted personnel, and the resulting bare metal hurriedly prepared for a new coat of navy gray by first applying a splotchy off-yellow primer. The ship resembled a multicolored open can of tuna. It looked helpless, unable to defend herself.

Leaning over the safety chains around the perimeter of the drydock, my chronic problem with heights kicked in. I was instantly dizzy watching civilian workers in hard hats far below on the drydock floor, looking up to inspect various sections of the belly of the warship. A second group of workers were peering at the two severely tarnished propellers beneath her stern. I staggered back from the edge, nervously looking around, hoping nobody saw me. Two sailors marched by, rendering casual salutes to me. I saluted each sailor as required, noting that neither bluejacket had displayed the military bearing of the Marine guard at the gate.

Moments later, striding up the prow towards the quarterdeck above without looking down, I arrived at the top of the metal grating. I stood at attention and snapped off two smart salutes, first towards the national ensign – the flag – flying off the stern of the ship, the other salute squarely directed at the OOD – the Officer of the Deck. With a firm voice, I announced, "Ensign Haynes reporting for duty. Request permission to come aboard." The OOD immediately returned the two salutes in succession, replying with exaggerated gravity, "Permission granted. Welcome aboard *John King*, Ensign Haynes. Can I have a look at them orders? We gotta make a log entry to make everything legal. And you want to take them down to the ship's office to get registered for payday next week. Look for Yeoman First Class Elliott. He'll fix you up." I nodded my understanding.

Once my arrival was officially recorded in the ship's watch log and my orders returned to me, I was escorted by the messenger of the watch to the executive officer – the number two authority aboard the ship – who quickly shooed me out of his office, ordering me to report back to the ship at 0700 hours sharp the following morning. The OOD nodded again on the quarterdeck and saluted me twice as I departed the ship, correctly rendering honors by saluting the OOD and stern ensign.

Taxis flock to pick-up stations outside Navy bases around the world. It was no different in Philadelphia. Hailing one, I tossed my seabag into its trunk and hopped in. The taxi did a fast, tight half-circle, pinning me against the passenger door, speeding north on South Broad Street towards the Stadium Hilton, a three-minute walk from Veterans Stadium, home of the Philadelphia Phillies. I was happy to see the ballpark was not far from the shipyard – perhaps one mile – while noticing how stifling, hot, and sticky the city was. I needed to cool off.

After checking in, I found hotel stationery and a ballpoint pen in my room. Pulling on my swim trunks and draping a bath towel around my neck, I grabbed a six-pack of icy Rolling Rock beer and headed downstairs to the outdoor pool. Sitting in the pool's shallow end and sipping from a green bottle of suds, I wrote a letter to thank my folks for hosting me in their homes for ten days following my commissioning. The stay at Mom's place in Providence was a brief, welcome respite from the ordeal of OCS, allowing me time to decompress and prepare for the real-world Navy. After mailing my letter to Limerock, I remembered my parents now had separate addresses. The letter would only be read by my father. I knew he would intentionally neglect to pass it on to Mom.

When I returned home from OCS, my three friends talked nonstop about how I had changed. It wasn't entirely clear if what they saw standing in "old Rod's place" was an improvement, as they saw things. It didn't matter. I was preparing to leave Rhode Island again. I needed to concentrate on my new future, not ponder the person I was before OCS. One fundamental life change was that the U.S. government dictated my daily itinerary. I was no longer calling the shots. I was both relieved and troubled thinking about it.

My letter home described walking around Manhattan in my naval officer's summer whites at midday. I attracted much attention in the Upper East Side, most of it positive. I relished my newfound status. Every five minutes, a stranger wanted to tell me about their military war story or buy me a drink. Two different women – they were both attractive – leered at me. I winked at them, not knowing what I was conveying to them. Less than a year earlier, I had traveled through Manhattan as a long-haired civilian in jeans bound for Seattle, in silence and anonymity. The situation had changed drastically, permanently.

In the morning, I arrived back at the shipyard an hour before officer's call. I was officially a stash ensign on USS *John King*, a guided-missile destroyer in extended overhaul in Philadelphia's Naval Shipyard. This destroyer class showed off its graceful, steeply rising bow designed to slice through rough seas neatly. They carried a fifty-four-caliber gun on the main deck forward of the pilot house, overlooking the bow from three decks above. *John King* was built in Bath, Maine. Bath-built ships had an excellent reputation among sailors for their ability to take a beating at sea or in battle and still deliver a nasty counterpunch against enemy aircraft, warships, or submarines. The primary mission of a guided missile destroyer was to attack enemy ships and, just as importantly, to shoot enemy fighter jets from the sky. *John King* was primarily an aircraft carrier escort platform. Her assigned station was twenty-five to forty miles from the carrier in a typical steaming formation of six or eight warships.

Back in the shipyard that first morning, I looked beyond the outboard side of an old destroyer and was startled to see a historic battleship from World War II, the USS *Iowa*, lying in stagnant, filthy water next to an old carrier. *Iowa* had been in mothballs for years, one of four battleships in her class. I quickly snapped a picture, unaware there were severe security restrictions within the confines of shipyards. Photographs of warships, old or new, were prohibited.

The day I saw USS *Iowa*, she looked mournful in her solitude. Large areas of gray paint flecked away from the ship's sides, running streaks of dark-red rust were everywhere, and the teak deck on the bow was dull gray,

U.S. Navy ships in mothballs, Philadelphia Naval Shipyard, August 1980

with individual boards drying up and pulling away from the deck. White and yellow bird droppings splattered around her bow. *Iowa*'s sixteen-inch guns were capped at the muzzle with a thick coat of navy gray paint, sealing them off from the corrosive effects of saltwater and general shipyard filth. I could not help but think of all the sailors who had walked those decks in World War II, never mind the great history and tradition *Iowa*-class battleships had witnessed in their day. What would they think of the ship now?

Several weeks later, I stood in the middle of *Iowa*'s muck in my service dress blue uniform, re-enlisting a young sailor extending his contract for four additional years of active-duty service. The sailor re-enlisted onboard *Iowa* as a tribute to his late grandfather, who served as a deck hand on the ship in World War II. Under my recent commissioning, I had the legal authority to perform re-enlistment ceremonies. I took on that responsibility with a gravity that surprised me. The tradition of re-enlisting was a time-honored ritual in the Navy, even with other sailors mocking the decision of a shipmate to "re-up" with the Navy.

The following day, I heard that the sailor I had re-enlisted went straight to the credit union on base to cash his reenlistment check. A good chunk of that money was frittered away that night in the seedy sailor bars on South Broad Street, close to the entrance to the shipyard. It was another time-honored navy tradition that seemed more foolish to me than anything else, but it was a habit among some sailors with a chunk of cash to spread it around with their friends. That night, the sailor bought multiple rounds of drinks for the same shipmates who mocked his signing up for another hitch in the Navy.

Philly Brig

A month after my arrival, Chief Bell stood by me at morning quarters, shaking his head. "Mr. Haynes, Seaman Powell's been gone for five days. Scuttlebutt is he's hangin' out at some cathouse on South Broad Street. It's located five minutes out the front gate."

A chronic slacker, Powell was known for leaving the ship for days on end without permission. Chief Bell and I thought it best to wait for Powell to return rather than sending out a Shore Patrol search party. The chief was certain Powell would return to the ship when his wallet was empty. Why give him special attention?

Dolphin Tavern, South Broad Street, Philadelphia

A week earlier, on payday, *John King* sailors on liberty watched Powell kick off another bender, buying endless rounds of drinks for his shipmates in the Dolphin Tavern, a notorious strip bar on South Broad Street. Before disappearing into the night, Powell picked a fistfight with a sailor off USS *Lawrence*, a sister ship in overhaul.

Almost on cue, the morning after deciding not to chase Powell around South Philly, he was spotted marching down the pier in the middle of the workday. The news quickly reached Chief Bell, who arrived on the quarterdeck just as Powell approached the brow. When Powell stepped onto the quarterdeck, the chief grabbed Powell by the scruff of his neck, hauling him down to "chief's quarters."

Powell's squawking wafted up from below. "Let me go, Chief! I have my rights," he cried as Bell shoved him along. I ran after them to prevent the chief from tearing Powell apart, arriving at Powell's rack to see Chief Bell brandishing a clenched fist inches from Powell's face. Powell had precisely five minutes to clean up and put on his service dress blue uniform, the chief roared.

Shortly, Powell stood at attention in front of Captain Cooper. Foregoing the usual asking for Chief Bell's input about Powell's work habits, the captain immediately sentenced Powell to thirty days in the Philadelphia Navy Brig and a permanent reduction in rank to Seaman Recruit.

"You are dismissed, mister," Captain Cooper told Powell. "Get your ass off my ship." Captain's mast lasted ninety seconds. Powell was not permitted to speak. When Powell was gone, the captain turned to me. "Ensign Haynes, I want you to share what happened at quarters tomorrow with your division. Understood?" The Operations Department consisted of two or three divisions, each with 25 sailors. The Engineering Division had larger divisions, some with up to 40 sailors and others as few as 22 sailors.

"Aye, aye, sir, consider it done." I saluted the Captain and struck below to ensure Powell didn't disappear again. A Shore Patrol van stood on the pier to transport Powell to the brig. Powell carried his seabag on his shoulder, and together, we walked down to the van where two Navy Shore Patrol petty officers stood waiting to transport him. Powell tossed his seabag in the truck before being handcuffed in full view of fifteen sailors watching from the ship.

From the back of the van, Powell turned towards me. Smiling broadly, he waved, "'Bye now, Mr. Haynes. See you in thirty days." I slammed the door shut. The van slowly drove down the pier, turned a corner, and was gone. The following morning, I asked my division if anyone wanted to join Powell in his new temporary home. All I saw was silent stares in response.

Division officers were expected to visit their sailors serving short stints behind bars. Twelve days after Powell's confinement, I was his first visitor. Two grim-faced Marines in immaculate uniforms standing at the parade rest met me just outside the brig entrance. Night sticks and cuffs hung from their belts. The edifice itself was a gray block surrounded by a barbed wire fence. Fear washed over me.

I knew Powell got precisely what he deserved, but I wasn't looking forward to performing this duty. I'd seen enough prison movies to know what was coming next, but nobody mentioned Navy brigs at OCS. I was anxious, almost nauseous, as I approached the entrance. The structure was an old World War II office building converted into a holding center of jail cells, temporary homes for sailors guilty of minor offenses.

At a checkpoint inside, a guard asked for two pieces of identification. A desk log recorded my military ID and driver's license numbers. I was patted down before moving deeper inside the brig with marine escorts on either side. I felt like an inmate. Everything was tightly controlled, all movements were closely scrutinized, and each procedure was exact. The guards were grim, all business. I was at their mercy if anything went wrong. I suspected terrible things could happen.

We marched through ugly, irregularly shaped sections of peeling green corridors. Shuddering, I figured I would maybe last five hours if I was sent here. The cacophony of shouts and the clanging of jail cell doors echoing up and down long, narrow passageways grew louder as we moved further into the complex. Sneaking glances sideways as I moved along, the faces of the prisoners behind bars showed either resignation or seething anger. I resisted the urge to leave. I must perform my duty and show I wasn't afraid, even though I was. Maintaining my military bearing the entire time I was inside the brig was what a confident naval officer would do. I put on a stern face.

We arrived at Powell's tiny cell. I saw the prisoner before he saw me. Powell sat alone behind steel bars, a miserable, forlorn look on his face. My first reaction was to pity him before I reminded myself he owned this mess. When I came into view, he leaped to his feet and stood rigidly at attention.

Powell screamed, "Attention on deck!"

I was stunned. *Who the hell is this guy?* I wondered. The guard unlocked the door, informing me I had exactly ten minutes to spend with the prisoner, no more. Inside the cell, I stood silently for fifteen seconds, looking straight into Powell's eyes, testing him to see how long he could maintain his military bearing. I saw terror and sadness in his eyes.

"Stand at ease, Seaman Recruit Powell," I growled, releasing him.

Powell grabbed my shoulders, sobbing, "Mr. Haynes, get me the hell out of here. Please, sir. I learned my lesson. I'm begging you, sir. I can't do this. It's crazy in here. I'm cured, honest, I am fixed."

I slowly removed his hands, replying evenly, "Easy, Powell. Get ahold of yourself." Walking further into the cramped interior of his cell immediately induced feelings of claustrophobia. He shuffled to one side as I passed him. I hated this fucking place. I hated this fucking duty. This was all Powell's doing.

"No, sir. I can't... this is... you don't understand, Mr. Haynes. I can't do another day in this hell hole." Powell was blubbering. "I'm sorry. Please tell the captain to let me return to the ship, sir. I'm begging you. I'm a new man now. These Marines... you don't know how they... please, Mr. Haynes."

I quickly became annoyed. "Powell, look. You're not leaving early so forget it. What, twelve days behind bars, suddenly you have a brand-new attitude? Mister, you screwed the pooch. You did the crime; you'll do the time." I couldn't help shaking my head. "You're pathetic, man, you are *pathetic*." I decided I was now royally pissed off.

Powell pleaded, "Mr. Haynes, please don't be making fun of me. I can't stand it. These guys play rough here. You don't know. I don't have a mark on me, but they know how to make me do what they say anyway, and there isn't any evidence. You don't know. You don't know."

"What did they do to you? Tell me," I demanded.

"Nothing." There was a moment of silence. "I don't want to say 'cause I'll get even more if I rat them out. These grunts are animals, Mr. Haynes, total animals. And they hate sailors the most, sir. We're fuckin' helpless in here."

"Seaman Recruit Powell, I will report back to the XO: you're doing all right, but you hate it here. The guards said you're trying hard to be good, so I'll tell the XO you're doing what they tell you. Don't ask for any favors. You've used them all up. You're a royal pain in the ass. And you're hanging by a thread with the Navy, Mister, just a thin thread." I held my forefinger and thumb an inch apart, leaning into Powell's face. "Quit whining. Suck it up."

"That's exactly what I am, sir. I've been acting like a jerk. But I can change. Can you ask the captain to accompany you next time so I can show him, too?"

"I'll be back when you get released. Forget the captain. He's got better things to do than to visit one of his dirtbag sailors in the Philly Brig. You've been cruising for this for a long time. You're doing thirty days, period, just like the captain said. Look, you're almost halfway there. Buck up, man."

Powell began crying again as I shook his hand and stepped outside the cell.

The guard stepped up to the cell door. "Sir, are we through here?" He asked this mechanically, without emotion.

I said, "Yes. I'm done." We quickly walked away.

I felt terrible about Powell. Later that afternoon, when I shared my guilty feelings with Chief Bell, he waved his arm, snorting, "Sir, please. You know how many chances that turd ball got? Screw him. Let Civ-lant deal with him."

"Civ-Lant?"

"Yes, sir. 'Civ-Lant' means civilian life. He's all done with the Navy. Mark my words."

Six months later, Powell was awarded a discharge for bad conduct, deemed unfit for future military service. It was a permanent blemish on his record that would likely follow him for the rest of his life. I suspected he just didn't give a damn either way. One day, he would regret the time he had wasted as a U.S. Navy sailor.

The Army–Navy Game

Every December, going back generations, the annual Army-Navy football game was played at JFK Stadium, a crumbling, horseshoe-shaped cement edifice built in 1925 in South Philadelphia. The game site was switched to Veterans Stadium in the early 1970s. The Vet was the modern multi-sports complex the baseball Phillies and football Eagles called home. Similarly designed and built stadiums existed in Pittsburgh, St. Louis, Oakland, San Francisco, San Diego, and other cities – the parks were barren, cold, and ugly. Players frequently suffered injuries because of the minimal padding beneath the cheap artificial turf.

These stadium complexes allowed owners to bring in larger crowds with minimal field maintenance costs. Unlike Boston's Fenway Park, where they were always close to the action, the fan seating at the Vet was set much farther back. The Vet was an unimaginative pile of steel, plastic, and cement, devoid of personality. It also lacked tradition. The Vet had an incredibly stark feeling to it when you looked around. Stadiums like the Vet made owners piles of money. The fans and players got the shaft.

In December 1980, the Philadelphia United Services Organization (USO), reserved a block of tickets for sailors stationed in the Philadelphia area. USS *John King* was given thirty tickets, twenty of which were snatched up by the crew. It was a frigid day, and wearing our full-length bridge coats over our working blue sweaters did little to quell the penetrating cold.

Before heading out to the game, Lieutenant Commander Greenfield asked, "All right, guys, who's got smuggling duty to get the beer inside the stadium?"

The group answered in unison, "Make George do it," pointing at me. "George" was the junior officer in the wardroom. As the "shitty-little-jobs-officer," at parties George had special assignments like ensuring all drinks were kept filled, cigarettes were lit, and coats were hung on coat racks and later retrieved. If someone wanted cheese and crackers, George was expected to fetch them or go to the grocery store and pay for them if necessary. He performed any demeaning tasks his fellow officers could conjure up, often in a very public way. George was a target of opportunity for senior officers seeking entertainment. It was how navy wardrooms welcomed their newest, least experienced comrades. Any complaints by George only compounded the abuse. George anxiously waited for a new arrival to take his place as soon as possible.

We had four six-packs in the car when we set out for Veterans Stadium. By the time we negotiated traffic and found a parking spot, one six-pack was gone, impressive considering the stadium was less than ten minutes from the shipyard. I stashed the remaining eighteen cans of beer in my camera bag, pushing a few down both arms of my coat. Resembling the Tin Man dance in *The Wizard of Oz*, I staggered towards the stadium gates, where the ticket taker wearily waved us inside without a second glance. Naval officers were not subject to security checks.

Our seats were behind a goalpost at the far end of the field. We had a decent view of the action when it was near us. I handed out the beer. Everyone got two or three. I nudged my buddy sitting beside me, nodding towards the row before us. Eight crew members of a cargo vessel, recently docked in the Philly shipyard, had just arrived. These merchant marine sailors focused on one thing that day: getting rip-roaring drunk as fast as possible.

On the field, Navy quickly put Army on its heels with its powerful running game. Army had no answers. Their defense spent most of the game on the field, steamrolled by a faster and bigger Navy offense. Army and Navy senior officers prowled their respective sidelines like caged panthers, unable to bear the thought of defeat by their arch-rivals. They acted like the fate of the free world hinged on the game's final outcome.

Thousands of young men and women stood packed together in the stands in their Army gray trench coats and Navy bridge coats. They chanted derogatory slogans towards their service rivals seated across the field while cheering on their gridiron heroes. Jumbled emotions engulfed the stadium crowd: patriotism, determination, institutional pride, dedication, and competitive spirit. The Army football team continued floundering on the field as the game reached half-time. Thousands of spectators stirred, making their way to restrooms and concession stands, all in simultaneous motion, creating pandemonium.

I wanted a hot dog. Amidst the throngs of cadets and midshipmen, I look down on the field, admiring the pageantry of the two military academy bands marching and playing tunes. I was transported back to OCS, grimacing, recalling Yankee Company's less-than-exemplary marching skills. I felt proud of being in a stadium crammed with patriots in uniform, something new. Service rivalry feelings aside, I joined over 60,000 people, celebrating American patriotism and military tradition. I belonged here. It was good.

On my way to the concessions stand, I discovered being a commissioned officer among thousands of midshipmen and cadets had a serious downside. The Vet was an open-air stadium; technically, everyone there was outside. Navy tradition held that while salutes were not to be rendered indoors as the Army mandated, all junior personnel must salute senior officers outside. Every five seconds, I returned a salute. The crook of my right arm ached, snapping off salutes to midshipmen buzzing by me in every direction, left and right and center, left and right and center. I passed inebriated midshipmen and cadets bent over, hurling their guts out on the concourse in the middle of the crowds. My buddies had wisely stayed in their seats, leaving me alone to experience robotic saluting during half-time at the Army-Navy extravaganza. It was my assigned duty to shuttle concessions to my shipmates.

When play resumed, the annihilation of the Army by the Navy continued unchanged until the clock ran out. Exiting the stadium, we watched sporadic pushing and shoving between midshipmen and cadets as the sun sank lower over the city skyline. The temperature plummeted; the scoreboard indicated twenty-four degrees without considering a 10-knot wind, making it much colder. We walked past three merchant marine friends lying sprawled in their seats. The ones who were still upright staggered to their feet and accosted their passed-out buddies, who otherwise might freeze solid in place.

The winning team's players were mobbed and hoisted on the shoulders of frenzied midshipmen, carried about the field as the grey-tinged sun dipped lower and lower over the city. A cold day had become arctic-like with the rapid disappearance of sunshine. We needed a warm place to thaw out; a nightcap at the officers' club at the Navy Yard was a good way to top off the Navy's big win over the Army.

In later years, I watched Army-Navy football games on television, wondering if the scuffles between Army cadets and Navy midshipmen in Philadelphia were a thing of the past. The rivalry between Annapolis and West Point was probably healthy for both sides. But I'd been in the Navy long enough to know alcohol saturated the social lives of more than a few sailors. Officers-in-training at the military academies were not immune from the problem. It was no different at OCS. Not everyone was a boozehound, yet everywhere I looked, including the military academies, at OCS, and all military installations, alcohol was always within easy reach. Was it any different than the civilian world the military drew its members from? I didn't believe so.

Imagine

It was bitterly cold in the Philadelphia Naval Shipyard that winter, a brutal, hurts-to-breathe cold made worse by a brisk east wind blowing in off the Delaware River. I was the Officer of the Deck.

The captain's orders prevented those standing watch from leaving our posts on the quarterdeck. I had to keep pacing repeatedly to stave off the freezing temperatures. With my binoculars, I scanned the dark, shimmering river. On the far side stood the lights of the New Jersey shoreline. The temperature continued dropping. In my mind, I saw General George Washington standing erect in his dress uniform, crossing the river in the dead of night in a rowboat. Jagged icebergs slowed the movement of the flotilla of boats led by the Continental Army's leader. Washington planned to surprise the Hessian forces slumbering in their winter quarters near Trenton, New Jersey. I shook my head and told myself to straighten up. I was on duty.

Later that morning, slowly recovering from my midnight watch, I consoled myself by phoning ex-college roommate Kyle, saying I needed to pay him a visit in Manhattan immediately. I had my fill of the filthy and noisy shipyard I now called home. Kyle chuckled. I was always welcome, but the weather wasn't any better in his neck of the woods. Less than two weeks later, I boarded Amtrak for New York City.

"So, how's the Navy treating you, buddy?" Kyle asked as we hunched over our beers in an Upper East Side bar on a Saturday afternoon. Chandeliers hung from the ceiling, and the mahogany tables and chairs reflected the tiniest bit of light. Only about a dozen other patrons were there, but I liked the quiet. Kyle and I had met at Grand Central Station an hour earlier.

"Like I wrote you, I get $16 daily for seven and a half months. That's $500 monthly on top of regular pay and living allowances while I'm assigned temporary duty in Philly. A year ago, I'm dead broke, hanging out at the Seattle YMCA. Today, I'm a commissioned naval officer driving a brand-new car. It's like I entered a parallel universe."

"You got nothing to whine about," Kyle answered. "How much of that money are you stashing away?"

"Not a red cent," I replied, sheepishly. Strangely, I still figured it wasn't fair. My fellow Naval Officer Candidate School colleagues were at sea. I was on shore duty in a god-awful shipyard, pissing away my money on beer and a car payment. But Kyle was right. I had it pretty good.

"I got something to tell you. It's so 'New York.' But you won't believe me."

"Oh, stop it," I said. Kyle was a superb observer of people, and, even better, a talented storyteller. "Well? Go on, I'm all ears."

"I'm down in the Village Tuesday afternoon, looking to cross the street. Suddenly, this dark-haired, stunning girl decked out in dark leather walks by. She's in her late twenties or early thirties and has a perfect figure, looking wild in a black-leather get-up. The girl had long, black hair. Her eye shadow was pitch black, like her lipstick," Kyle told me, his eyes wide with excitement. "She looked like a Dragon Lady or Morticia from the Addams Family. She was hot. I was in love."

"More like lust. You get her phone number?" I raised my eyebrows.

"Be serious. Suddenly, out of nowhere, this guy dressed in a coat and tie walks up and stands between me and the Dragon Lady. He looks her up and down once, twice. Then, unbelievably, he says, 'Hey lady, where's your whip?' I mean, it was priceless. I turned aside so she couldn't see me bust a gut."

I laughed, spraying a mouthful of beer onto the floor. "Stop it. You're making this up. Now look what you made me do."

"No, I'm not. I knew you wouldn't believe it. There's more." Kyle continued. "So, she throws him a nasty look and says, 'Up yours, Romeo.' Then, she knees him right in the balls. Hard. He falls to his knees, then on his side, grabbing his crotch, groaning. The pedestrian light flashes WALK, and she nonchalantly takes off, leaving him sprawled on the sidewalk without looking back. People are stepping over and around the dude like he's invisible. Now that's New York."

We laughed, clinking our beer glasses together. Catching up with my old friend was terrific. He asked what I had in mind for the rest of my time in the city. I hesitated. "There's something I've wanted to do every time I come to town, but I never told you. I want to go up to the Dakota."

Standing on West 72nd Street and Central Park West, the Dakota was over one hundred years old. An imposing brick edifice with Victorian trim and ornate black balconies adorned its exterior. The building occupied an entire city block. A number of celebrities called the Dakota home, including John and Yoko Lennon. Since meeting Kyle in my freshman year, I made it clear I worshipped John Lennon. I enjoyed spinning his records on my college radio show and playing Beatles records in our dorm room, over and over. I was obsessed. That weekend in New York, I wanted to head up to Central Park West to see John Lennon and Yoko Ono. I could tell my grandchildren about it. Kyle was indifferent. Celebrity sightings were no big deal around town. But he agreed to take me the next day.

On Sunday afternoon, we walked down East 51st Street to the Lexington Avenue subway station to catch the "F" train uptown. I watched the overhead lights in the rail car blinking on and off as we sped north under the streets of New York towards the 72nd Street subway station. The subway made me uneasy because it was shaking and screeching. The cars slamming into each other in the dark tunnels made me think a crash happened every two minutes. As a kid, I never relaxed riding the subway in Manhattan when it should have been fun.

"What's with this John Lennon fixation, anyway?" Kyle asked as we sat in the train's cheap plastic seats, scanning the filthy graffiti that covered the car's interior. It felt like we were riding inside a kaleidoscope, surrounded by swirling colors and bizarre designs. "I thought you'd be over it by now."

"Not now, not ever," I replied. "Like I told you, freshman year, it all started on The Ed Sullivan Show when I was a kid. We were eating popcorn in the living room watching TV, staring at these four guys from Liverpool with long hair. All the girls in the audience were screaming and jumping up and down. I was a confused eight-year-old, asking my parents, 'Who are these guys?' and 'What's wrong with those girls?' Nothing was the same after that. Nothing."

Kyle sat silent for a moment. "You always were sappy about the old times, especially the Beatles," he conceded. "Not me."

"It's true," I agreed. "I'm buried in the past. After Ed Sullivan, Mom and Dad took us to the Lonsdale Drive-In to see *A Hard Day's Night*, then *HELP!* A few years later, *Yellow Submarine* came out. We were the first family in Limerock to buy *Rubber Soul*, *Sergeant Pepper*, and the *White Album*. My friends came over, and we played those albums non-stop. We did the same thing freshman year. I gotta meet Lennon at least once before I die."

Kyle snorted. "He gets bugged by fans every time he steps outside. He'll probably tell you to leave him alone."

Imagine

"That's possible," I said. "Just seeing him in person would make it worth it. Will he say something nasty 'cause I look like military?"

Kyle shrugged indifferently.

The subway slowed to a stop. Our ride was over. We scampered up the stairs and into the sunlight of mid-afternoon New York. The wind whirled through the canyons of downtown Manhattan, haphazardly tossing hot dog wrappers and newspapers around us. Kyle and I jaywalked across the street, avoiding the frozen slush and snow from passing vehicles, then returned to the sidewalk.

"What's your favorite Beatles song, anyway?" Kyle asked. I understood he was just making conversation.

"I told you a long time ago. 'In My Life,' from *Rubber Soul*. Lennon wrote it when he was twenty-four. Remember when I got those complaints 'cause I overplayed it on my radio show? It's a classic, like 'A Day in A Life.' McCartney can't hold a candle to Lennon."

Kyle pulled his collar up around his neck. "One of them couldn't have done it without the other."

He had a point. We walked across Central Park South towards the Dakota. There, in the deepening shadows of winter, a solid brick fortress stood. Its mammoth size and stylish exterior dominated the setting.

"Do you know they filmed the exterior of *Rosemary's Baby* here?" Kyle asked.

"I heard that somewhere. I still wouldn't mind living here," I replied, "even if it is scary."

Forty-five minutes went by. "Well, I don't see Lennon or Yo-Yo around," said Kyle, blowing on his hands. He had left his gloves at home.

"Go easy on Yoko. I never understood why Lennon had gone for her, but I don't blame Yoko for breaking up the group. It's Lennon's life, and he wanted Yoko. He just outgrew the Beatles before McCartney did. All Yoko did was speed up what was happening, anyway. Man, it's cold, worse than Philly."

"Told you." Kyle stamped his feet and tugged his wool cap down over his ears. "What should we do now?"

"Let's hang out here and then head over to Grand Central. My train leaves at 1830 hours. I'm a dead duck if I'm not on board ship in uniform, clean shaven, at 0630 tomorrow morning."

We withstood forty more minutes of the windy chill on that December afternoon. As daylight quickly slipped into twilight and then darkness, we headed downtown. I thanked Kyle and jumped on the train with minutes to spare. The trip was just what I needed, even though Kyle was right: the weather wasn't any better in New York than in Philly.

Late Monday afternoon, I left the shipyard to return to my West Deptford, New Jersey apartment. It was December 8, 1980. I enjoyed preparing dinner while watching Monday Night Football. The New England Patriots played a crucial game at Miami, and the score was tied late in the contest. Football broadcaster Howard Cosell abruptly broke into the broadcast, gravely announcing, "An unspeakable tragedy... one of the leaders of the Beatles, John Lennon, was shot multiple times tonight. He was dead on arrival at Roosevelt Hospital."

I immediately started flipping through TV channels when a familiar scene appeared on the screen: the Dakota. It looked vastly different now. People were gathering around the building, holding candles and singing. A reporter stared into the camera, announcing, "In the past hour, an assassin shot and killed former Beatle and world peace activist John Lennon. The shooter is now in police custody; he surrendered at the scene. Lennon's wife, Yoko Ono, was by his side when he died."

My knees shook, and my mind went numb. I turned off the television and called Kyle, crying into the phone. He said he had to go, blurting out a quick goodbye. I switched off all the lights and slipped my *Rubber Soul* cassette tape into my boom box. Sitting cross-legged on the living room rug, I cracked open a cold beer and replayed the Beatles' music over and over. I felt lost and hurt. Then, anger took over. A man of great creativity and peace – an iconic rock figure – who had accompanied me from childhood into young adulthood, was now dead. It wasn't true. It couldn't be true. But it was true.

Thousands of fans gathered outside the Dakota, carrying flowers and chanting for peace. I recalled the Beatles' live broadcast on BBC radio, accompanied by the London Symphony Orchestra, singing "All You Need is Love." Millions of listeners around the world had tuned in.

Not everyone had received the message.

Leaving Philadelphia

April finally arrived. It was time to report to SWOS Basic in Newport. Departing USS *John King* triggered my first Officer Fitness Report, which was generated annually or whenever an officer changed duty stations. There were multiple leadership elements and skill-set categories contained in "fit reps." They could make or break an officer's career.

I knocked on the bulkhead at the captain's cabin, loudly requesting permission to enter. A muffled response directed me to come in.

Captain Cooper said briskly, "Grab a chair, Ensign Haynes. Here. Look this fitness report over carefully before we talk about it."

Quickly scanning the document. I noted being ranked in the top ten percent, one out of one ensign, which meant very little because I was not ranked against any other ensign. Since this was temporary duty, it was not a consequential document unless it contained adverse information.

My eye caught one key category on the sheet, losing track of time. The captain finally spoke. "Comments, Mr. Haynes?"

"Ah, no, sir. It's just that the 'C' grade—"

"For Judgment," Captain Cooper said. "Yes, I hoped that might catch your attention." He grew serious.

"Captain, what did—"

"Ensign Haynes, it was a pleasure having you aboard *John King*. The officers in the wardroom and the crew generally have positive things to say about you. They like you, which you can consider a good thing, although it isn't necessary to be liked to perform your duties well. You have excellent potential. Lots of energy. You work hard."

"Yes, sir. Thank you. But how—"

"You're a young officer, with a bright future ahead if you desire, like I wrote in paragraph two. I meant what I said. I'd gladly welcome you back aboard *John King* as a permanent billet assignment. All that said, I want you to take something from your experience here in Philly, something you must clearly understand as you head off to SWOS and then go on to your first at-sea assignment."

"Yes, sir?"

"I found your slapping a *John Anderson for President* sticker on my car last October unacceptable. Frankly, I'll say it straight out, that stunt pissed me off."

I froze, wanting to duck under the table. Who snitched? How did—

"This is not a college fraternity," Captain Cooper said. "I'm the commanding officer of a U. S. Navy warship. You are a brand-new junior officer. Certain 'pranks,' for lack of a better word, do not belong here. Where did you get the idea that you could do this and it would never get back to me? Are you that stupid?"

"Captain, please...can I—"

"No, you can't. I'm talking. You sit, and you listen. Did you know I'm a Mustang?"

"No, sir. I wasn't aware of that."

"I rose through the ranks after reporting to boot camp at Great Lakes in 1961. I served in the brown-water Navy in 'Nam and got selected for OCS. I've been in this man's navy a long time. I was a senior chief once. There are times for laughs. There are other times when shenanigans just don't cut it. There are traditions in the Navy. One of the most important things is respect for the commanding officer, not for me, but for who I am, what I represent, and the ultimate authority I hold. The grade I awarded you for judgment was not out of anger, Ensign Haynes. It is intended as a warning. You must conduct yourself with a little more discretion. No, I mean much more discretion. Grow up."

"Sir, I made a bad mistake. I apologize."

"Wrong. It wasn't a 'bad mistake.' This was more along the lines of being disrespectful towards a senior officer. It wasn't very smart on your end. You meant it as a joke. But you chose the wrong person to tangle with. A 'bad mistake' is slamming a ship at sea into an oiler while taking on 110,000 gallons of DFM at thirteen knots in heavy seas, eight hundred nautical miles from land, at 0300 hours in the dead of night, then losing two sailors over the side, in February. That stupid bumper sticker caper was more like beneath an officer's dignity. It's akin to a deck seaman getting thrown in jail for being drunk on the street after getting nabbed pissing in a gutter. It's an unforced error."

"Yes, sir, I understand. It's not satisfactory."

"It is *not* satisfactory. Take this one as a freebie. It's your first report card. Don't overreact, but I want you to seriously think about what I'm saying. Exercise some *discretion*, for Christ's sake. All right, I want to change the subject. Tell me something you experienced over your seven months here on *John King*, that made an impression."

"Well, sir, there are a couple of things. I will always remember this ship. I intercepted that beer cooler the first week I stood watch, and you wound up distributing it to the crew. I thought that was cool; the commanding officer distributing the contraband I caught coming aboard the ship. The crew was impressed when you did that."

The captain smiled slightly and nodded. "You reacted well in that exchange. It was good. Some of the crew enjoyed some cold ones on a hot summer day. Anything else?"

"Sir, do you remember sending Seaman Powell to the Philly brig in October?"

"Of course. Sonofabitch went UA three times, and Master Chief Ruiz and Chief Bell both said it was time to make an example of him, so we did. We're gonna shit-can the kid. He doesn't know how a bad conduct discharge will impact his civilian life, but he'll find out. Maybe he won't. Doesn't matter to me either way. If a sailor doesn't respect himself or authority, I can't help him."

"Yes, sir. Powell deserved what happened. You know, going to the Philadelphia Brig and watching those marine guards in action scared the shit out of me. It wasn't the movies. It was real. That's something I will never forget."

"The brig is supposed to get the attention of sailors sent there. The Philly Brig has a nasty reputation, so does the one in Portsmouth, New Hampshire. Sailors don't belong in brigs. The more they hear about them, the more they'll avoid going there, that is, if they're smart. Powell didn't get the message. He's not on the ball. Like I said, he'll probably pay a big price down the road, and, sadly, he doesn't know it. Yet."

I wondered if the captain knew about his two naval academy officers in the wardroom who regularly partook of their bongs at their apartments across the river in New Jersey, scoring their pot from an anonymous enlisted sailor on *John King*. Sooner or later, a surprise urinalysis test would do them both in, but they kept on anyway. The other incident was more personal: I rebuffed the sexual advances of a senior officer assigned to the ship, a man who was married. I decided not to cause any more trouble. I was leaving and I would not be returning. Best to move along quietly at this point.

"Escorting the Miss America contest last September in Atlantic City. And meeting Miss Wisconsin backstage," I said. "That was great. Oh, and sir, enlisting Petty Officer Plummer aboard *Iowa* was another special time. It's sad to see the terrible shape the ship is in. Plummer's grandfather was aboard her in World War II."

"Yes, well, if the scuttlebutt I hear is true, the Defense Department has plans to refurbish the old World War II *Iowa*-class battlewagons, maybe all four. Wow, that might get the bad guys' attention! But you're right, sorry to say. Every day we report to work, we have to walk past *Iowa*. It's depressing." The captain glanced at his watch and stood up. "Time's up. Got a meeting in five minutes. Rod, your fitness report is not spectacular, but understand it's better than other first-time fit reps. This one's not as good as it *could* be. You have a choice. Pick one of two directions: up or down. It's your choice. There's a little time for you to grow and improve some more, but you need to take this business with the gravity it deserves. I suspect you'll do all right when you get more seasoned. Use your head. Good luck, Ensign Haynes."

"Aye, aye, Captain. Thank you again." Clutching my paperwork, I stood up, came to attention, spun around on my heels, and quickly exited his cabin, softly closing the hatch behind me. I later learned that Captain Cooper was diagnosed with brain cancer out of the blue, not long after I detached *John King*. The prognosis wasn't good. He died six months later.

Lighthouse Tavern Newport

During my six months of training at Surface Warfare Officers Basic School, I called the bars in downtown Newport home. Several shipmates joined my escapades on Thames Street, but during the workday, in class, they held their own. Their extra-curricular fun did not tarnish their grades. The temptation of wild romps among the beautiful people on Thames Street in Newport's historic district was great – as I discovered during my last few months of OCS. Having steady paychecks in my checking account and starting training in Newport in May only worsened the temptation to play. Summertime was right around the corner. Downtown Newport was about to become a non-stop carnival of pretty white people under the influence, many of whom were Ivy League college graduates.

Yard Patrol Training, SWOS Basic, Newport RI, 1981

SWOS was more challenging than it had to be for me. I preferred socializing in Newport over learning to be a competent naval officer at sea. For years, the Lighthouse Tavern stood high on a hill overlooking the Newport Navy Base, a blinking beacon on its roof welcoming thirsty sailors home from the sea. The tavern doubled as a popular, cheap seafood restaurant with plastic lobsters, boat oars, and fishermen's nets hanging from the walls in between narrow booths. An old bar dominated the interior, which was reeking of stale beer and defaced by patrons openly carving their initials into polished wood.

Pretentious was not welcome at the Lighthouse Tavern. With Buck Owens or Patsy Cline crooning in the background and amidst boisterous crowds, retired shipmates renewed old acquaintances. Ship parts were bartered without fanfare, and cash was loaned at usury rates, old debts were settled, and disruptive fights occasionally erupted as closing time approached. Violence at the Lighthouse Tavern was a distinct possibility whenever multiple warships from Norfolk or Charleston pulled into Newport for a few days of unrestrained liberty, especially on paydays when everyone came in flush with cash. On Friday and Saturday nights, horny sailors sweet-talked the wives of sailors currently at sea. These same sailors were aware that the tables would be turned when it came time for them to set sail.

The latest news from the destroyer piers on base was easily obtainable at the Tavern, particularly when the partying extended past midnight as it routinely did. A popular Navy slogan during World War II read, "Loose Lips Sink Ships." Tipsy sailors inadvertently divulged classified information like ships' schedules. Waterfront rumors – some accurate, some not – were always floating around, scuttlebutt about which ships favored the local commands, whose departure for sea duty was imminent, or which ships were arriving in port. Ship reputations, legitimate or otherwise, often sparked sailor brawls.

During liberty hours, I slipped into the Tavern unnoticed in civilian attire. Slapping a five-dollar bill down on the bar, I'd order a bottle of cold Narragansett Beer, Rhode Island's native brew, and a sloppy meatball sandwich for dinner. Most of my peers would not consider drinking at the Tavern, knowing it was an enlisted sailor oasis. On weekday nights, I typically found a quiet booth in a corner to watch the drama that evening. It was cheap entertainment.

One Saturday night, when I entered the Tavern, I sensed something was wrong. The atmosphere was uncharacteristically subdued. There was only a scattering of people, not close to a typical weekend gathering. Two middle-aged women – I recognized them as regulars – sat at the far end of the bar, hugging each other, sobbing. Across the bar sat two older men with crew cuts, one shaking his head, the other with three loaded shots of brown booze in front of him. He quickly drained the shots, one after the other. Several other guys stood next to him, whispering. The jukebox was shut down. There was no loud talk, rabble-rousing, rowdy dancing, or bantering.

I quietly approached the bar, ordered a beer, and slid into an empty chair, recognizing the sailor next to me as another Lighthouse regular.

He slowly shook his head. "Heard the funeral's Tuesday at 1700 hours downtown," he told his buddy. "I think the Old Man's gonna let everyone who wants to go. You going, Larry?"

The man's acquaintance said, "What do you think? Shit, I served with him for seven years. He was my shipmate. How 'bout you, Steve?"

"Absolutely." The regular drained his beer, immediately signaling for a refill.

Larry turned to the barkeep and asked, "Joe, what time you say he left last night? Was he stewed as bad as I heard?"

I barely made out the bartender's whispered reply. "For the last time, God damn it, I ain't supposed to talk about it. The investigation just started today. The detective was here an hour ago. All kinds of legal shit's going down that we don't know nothing about. Billy was here 'til about 2330. He was waxed through and through. I told him twice let me call a cab, but he wouldn't listen. Don't say nothin' to nobody, okay?"

One of the ladies at the end of the bar sobbed, "Billy, Billy, my God, what happened? I can't stand this. Please, Jesus, please." Her friend again hugged her closely.

I tapped Larry's arm. "Excuse me. Sorry to interrupt, but what's going on here?"

"Who the hell are you?" someone from behind me barked.

I knew that voice, someone I feared back in time. I turned around while replying, "Nobody. I'm a student at the base. I'm just trying to understand – Senior Chief Sherman? Holy shit, it *is* you. How you doing?"

The senior chief leaned towards me, looking me over once, then twice. "I don't recollect knowing you."

"Sure you do, Senior Chief. You threatened to make me repeat OCS back in the spring of 1980. I'm Rod Haynes. The OC you hated until the week when you told me I might make a decent officer one day. Don't you remember? I damn sure never forgot *you*."

The senior chief broke into a broad smile. "Officer Candidate Haynes? Yankee Company, right?" He wagged his index finger at me. "Yeah. Yeah, I remember you. You were one sorry sack of seaweed. Well, son of a bitch, the navy didn't eat you alive yet? I'll be double-damned."

The senior chief leaned back and shook his head, laughing uncontrollably. "I thought you'd be shark bait by now," he boomed where everyone in the place could hear him. He signaled the barkeep to bring me a beer. As we shook hands, I noticed that his eyes were bloodshot. He looked deeply troubled despite his bravado. Senior Chief Sherman chuckled weakly for a moment before growing serious again.

Larry interrupted, "Well, even though you're a zero, you know Tommy, so I guess it's okay. See, a good shipmate we knew for a long time, a chief, retired yesterday. Had his retirement ceremony at the chief's club. I was there, and so were most of these guys. He did twenty-one years of active duty. Good man, even better sailor." Sailors sometimes referred to officers as "zeroes" when officers were not around.

"Right," I said solemnly, then nothing more.

One of the guys from across the bar piped up. "Let me tell it, Larry. So, he's at the chief's club and has a few pops for himself with the rest of the old goats who came to see him off. Musta been there three hours raising hell. It got crazy, so I got outta there."

Larry's other friend said, "You didn't say about his new truck, Larry."

"Shut up, Steve, I'm telling it," Larry snapped. "Okay, for a retirement present to himself two days ago, Billy runs out to the Ford dealer on Route 114. The guy drops ten Gs on a brand-new truck. This ride was loaded, jet-black with big tires, pinstripes, a big fuckin' monster motor, a cassette deck, and the whole works. Beautiful. Billy even let me try driving it in the Commissary parking lot the day he bought it. Nice ride, that truck. It had padded roll bars, too. Smelled clean and very nice. 'Least it *was*."

The bartender leaned over. "Keep it short, Larry. The cops said we shouldn't—"

Larry nodded. "So, Billy drove over here for a nightcap last night. Joe, here, was the last guy who saw him before he headed home down West Main Road."

I interrupted, "Hold on. You all talkin' about that wreck on West Main Road, where the sailor hit a stone wall full speed after midnight?"

Senior Chief Sherman interjected. "Yeah, that's him. I met Billy twelve years ago, on a mine-sweep outta Norfolk. Good guy and a solid boatswain mate. Terrible, terrible thing."

Earlier that night, a Channel 6 news broadcast from Providence showed a film crew reporting from the scene. Viewers couldn't tell if the wreck was once a truck or a car, never mind that it was brand new. The

Rhode Island State Police spokesman said the truck hit the stone wall at seventy miles per hour. It flipped over twice before coming to rest on its roof in the middle of a muddy field. The truck burst into flames on impact. A police vehicle was in pursuit after someone reported seeing a vehicle swerving all over the road to a patrol car parked at Chicken City. The driver, traveling alone, was thrown from the cab. Airborne, his head struck the stone wall. He was instantly killed.

"Did he have a wife? Kids?" I asked the senior chief, slowly shaking my head.

"Billy got divorced a long time back. He got two sons, both teenagers. Talked to them yesterday afternoon. They're in college, doing good. Feel bad for 'em. Third time I've seen this kinda tragedy since I got out of boot camp all those years ago. Gotta piss." The senior chief's eyes were still red, as he blinked back tears and turned away, slowly walking into the shadows, away from the rest of us. His shadow worked its way around the bar towards the back.

Early in my career, I learned that when sailors retire from the Navy, some don't live long trying to adapt back to civilian life. Something inside sailors withers away at retirement. Call it love of the sea or professional pride that kept them motivated while in uniform. More than a few retired sailors didn't get to enjoy their retirement because the navy was their life. They passed away far too soon. Senior Chief Sherman's friend had joined the long list of that unfortunate group.

Brooklyn Navy Shipyard

Three days after graduating from SWOS Basic, I reported to the USS *Joseph Hewes*, a Knox-class fast frigate in overhaul in the Brooklyn Navy Yard. *Hewes* was scheduled to return home to Charleston, South Carolina, the following May for one month, then steam south down through Windward Passage to Guantanamo Bay, a small U.S. Navy base located on the far southeastern side of the island of Cuba.

Crossing over the historic Brooklyn Bridge into the borough of Brooklyn, I drove my new Datsun 210-SL northward towards the shipyard through potholed cobblestone streets, passing abandoned warehouses and trashed-out grassy lots along the eastern shore of the East River, an area of the city adjoining the infamous Bedford-Stuyvesant projects. The car's undercarriage bottomed out twice, despite the car's upgraded suspension system. Cringing with each slam, I was worried the transmission would drop onto the street, leaving me riderless for a month. *Spooky place*, I told myself. *Don't be here after sundown.*

I slowly approached the gate. A uniformed officer stepped out of a guard shack and raised his hand. I produced my military ID. He glanced at it and waved me through after telling me where I could find *Hewes*. I drove around a corner and saw scaffolding encasing a small warship's mast off to the right, a quarter mile away. I crept past a long line of yardbirds and sailors carrying tools and swapping insults. It was a Tuesday afternoon, 1400 hours. Nearing *Joseph Hewes*, I parked at the designated spot for officers. I strode towards the ship; my seabag slung over my shoulder.

At the edge of the drydock, I leaned over two parallel rows of rusty safety chains to see the ship's keel balanced precariously, seemingly suspended in the air. Just like in Philadelphia, I instantly became dizzy and stepped back. *Hewes* was perched upon a long row of wooden blocks anchored to the floor of the empty drydock adjacent to the East River. And like USS *John King* on the blocks in the Philadelphia Navy Shipyard, it seemed like a stiff wind blasting in off the water might knock *Joseph Hewes* onto her side inside the drydock, but that would not happen. Then it dawned on me: *Joseph Hewes* was my home for the next few years. A

USS Joseph Hewes, FF-1078, Brooklyn Navy Yard, 1982

new feeling sprung up inside me: a connection, a deep, instinctive sense of pride and fierce protectiveness brazenly proclaiming I would allow no harm to come to this ship, *my* ship. I hadn't felt anything remotely close to this aboard *John King*. I had a significant stake in bringing this warship back to life. I felt ownership here. On *John King*, I felt pride in myself and the ship I served on, but compared to *Hewes*, I was simply marking time in Philadelphia. *John King* was a temporary duty station. *Joseph Hewes* was my permanent home for the next two or three years.

Clouds of dust and gray paint chips hung everywhere as grimy sailors outfitted with dust filters and hearing protection leaned on their paint grinders and needle guns, methodically removing layers of salt-encrusted gray paint and running rust from the ship's exterior in the sticky, sooty heat of a hot summer afternoon in downtown Brooklyn. Out of every five sailors, three of them had cigarettes dangling from their mouths. Yardbirds carrying fire extinguishers and toolboxes were moving in and out of various openings all over the ship like a colony of ants frantically building a new habitat. I felt both saddened and exhilarated by the hyperactivity surrounding me; depressed because the ship lay in thousands of pieces, happy knowing the ship would be reassembled and eventually go back to sea, where she belonged. This was true in Philly, but I never thought much about USS *John King*'s life after I left the shipyard. It didn't matter to me.

Yardbirds had sliced gaping holes in both sides of the ship, feeding dozens of wires of all sizes and colors into the openings, along with ventilation ducts and acetylene torch feeds, all carried deep inside the skin of the ship. Scaffolding sprung up around the mast hours after the gear was removed. My ship lay gutted like a freshly caught and cleaned out tuna fish with all her entrails – electrical rigging and high-pressure hoses for cleaning fuel tanks – laid out on the pier. I kept reminding myself this ugly chaos was temporary; everything would be back in place, and we would be rejoining the Atlantic Fleet to start our workups toward deployment. Overhaul was an ordinary part of a warship's life cycle, regularly scheduled to prolong the ship's life in the Fleet.

The nonstop cacophony of noises engulfing *Joseph Hewes* was painful, again reminiscent of my stint in the Philly Shipyard. I marched along the perimeter of the drydock dressed in my freshly pressed summer white uniform, my heart pumping furiously, anticipating my arrival on the quarterdeck. On the far side of the dock, the black-green East River slowly rolled westward towards New York Harbor on a slack tide, with barges, sailboats, and tugboats skittering around haphazardly like water bugs on a country pond. Further downriver, the Manhattan Bridge loomed in the foreground of the magnificent lower eastside skyline of New York City. Dominated by the Twin World Trade Towers, the outline of Manhattan against a summer sky was stunning. I felt dwarfed by the historic structures looming up around me and all that watercraft activity leading into New York Harbor.

Manhattan Skyline Post-9/11, Author photo.

The heat of the day, mixed with my sweat and airborne particles of the shipyard, caused my face to become streaked with soot. I stopped and lowered my seabag to my feet. Lifting my cover, I mopped the moisture off my face with the crook of my elbow and tugged my hat back on my head. My brand-new white shoes were severely marred by greasy black scuff marks while stumbling over a boa constrictor-sized electrical cable on the pier. I felt like a character from an old Marx Brothers movie.

I approached the ladder leading up to the ship's quarterdeck for the first time. A middle-aged sailor in a khaki uniform came directly before me, descending the brow, his head down, frantically scribbling on a notepad. Standing back, I quickly shifted my seabag to the other shoulder, freeing my right hand. I immediately popped a crisp military salute, only to discover I was saluting a chief boatswain mate, a senior enlisted man. He was inferior in rank to me. Stepping off the brow two feet from where I silently stood, my face turning beet red, the chief frowned and spun to his left, ignoring me and my salute.

Watching him stomp down the pier, the chief loudly sputtered, "God damn it, not another one. When will they stop sending these chickenshit boots to us?" Like acid on tin foil, the incident remained etched in my memory for years.

Climbing to the top of the brow, I turned to my left and saluted the national ensign lazily, flapping off the stern of the ship. I spun to my right and, snapping off a second salute to the deck officer, announced, "Ensign Haynes reporting as ordered. Request permission to come aboard."

The officer of the deck was a first-class sonar technician named Summers, whose stomach spilled over his web belt. He returned each salute in succession, replying with a smile, "Permission granted, sir. Got your orders there? I'll have a look-see, sir. Thank you."

Dropping my seabag onto the deck with a thump, I withdrew my official Navy orders from the top of the bag, handing them to the OOD. He motioned his petty officer of the watch towards the deck log as he opened a sealed manila envelope with his thumb. "Petty Officer Moore, enter Ensign Haynes' full name, Social Security number, and orders number in the deck log. Write, 'Reported for duty 1440 hours,' real clear." His forefinger thumped a spot in the deck log. "This is an official entry, Moore. It's the ensign's first time aboard the Joey Boat. This here is the numbers you write in the log. Right there."

"Alright. Uh, Mr. Haynes?" The young man writing in the log looked up at me.

"Yes, Petty Officer Moore?"

"I, uh, I know you're brand new and all that but look." He pointed out that I had parked my car on the pier.

"What am I looking at?" I was puzzled.

"Well, sir, you just parked in the captain's parking spot."

"What? Goddamn it!" I saluted, then hurried onto the brow, my heart racing. "Give me a minute. I'll be right back!"

"Hold on, sir! You might wanna take your seabag with you. You don't need it aboard, not yet, anyway. Maybe throw it in the car trunk for now?"

"Good idea." Stepping onto the brow, my foot caught a grating, and I fell forward, catching myself before I landed on my face. Standing up, I came face to face with the chief I had crossed paths with on the pier moments earlier. I waited for him to salute me. Drawing closer, he swiftly snapped off a half-hearted salute with a muttered, "Harumph." Brushing past me. "'Scuse me, sir," he said barely audibly. I made my way down to the pier. I drove the car to a designated parking lot for officers a hundred yards away and hurried back to the brow, reporting aboard a second time.

The OOD welcomed me back, explaining the log entry was completed correctly. Pointing at two sailors standing on the stern of the ship, the ones who had been laughing at me moments earlier, the OOD barked, "You two knuckleheads, Sparks and Johnson, front and center. Sparks, escort Mr. Haynes to the XO's stateroom. Johnson, you strike below and get a haircut. Move!" The OOD turned around to face me again. "Mr. Haynes, you need to report to Commander Gaffney's stateroom, he's our XO."

"Thank you." I nodded.

Summers smiled broadly. "Aye, aye, sir. Welcome aboard the Joey Boat, best damn ship in the United States Navy." He saluted a final time, snatched up the 1-MC microphone, and, in a deep voice, announced, "Men are working aloft on USS *Joseph Hewes*. Do not operate or rotate any electronic gear without first checking with the officer of the deck on the quarterdeck. Men are working aloft."

Summers resumed his position as the leader of his watch team. It seemed official. I liked it. Sparks and I slowly made our way down the ship's port side on the main deck, stepping over a jumble of wires and exhaust ducts as we moved along.

"You got to be looking where you're going, sir, mostly downward," Sparks said. "But always look overhead, too. You could bang your head, trip over something, or fall into an open hatch. I took a trip and got a real bad cut on my first day here. See?" The young man showed me a lengthy, ugly scar on his left forearm. "Got it two months ago and it still ain't completely healed up, yet."

"Yeah, I know," I said. "Spent almost a year in the Philly yards recently. It's just as bad there. I got one of those cuts on my left ankle, a permanent scar. Sorry 'bout that."

After taking a quick left, we ducked inside a hatch and walked forward fifty feet before snaking our way to the right and then immediately left, passing through two more hatches in the process.

"What division you got, sir?" Sparks asked.

"I'm the new CIC officer."

"That's the operations intelligence division. Chief Sanchez is your chief petty officer. He looks out for his people. Tough to work for, though." Sparks sighed.

We moved forward through the center passageway towards an opened space ahead. Sparks rapped twice on a bulkhead. A grunt came from inside the space. We entered the XO's stateroom.

"Sir, Seaman Sparks is requesting permission to enter. This is Ensign Haynes, XO."

An officer with short gray hair and round wire-rimmed glasses glanced up from a personnel file he was scribbling in. "Very well, Sparks. You are dismissed. I'll take it from here."

"Aye-aye, sir. Thank you." Sparks stepped out of the stateroom and disappeared.

"So, you're Haynes?" the XO asked, extending his right hand toward me.

I shook it firmly. "Yes, sir. Reporting for duty from SWOS Basic."

"Right. Grab a seat."

The XO pulled a chair out from behind him. "I got just a few minutes before meeting with the skipper in the engine room. We're checking on a few problems in Main Control. Welcome aboard. Where'd you come from today?"

"Rhode Island. I drove my new car, sir. My parents live there. Took five hours."

"Right." The XO reached for his pack of Winstons in his shirt pocket, shook a cigarette halfway out, and offered it to me. I accepted it. He snatched a second butt from the pack with his lips. Then he snapped off a flame from a silver-plated lighter, lighting both cigarettes. "Now, what I usually do with new officers is have them meet with the captain immediately. For you, that means either tomorrow or the next day 'cause I want you in on that fire-fighting training in Bayonne this week, about 40 minutes west of the city in New Jersey. Did you get any training like that in Philly?"

I shook my head. "Negative, XO."

"Too bad. Anyhow, the captain decides when he will meet with you, depending on his schedule. I'll ask him. Have some coffee."

The XO poured half a cup of black coffee into a mug and handed it to me. I took a large gulp. It was cold and rancid. I made an ugly face.

A smile flitted across the XO's face as he said, "Like I said, I know you were in the yards in Philly, but I give the same speech to every officer reporting aboard regardless of rank. On this ship, we dress in working khakis unless we have a special ceremony or some senior big wig coming aboard. Got it? Always wear your hard hat and ear protection. I will tell you this just once in a nice way: always wear your hard hat and keep earplugs handy or wear them whenever you are on board this ship. *Always.* If you see any bluejacket grinding out there on a deck and he doesn't have his ear plugs in, you stop him immediately and make him find some plugs. If he repeats the behavior several times, write the sonofabitch, up. He'll see the captain. We play hardball here with safety. And a lot of other stuff, too. Understood?"

"Yes, sir, understood."

"Now, I also say this to every junior officer coming aboard for the first time. Don't even consider getting drunk some night and missing quarters in the morning 'cause you're hung over. You don't put up with it from your division: you set the example. I won't say that twice, either. You hoot with the owls at night. You damn well better soar with the eagles in the morning. Every morning. No excuses. Got steel-tipped boots?"

"No, sir, I—"

"Well, get them. Right away. Yesterday, the captain said something about you being the Safety Officer here in Brooklyn. You'll walk all over the ship with the Shipyard Safety officer every afternoon looking for safety hazards. The boatswain mates issue steel tips; the first pair are free."

"Yes, sir."

"Okay. Go ahead and head over to the Officers' quarters and get settled. Take the rest of the day off. Hit the decks running tomorrow morning, ask questions, and take notes. I gotta go down into the hole with the captain and see what's what. Welcome aboard the best damn ship in the Atlantic Fleet."

"Thank you, sir. See you soon." I shook his hand again.

"Don't forget those earplugs and hard hat." He turned back to his paperwork. "And those steel-tipped boots, too!" He barked in the direction of the forward bulkhead.

"Yes, sir. Thank you." The XO didn't look up as I left.

James Lee

I departed the ship to find the officers' quarters, a red brick building with a large concrete landing area leading to the entrance. It was close by. Snatching my seabag from the trunk, I walked inside and immediately headed upstairs. At the top, I entered what I understood to be my assigned space.

A calm, cheery voice from behind said, "Hey, man, what's up? I'm James."

I turned and stared up at a tall black man holding in place a towel wrapped around his midsection with his left hand, his right hand extended in greeting. He had a Southern drawl. I liked him right away.

"Uh, Rod Haynes," I said, shaking his hand. "Just got here. If I'm in the right place, you and I are roommates."

It never occurred to me that my roommate would be black. Then I wondered why it mattered. It didn't.

"Cool. Yeah, this is your space. XO told me you were coming in today or tomorrow. Hope you don't mind, I grabbed this rack. Doesn't matter to me, either way."

"Fine. Whatever. A rack is a rack, right? Everything's cool, thank you."

Tucking his towel into his waist, my new roommate reached over to the stereo sitting on top of his bureau, flipped a switch, and a mellow jazz tune wafted out into the room. He slowly nodded his head in time with the beat of the music.

"Do you like Miles? *Kind of Blue* is his best."

"Sure. How long have you been aboard *Hewes*?"

"Since May. I just got back from gunnery school five days ago. Went home for a week after, so that was good. Nice beaches in Dam Neck, Virginia."

James searched the closet for a new set of khaki trousers and a shirt while we talked.

"So, you got Second Division?," I asked.

"Yeah, twenty-eight squids, plus my senior chief. Hoping to be assigned navigator for my first sea tour, but needs of the Navy and all that, right?"

"Yup. Just got out of SWOS Basic. Where you from?"

"Charleston. My people go back at least five generations down there. Got a degree in chemistry from the University of South Carolina. Graduated from OCS in the class right after yours." He rubbed his hair dry with a towel and started pulling on his uniform. "First in my family ever to go to college. Three brothers and seven sisters at home."

"Want to go grab a beer?" I asked.

"I got thirty minutes of paperwork to plow through. Then we could go catch a drink up in Brooklyn Heights. It's only fifteen minutes up the hill. We found a good watering hole up there Tuesday afternoon. Michaels Pub. My wheels are right outside. What do you say?"

Thirty minutes later, we were leaning over a black wrought-iron fence and gazing westward toward the Lower East Side of Manhattan. The World Trade Towers and the rest of the magnificent skyline below them stood imposing in the late afternoon light.

"I've been to New York a bunch of times. My old college roommate is from midtown Manhattan. His dad is a bigshot attorney in the city. School trips to Broadway plays, the Museum of Natural History, the United Nations, and the Statue of Liberty. Love the place, at least to visit. Not sure I'd want to live here permanently, though."

"Tell you what, Rod. I plan to take in a bunch of jazz while I'm here and some museums. Sweet Basil is a cool jazz club just north of the village. I spent three hours there last night. It cost me ten bucks to get in. It was worth every dime. The Village Vanguard's got good jazz, too."

"Count me in, James. We can go see the Yankees play, too."

"Right on." We slapped our palms together again.

James pointed his right thumb back towards the tree-lined streets of Brooklyn Heights. "C'mon, man. Let's go get us a bite."

Michaels was a pub below street level on Montgomery Street, five minutes from where we had been looking at the lower East Side skyline. It was a charming section of Brooklyn, especially in a summer day's leafy green, late-afternoon sunlight. The stately brownstone buildings with black iron railings and brick sidewalks reminded me of the Back Bay section of downtown Boston. We parked on Montague Street, a block north of the pub.

Minutes later, James and I sat hunched over two frosty beer mugs. In the months ahead, Michaels would become the USS *Joseph Hewes* wardroom's after-hours destination. Inside, an aroma of grilled onions and steak enveloped us. I noted red leather chairs against a polished bar adorned with brass trim and small tables with white linen cloth lined up along the walls in the dining area.

I asked, "Tell me about the CO. What's he like?"

"Commander Beckham came aboard three months ago. The ship just got off deployment in March. Word is the last CO, Captain Fitzberger was a total screamer. You're gonna hear endless horror stories about that guy. I heard the crew still had a decent cruise despite him and his shit. The ship spent a lot of time at sea. Everyone celebrated at the change of command ceremony. This captain is pretty high-strung, too. I saw him go full blast this week at captain's mast. A seaman apprentice was caught smoking pot down in Electrical Central on the ship. That space was supposed to be off-limits for the next three months, sealed up in plastic sheets. The kid snuck in and thought he could get away with it. Nope. The captain busted him a rank and restricted him to the ship for a month. But, you know, Captain Beckham carries himself well. He's tough, and the men say he's a good ship driver. Somebody told me the skipper made the commercial pilots coming into New York stand back and let him handle the ship until it got close in before he let the pilots bring the ship pier side. He's old Navy all the way. I'd go to war with him any day."

"Commissioning source?" I asked.

"OCS. Oh, and there's one thing you need to know about him. Listen up. You never, *ever* say anything nice about Jane Fonda." James struck his index finger down on the bar emphatically. "In fact, don't bring her up. Ever. Let's say he's not enamored with her."

"I can remember that."

"You better. You know that photo of her in *Life* magazine?"

"Yeah, I do." Fonda was wearing a helmet sitting in an anti-aircraft gun pointing at the sky, where American bombers were regularly flying with their deadly payloads. As James suggested, she seemed to have the time of her life. The North Vietnamese propaganda machine had a field day with the photo. It was something Fonda would have to carry with her for years. It electrified political conservatives in all corners of the country. In their eyes, Fonda was a traitor to her country.

"Captain Beckham hates Fonda more than almost anything, and he won't have anyone discussing her at the meals or anywhere else."

I nodded soberly. I sensed I'd found a close ally and friend in James Lee. He gave off good vibes. His advice seemed spot on, as well.

Learning the Ropes

A few days later, the XO pulled me aside at officer's quarters to remind me that my job was to learn the ship's layout as soon as possible. Just because I was the Safety Officer didn't mean that that was the only way to familiarize myself with the insides of *Joseph Hewes*. I had to take the initiative and explore all the nooks and crannies of the frigate – from the chain locker in the bow to the aft-diesel space near the stern where the emergency ship's diesel engine was.

An hour before lunch, I made an excuse to visit the engineering spaces. Two technicians, one a senior petty officer, offered me a quick tour through the boiler room. He said, "Ensign Haynes, I bet you can't show us the de-aerating feed tank."

In the Navy, "snipes" were enlisted sailors assigned to any engineering department. "Deck apes" were in First Division: they painted everything on the ship and were line handlers when the ship tied up to the pier. "Twigets" referred to the Operations Specialists (they were also derisively called "ops pussies") and Electronic Technicians in the Operations Department. The "mess cranks" were mess specialists, the cooks aboard the ship. The Chief Petty Officers' living quarters was called "the Goat Locker."

I pointed to where a third sailor was removing bolts from a tank's manhole cover, "I believe that's the DFT right there."

One of the sailors said, "That's right, sir, you got it. Maybe you'd like to see the tank from the inside? Rare chance there. Go ahead and try it, Ensign."

I looked at the three grimy sailors and decided I wasn't about to show them I was afraid. "All right, one of you guys help me up here."

"Here you go, sir." One of them interlocked his fingers, and I stepped up and into the tank. It was a tight fit, but I crawled inside, folding myself into a fetal position as I inched further into the void. Once inside, the senior sailor laughed as he placed the cover plate back on and twisted two bolts into place.

My neck was bent over, forcing my chin into my collarbone, and my legs locked at an angle, causing my muscles to cramp up. "Okay, fun's over. Get me the hell out of here," I said, banging at the inside with my palm.

There was no reply.

"Hey, I mean it!" I shouted. "Cut the shit. I want out. I'll write you guys up if you don't obey me. C'mon, the comedy hour is over! That's an official order, guys!"

I spent the next six or eight minutes in the damp darkness of the DFT, begging to be let out. The terror I experienced in those brief minutes I would never forget, not only because of the extremely tight surroundings. I could not shift my position to the left or right. I didn't know these men, the only ones who had seen me enter the DFT. How long would I be left there? I had never experienced claustrophobia before. My legs began to cramp. I was unable to shift onto my back or flip over. In my panic, I began to hyperventilate. It was extremely frightening. I'd never felt so helpless before. It shook me to my core.

One of the jokers finally uncovered the plate, reached in for my legs, and slowly dragged me out horizontally until my arms could grab the edge of the tank, allowing my feet to barely reach the deck plates.

Hopping down, I looked at each of them and smiled the bravest smile I could muster. "Well, that was cute, gentlemen. I hope you had fun. I know I did."

Inside, I was shaking with anger and fear, but I had asked for it. I always trusted people far too much. I felt ashamed.

The sailor who had pulled me out grinned. "Ah, sir. Just a little joke to welcome you aboard the best damn ship in this man's Navy. You made it out. I heard not everybody does, you know."

"Oh, so you're a joker *and* a boiler tech. Don't quit your day job," I said through a clenched jaw, still furious.

They quickly returned to their work. I climbed out of the Fire Room, taking two steps at a time up the ladder. Emerging onto the main deck, I gulped fresh air and blinked in the sunlight, rejoicing in my freedom. I knew I had screwed up.

After lunch, Chief Sanchez, my division chief, pulled me aside and handed me a cup of hot coffee. The chief looked down at his cover, which he twirled between his hands. Then he looked into the distance and slowly said, "Look, Mr. Haynes, I'll gladly answer your questions and show you the ship wherever you want. I know the XO told you about learnin' it quick like he does every new boot reporting aboard." He fixed his eyes on me. "But damn it, sir, please leave the men alone for now, okay? Don't go doin' nothin' they tell you to do until you check with me first. Let me know what you want done and I'll make it happen. And most of all, God damn it, sir, steer clear of them snipes. They seen you coming a mile away and now everybody is talking about it, sir. You can't be doing that kinda shit with the engineers. They don't play nice. Officers and chiefs don't fall for those silly ass games out here. You're in the *fleet* now, sir. It's time to act and think like a leader. With all due respect, sir, you looked like a fool this morning. These next few weeks are important. I'll help you if you let me. But you got to talk to me, sir. Not after, but before you do shit like this."

"You're coming off strong, Chief. Don't you think you're overstating things just a tad?" I responded, my face red. How dare this subordinate talk to me like I was six years old? It's time to assert myself.

Chief Sanchez looked me straight in the eye. "No sir, I don't. I told you when I met you the other day if you let me help you, I'll do it. But you and I gotta trust each other and that starts now. You said you spent some time in the Philly yards. Well, I got twenty-two years in, fifteen of 'em at sea. Take my advice or toss it over the side. It's up to you. You ensigns kill me with your innocence about things. You do."

"Okay, okay, I hear you. I got it, Chief Sanchez." I chuckled, but the chief never smiled. He jammed his hat back on, came to attention, and saluted. I saluted him back. Then the chief stalked off to inspect a paint job his men were finishing up.

Later that afternoon the commanding officer sent for me to conduct my welcome-aboard interview.

Outside his stateroom, I knocked twice on the door before opening it. "Ensign Haynes requesting permission to come aboard, sir."

"Come in, Ensign Haynes. There, grab a seat." A middle-aged officer wearing the silver oak leaves rank of commander on his collars glanced up from his desk. He finished his writing and then put his pen down with some emphasis. His eyes bore into mine. "I hear you've already made a mark for yourself with the boiler techs," Captain Guy Beckham told me. "Congratulations." While he wasn't smiling, the captain didn't seem overly annoyed. He lit a cigarette, inhaling the smoke deep into his lungs.

"Sir, I can explain that—"

Exhaling the smoke through his nose, the captain shook his head, waving his hand. "No need. Maybe it's a good sign; you're showing initiative in going down into the holes while they're all torn up. A new officer can learn a lot in an overhaul if he wants to, like you did this morning. I am concerned you were foolish enough to crawl inside that tank on the word of those snipes. My officers must exercise better judgment than that, even new ones. You could still be down there if they didn't like you. Do you understand me, Ensign Haynes? I'm talking about judgment, of which you demonstrated absolutely zero today."

"Yes sir, Captain. Won't happen again." I looked back at him, vigorously nodding my head. He seemed firm but not angry. His eyes were locked on mine.

"Remember, the bluejackets are always looking for their leaders to set an example, even though they might not say so. You are not here to be their friends, drinking buddies, or a clown for their jokes. Your job is to take this ship to sea, fight the enemy, and win, then return in one piece. Most importantly, you bring your men back to port in one piece. Is that clear?"

"Clear, sir."

"Ever been to sea before?"

"Not aboard a Navy unit, sir, only day sailing with family and friends. I was stationed on *John King* in the Philadelphia shipyard for six months, just after I got my commission last year. This is my second overhaul."

"Is Jack Cooper still the CO on *King*? He's an old friend."

"Aye, sir, he sure is."

"I think he rotates off the ship in a few months." The captain tipped the ash of his cigarette into his ashtray. "Someone told me he might have cancer."

"Really? Sorry to hear it, sir. He's a good man, I mean a good captain. Tough but fair."

"Yeah. I'm guessing you feel unlucky 'cause you pulled another repair period at the start of your career, right?" He stared at me again through a cloud of smoke.

"To be honest with you, Captain, I want to go to sea soon to get my warfare qualifications going. Some of the guys I went to OCS with are almost SWO-qualified now. I feel like I'm behind the curve, spending all my time on shore. I feel just a bit unlucky." Surface Warfare Qualifications required junior officers to earn their SWO pins, the equivalent of the "air wings" pins naval aviators wore on their uniforms.

"Don't you worry. This ship was built to go to sea. That's what we'll do next spring. Then you'll be wanting to be back on the beach." The captain stroked his chin thoughtfully. "Sometimes, our junior officers are sent on temporary duty orders over to other ships underway while we're in the yards. What would you think about that?"

I sat up, excited. "Sir, I'd love it. Just say the word."

"Hold your horses. I can't promise anything. But we'll look at you riding a Knox class for a few weeks in GITMO [Guantanamo]. I have one in mind, but first, let me talk to XO about it. Meantime, you stay out of trouble. Stand your watch and learn your job. Listen to Chief Sanchez. He's been in the Navy for a long time."

"Aye, aye, Captain."

"That's all for now."

"Yes, sir, thank you." I stood up at attention to show my respect. Then I moved towards the hatch.

The captain said, "Remember, Ensign Haynes, this is a United States Navy warship. The men don't need friends. They need leaders. I expect my officers to act like they know the difference."

"Yes, sir, Captain. Understood. Thank you." I quickly stepped outside his stateroom, quietly shutting the door behind me. I went looking for Chief Sanchez.

Gay Pride Parades and Blanket Parties

Things happened quickly during the first two months aboard *Joseph Hewes*. I became embroiled in an incident involving a married second-class petty officer who marched in the annual Gay Pride parade on Broadway in his dress white uniform, which was strictly against Navy regulations. The situation became stickier because the commanding officer had seen Petty Officer Garrett Ferguson on the evening news, in the middle of the festivities in downtown Manhattan. Ferguson was grossly overweight, his belly held together by a belt and buckle that looked like it was ready to snap. In the parade, he wore a wig that included extended blonde pigtails and red ribbons. He had a white cape wrapped around his shoulders. His sparkly sequin-rimmed sunglasses did not disguise his identity for anyone who knew Ferguson; his physical profile was a dead giveaway.

At lunch the following day, I disgustedly told my roommate James Lee that as Ferguson waddled down Broadway, drawing appreciative cheers from the crowds lining the street, he looked like a bloated nursery rhyme character from a Mother Goose children's book. And wearing a goddamn United States Navy uniform, to boot. James leaned back from his chicken curry and laughed out loud while waving his fork around and around, drawing a disapproving frown from the XO at the far end of the dining table. I was not amused. James kept smiling.

The next day the XO said the CO debated filing a formal incident report with the public affairs branch at Surface Force Atlantic headquarters in Norfolk. The captain decided to forego sending the report, but he was plenty steamed. He had not calmed down much in the days following the incident. Neither had Chief Sanchez, whom I had to persuade against tossing Ferguson into the East River to settle the matter. I explained to the chief that it wasn't a good idea; he would only be playing into a young man's attention-seeking behavior. We both knew that Ferguson needed to face discipline. The rest of the division was watching closely. It was announced in front of the men that Ferguson would remain on duty for two hours beyond liberty call to update all the warfare publications in the combat information center for the next two weeks – a task that everyone loathed. Public humiliation of subordinates was a favorite tool of persuasion by chief petty officers in the United States Navy. Naval officers were not immune from similar treatment by their superiors.

While Ferguson dodged the wrath of the captain, later that week, with Chief Sanchez's buy-in, I warned Ferguson the next time he did something anything like that parade nonsense, there would be hell to pay. "You appear on the fucking nightly news again, Ferguson, and I mean in any goddamn capacity, you'll be standing tall before the captain before the next television commercial runs. I don't even want to see you rescuing a cat from a burning apartment on the nightly news. Understand?"

Ferguson stared back at me defiantly, then reluctantly nodded.

"You know the one you need to be afraid of, Ferguson, isn't the captain. It's your chief. Stay out of his sight. The man's gunning for you right now and I can't prevent him from tossing you into the river."

"That's illegal. I'd sue."

"Yeah, yeah. You'd sue the chief after they fish you out of the filthy, stinky East River. That makes perfect sense. You do what you're told and keep your nose clean. Or I'll tell the chief your ass is his to do *whatever* he wants. And you go right ahead and sue Chief Sanchez after you take your plunge. See what that does for you."

Ferguson gritted his teeth. "Yes, sir. Anything else?"

"Yeah. Now, listen to me and listen closely, you two-bit clown." I drew close to Ferguson, my right index finger right in his face. "You are a second-class petty officer in the United States Navy. *Not one more misstep.* I'll ask the captain to take one of those stripes away from you, bust you down to third-class. I dare you to try me. Consider yourself warned. Get back to work." I stared him down as he stomped off in a huff.

One morning at quarters my eye caught the face of a young midshipman from Annapolis who had reported aboard a week earlier for his first experience with enlisted life on what was known as a "summer cruise." He was standing in the back row, trying to hide. His face was puffed up; one eye was black and blue. His mouth was also bloodied. Welts crisscrossed his face. The rest of the division stood away from him like he had a disease. I didn't grasp what was happening.

Chief Sanchez quickly pulled me aside. "You need to know about this cluster-fuck Olsen got himself into last night. Like, right *now*, sir." Chief Sanchez turned and dismissed the division. Then he faced me again. "Sorry, sir, that's your job to dismiss them, not mine. I just didn't want to go over this in front of the men, Mr. Haynes. A few of 'em had a blanket party for Olsen last night."

"'Blanket party?' Translation for the boot ensign, please. Once again."

"Yesterday afternoon, when the crew knocked off, some of the men returned to the barracks to take showers, like usual. So, Davis gets ready to jump in the rain locker to clean up, and being the dumbass he is sometimes, he leaves his wallet on the rack out in the open while he's in there. It's in plain sight, ready to be snatched."

"Oh, no. Don't tell me." I removed my cover and scratched my head, frowning.

"Yes, sir, it happened. Olsen was inside the space and when he thought nobody was looking, he grabbed Davis' wallet and stuffed the money from it in his shirt," The chief added, "Saltzman was secretly watchin' from the other side. The kid got caught red-handed, Mr. Haynes. Stole forty-two dollars cash."

"Then what?" I sensed what was coming.

"Last night after lights out, four guys threw a blanket over Olsen's head while he was asleep, so he can't see who done it. They dragged him out of his rack, beat the living shit out of him, and left him there lying on the deck. I don't know who they were and I ain't askin' for details, sir." Chief Sanchez exhaled loudly and folded his arms. He stared off to the side, refusing to look me in the eye. "If I was you, I wouldn't ask, neither."

I sighed. "God damn it. What should we do?"

The chief shrugged. "Your call, sir. Olsen got no bones broke. He didn't need no stitches, far as I can see, just got some deep bruises, the lucky motherfucker. Olsen gave me half the money back. He promised to return the other twenty he spent in town last night on payday. I'm sorry, Mr. Haynes, but you know sometimes the crew takes care of these things. That's the old navy way."

"Chief, I have to talk to Lieutenant McDonald," I said. "If I don't, he'll think I don't know what the hell is happening around here. Or he'll think I'm withholding information. Take Olsen to the corpsmen to look him over for anything serious. What else, Chief?"

"The kid already knows that if this gets back to the Naval Academy, he's gone, expelled, no discussion, no nothin'. Annapolis don't like their midshipmen being thieves. But I don't want nobody there to hear about it. Unless the command decides to tell 'em, I think that's too much heat for the kid. It just ain't right."

"Are you saying—"

"Sir, justice was given out last night on a temporary bluejacket who screwed with his shipmates," Sanchez said. "It's over and done. I don't think losing his future in the Navy over this is right. I don't. Even for a guy who wants to be a zero someday."

"Like you said, this is a future officer with character issues. Am I right? I mean, this fuckin' guy is ripping off enlisted men. That's a line no officer can ever, ever cross. It's bad. Tell me I'm wrong."

"That might be the case, okay, but if you go tossin' every criminal standin' in the ranks out of the Navy, we wouldn't have much of a navy *left*, sir. That's why we have blanket parties, sometimes. The crew knows what happens if they get caught ripping someone off, so most don't try it in the first place. No one wants to get pounded into the sand, leastways by their shipmates."

"I don't go for vigilante justice if it's old navy, new navy, or *any* navy. All right, Chief. Please get the kid to sickbay, like we agreed." Chief Sanchez saluted and left.

I quickly reached the executive officer through Lt. McDonald, my department head. I later discovered that the captain was told five minutes after the XO got the word. Olsen was restricted to the Navy yard for the balance of his six-week summer cruise by the XO. It was decided the Naval Academy would not be briefed on the incident, at least not yet. I had mixed feelings about the decision. But I knew the XO was an Academy graduate, and he knew best, so I left the decision to him.

A week after my arrival, two electrician mates approached me to invite me out for a beer after work. I went against my better judgment and quickly became friends with the two sailors. One month later, I lent one of them my brand-new RX-7 sports car. I'd recently traded in my Datsun 210 SL for the RX-7, taking on a substantial monthly car payment. They drove it out to Massapequa on Long Island, got drunk, and wrapped my car around a telephone pole on the return trip to Brooklyn. They walked away from the crash unharmed. The XO went batshit crazy when he learned about it later that day. He could not fathom one of his newest officers casually tossing the keys to his new car to two subordinates. The word quickly spread among the crew. Chief Sanchez said the only good thing is that it did not involve any men from OI division. The bad news was I would be left holding the entire $5,500 repair tab unless I sued the two sailors, which wouldn't happen. My insurance rates skyrocketed after I filed a claim. The captain had explicitly warned me that he did not take kindly to junior officers making friends with enlisted sailors. I was

RH, Emergency Repair Locker Training, FF-1078

disgusted with myself and afraid of the impression I had made with the captain and the XO so early in my career. Here was, one more time, a serious lapse of judgment. I kicked myself.

Despite being thoroughly pissed off, the XO was mostly tight-lipped about the incident. A month later he said, gritting his teeth, that my lack of decorum was not a good look for me. It took the XO a long time to settle back into his old ornery self. Somehow, I was never called to account for my mistake by the captain. The command probably figured $5,500 worth of lessons learned and having no car for two months, was punishment enough, but I never knew their strategy. I just thought once again the captain got wind of what happened five seconds after the XO learned of my indiscretion, deciding to keep his disapproval to himself. I wondered if I would read about the matter in my upcoming Fitness Report. I recalled my first Fitness Report discussion with Captain Cooper about my lack of judgment when I left *John King*. I chided myself for my stupidity.

Although we had lengthy discussions in the leadership classes at OCS about how to interact with enlisted personnel, it took time for me to grasp that respect could not be earned through leniency or granting favors to subordinates. Fraternization rules in the military existed for a reason. Still, because of my poor self-image and a desire to be liked by others, these leadership deficiencies impaired my reputation aboard *Joseph Hewes*, at least early on. Hoping to lower my profile, I practiced damage control drills, cranking out my daily paperwork, and just trying to avoid drawing more attention to myself. Back in college, I read a piece about General George Washington, who warned his junior officers in writing against fraternizing with their soldiers during the worst days of the Revolutionary War. Washington's principles of proper military protocol came into play here. There was no excuse.

KKK

Two months had passed. On a sunny fall day, while gazing across the East River from the ship's flight deck, I dismissed the men from our daily gathering at the start of the workday. Then I called Chief Sanchez aside.

The chief finished issuing the men his work orders for the day and sidled up next to me. "You wanted to see me, sir?"

"Yes. I was up on the O-1 level portside weather deck, yesterday afternoon, just before the liberty call. I saw something alarming up there. Graffiti." The O-1 was the first deck above the main deck of the ship.

"Graffiti?"

"Yes, *graffiti*. Some fool with a needle gun carved KKK FOREVER into the bulkhead next to the hatch leading into CIC in big block letters, plain as day."

"Aye, sir. I had Michaels take a needle gun and gray paint to that spot about 1600 hours last night. It's gone now. Good as new."

"Well, that's fine, but it doesn't fix what concerns me."

"What's that?"

"You're a smart man, Chief. Do I need to spell it out for you?"

The Chief frowned. "Sir, like I said before, I'm approaching twenty-one years in the Navy. I seen bullshit like that and worse. It's better now than it was when I got in. And you don't know if a civilian did it, anyways."

"No, you're right. A yardbird might have done it." I hesitated before continuing. "Uh, what's better now in the Navy than before?"

"Relations between white sailors and ones like me who ain't white."

"And that's it?"

"I don't follow you, Mr. Haynes. What are you asking me? You want the Naval Investigative Service to launch a probe about some stupid initials on a bulkhead?"

"Will you stop being dramatic, Chief? I want to know, was it someone in the OI division who did it? That's what I'm asking you."

"Can't say, sir. I never asked who done it. I got bigger fish to fry than chase down shit-birds who act stupid, less they killed somebody."

"I thought that's what chiefs do every day. They straighten out the sticky problems with the assholes in the ranks, right? Why didn't you ask who did it? Chief, I'm not gonna play twenty questions with you. Do you or don't you know the one who put the graffiti up there?"

"I don't know for sure, sir. Yeah, I got my suspicions, but you can't hang a man on what you think he done wrong. Right?"

"Agreed. Here's the thing, Chief. Seaman Apprentice Michaels wears that stupid Stars and Bars patch on his jeans whenever he goes on liberty, almost religiously. I think it's too bad a sailor in the United States Navy is running around town displaying that symbol. Some might consider it subversive. I'm not pointing blame, not yet. But my thought is that Michaels could be responsible."

"Subversive? Not sure Michaels knows what that means. I know what it means. He probably don't. And he ain't alone wearing that shit. Bunch of 'em do it, you know that, sir. There's a kind of gang of Confederate sailors running around these decks. It ain't just Michaels."

"Once again, we agree. Michaels isn't the only one wearing that trashy symbol. Some people, and I'm one, consider the Stars and Bars anti-American. I don't like to see it promoted by our sailors. It bugs me, Chief."

"Oh, I don't know, Mr. Haynes. Yeah, there's a dress code when our sailors hit the beach at night, but I never seen anything in writing that says you can't wear that rebel flag. Where do you think most of our sailors come from, anyways? I mean, which states do most call home?"

"Never saw a demographic breakdown of where our sailors come from. On a wild ass guess, I would say at least sixty percent are Southerners, but I don't know. I don't think about it."

"You're probably pretty close there," Sanchez said. "A lot of our sailors are southern, like me. I'm from Texas, you know."

"I didn't know you were a Texan. The captain is from Florida, and a bunch of other officers and chiefs are from the South, too. What's your point, Chief?"

"I recommend you don't broadcast your opinion of the rebel flag. There's plenty who support it."

"That's exactly what I mean. Too many believe in that bullshit. Hey, I don't want to refight the Civil War on *Joseph Hewes*. If nobody objects to it, it becomes normal attire. I don't like it. But I want to talk to Michaels today after liberty goes down."

"Who said it was Michaels? I never said—"

"I know you didn't. I *think* it was him, but he's not the only sailor who wears that in plain sight. I'm talking to him 'cause he's in the OI division, and I already spoke to him about it before, a couple of weeks back. Tell him to report to the wardroom at 1500 hours after liberty call goes down, okay?"

"Me, too? Want me there?"

"No. Tell Michaels to bring his lead petty officer with him when he comes."

"Why bring Petty Officer Matthews and not me?"

"I have an idea, Chief. I'll tell you what happens after I talk to those two, don't worry. I want Matthews to hear me when I speak to Michaels. I'm sure Matthews will talk to the rest of the men later after I ride Michaels' ass a little bit. This is a leadership opportunity for Matthews, get it?"

"Hmmm. Maybe you're right. Matthews is new in his LPO [Lead Petty Officer] role, so it's good that he hears this and then relays it to the guys. But I don't want you goin' around me to get to Matthews and the rest of OI division all the time."

"Just a minute, Chief, hold it right there. Do I *ever* go around you? Do I disrespect you? Here I am strategizing with you, and you're afraid I'm undercutting your authority? C'mon, lighten up a little."

"Alright, Mr. Haynes. You want Matthews to start feeling his oats, to act like someone in charge. He'll be a chief someday, right?"

"*Bingo!* My point exactly. See? It's called exercising leadership. You get it. Matthews needs to take on this stuff, not just let his crusty old chief handle the discipline around here. It's time he steps up. All Lead Petty Officers should get a chance at handling this kind of personnel bullshit, right?"

"Got it. Okay, I'm in. 1500 hours. Michaels and Matthews at the wardroom."

"We'll meet there, then move to CIC. I want to start in officer's country. I'll brief you later on what goes down."

At precisely 1500 hours that afternoon there was a knock on the entrance to the wardroom. Petty Officer William Matthews stuck his head through the hatch. "Ensign Haynes? Permission to enter?"

"Yes, Petty Officer Matthews, come on in." The two sailors entered the space. Both had plastic safety goggles dangling from their necks.

"Jerry, take off that goddamn cover. You're in officer's country," Matthews growled to Seaman Apprentice Jerry Michaels, snatching the

Dixie cup cover off Michaels' head and shoving it against his chest, who clasped it.

I stood up. "We gotta relocate. There's a meeting here in five minutes, guys. Is CIC available for us, Petty Officer Matthews?" I asked.

"The space should be empty. Liberty Call just went down, sir," Matthews replied.

We moved quickly down the passageway in the ship's interior, carefully stepping over electrical wiring and other hazards. CIC was in the forward section, one deck above the main deck, on the O-1 level.

Combat Information Center

We climbed one flight of a ladder up to the O-1 level weather deck, just outside the hatch leading into the combat information center. I decided to speak to the men at the exact spot where I found the graffiti the day before. I pointed to the bulkhead. "Petty Officer Matthews, your men did a nice job painting this area and getting rid of that graffiti."

"Aye, sir. First, we needle-gunned the area down to bare metal and primed it good. Then we let it dry and then applied two coats of navy gray over it yesterday afternoon."

"Shows good work. Seaman Michaels, you know anything about this?"

"Yes, sir. I got the primer and paint from the bosun locker. It took us about ten minutes to needle-gun it, prime it, and then we painted it after the primer was dried."

"KKK," I said. "Wonder how that got put here in the first place?"

"Couldn't say, sir. It got fixed, though. No problem," Michaels replied absentmindedly.

"Michaels, where do you call home?"

"Dalton, Georgia, Mr. Haynes."

"How 'bout you, Petty Officer Matthews?" I looked over at him.

"Hendersonville, North Carolina, born and bred," Matthews said proudly.

"No kidding? Hendersonville? You must know where Clyde is, don't you?"

"Sure, sir, it's about thirty-five minutes west of Hendersonville, closer to the Smokies. I have an aunt who lives there. Nice little town."

"My dad's side of the family is from Clyde," I said. "Haynes kin all over the place there. Lots of inbreeding is going on. When I was a kid, I went to Clyde in the summertime. Michaels, you sure you don't know anything about the KKK graffiti from yesterday?"

"Not a thing, sir."

"Got any opinion about the Klan, Michaels?"

"Huh? Why do you ask, sir?"

"Well, your favorite liberty attire includes a Stars and Bars battle flag on your left back pocket. I saw it three separate times this week at liberty call. You know that the Ku Klux Klan uses the rebel flag as a calling card. It's seen at Klan rallies all the time."

"I heard about that, too. I got this tattoo when I was home last Christmas on leave." Michaels rolled up the sleeve of his working blue uniform shirt, revealing a sizeable red rebel flag tattoo rippling in the breeze, crisscrossed by a banner reading "Southern Pride."

"Nice," I said, scowling. "Ever asked Petty Officer Tatroe what he thinks of that artwork on your arm?" Petty Officer Harold Tatroe was a second-class petty officer responsible for handling all classified material in CIC. He was Black.

"Never have, sir. Didn't think to ask that."

"Let me ask you this hypothetical. That means I'm gonna give you a pretend scenario, a situation I'm gonna make up. Say we're operating in the North Atlantic next January, and we just pulled alongside a British tanker to take on 150,000 gallons of DFM at 0100 hours in the morning in the middle of a bad gale. We're going at twelve knots, and about 110 feet separate us from the oiler; we're beam to beam, side by side. Okay? You're out on the O-1 level handling the line that's bringing the fuel nozzle from the tanker over to our ship so we can start taking on gas. Suddenly, the two ships hit a big wave, they each take a heavy roll. You slip, lose your footing, and go over the side, right over the lifeline, straight into the water. The only squid to see you fall is Tatroe. So, let's just say that happened. Bad situation. With me so far?"

"Aye, sir, I follow you," Michaels answered, eyeing me warily.

"So, you're in the water, and the temperature is barely above freezing. The ships are now 100 yards ahead and opening distance from you, real fast. You need to get the hell out of there before hypothermia takes over, and you're dead. You got less than five minutes before you're a dead man. Know what, Michaels? If I'm you in that water, I don't give a flying fuck about what color skin my shipmate's got, just as long as he saw me go over the side and he can get his hand on a life ring and toss it to me and sound the alarm to the pilot house and haul my ass back aboard."

"Now hold on, Mr. Haynes, I want—"

"No, Michaels, let me finish. Then you get your say on this. So, if I'm down there in the freezing water and my name is Jerry Michaels, and I never much liked black people, and I look up and all I know is that a black shipmate is the one person who saw me go over the side, I got a serious problem. I realize my ass, if it's gonna get saved at all, gets help from someone with a skin color I never much liked. And that guy knows I don't like black people. Why should the black guy toss me a life ring?"

"Sir, I did not scratch that KKK in the bulkhead. I don't hate colored people. You can't prove—"

"Who *said* you did anything? Not me. Not your chief. Not Matthews. Nobody accused you of doing anything. Nobody. All I'm saying is that if you get in a jam at sea, or in an alleyway in Naples, Italy, someday when you're pie-eyed drunk, and you need a shipmate to help you out because some asshole just pulled a knife on you and he wants your money, and that shipmate you need help from isn't white, what fucking difference does his skin color make? If you don't like black people, maybe black people will remember that just when you need any shipmate to give you a hand, to maybe save your life."

"Sir, I—"

"Look, Michaels, the captain can't legally make you stop wearing that rebel patch. We can't order you to lose that stupid tattoo you wear. You got the legal right – and I will say it out loud – the stupidity to show it off if you want. All I can say is if I was a black guy, seeing that rebel flag symbol in the shower every other day would make me mad. That's all, I'm done. You're dismissed, Michaels. Let me talk to Petty Officer Matthews a minute."

"Yes, sir." Michaels saluted me, clearly unhappy. I returned the salute.

"I still didn't do it," he whispered as he descended the ladder towards the main deck.

"I don't know who's responsible for it, Mr. Haynes. I don't know," Matthews said once Michaels was gone. "So, don't ask me. I'd tell you if I knew. And you never let Michaels explain himself like you said you would."

"No, you're right, I didn't let him speak. I did that on purpose. I wasn't very nice. Too bad. He pissed me off with that tattoo of his. As LPO, it's your job to know about these things. Keep your eyes and ears open. Look, I'm not launching an investigation. It's a waste of time. There are twenty or more Michaels-types on this ship. I know it. What I'd like you to do is get with your chief and figure out how to talk to the division about this KKK stuff. You with me on this?"

"Mr. Haynes, I grew up in Hendersonville, attending a Southern Baptist church with mostly black folks. My pastor was black for the first twenty years of my life. I ate Sunday potlucks with my church family the whole time I was growing up. I never wore that Confederate shit any time in my life, but I saw a lot of it around town. It's big in North Carolina, you know. But I hear what you're saying, sir."

"Okay. Did I get through to Michaels?"

"Oh, I doubt it, sir. I seriously doubt it. It takes more than a new division officer giving a sailor a hard time to change his mind. You must know that sir."

"Hmmm. I want you to get with Chief Sanchez and tell him what all went down here, do you understand me?"

"I understand, sir. I'll get with Chief Sanchez later today." Petty Officer Matthews saluted me and struck below deck. I stood on the weather deck alone for ten minutes, mulling things over. I wondered whether I handled things okay this time, or was a different approach called for? I wasn't sure I knew.

Adventures in GITMO

One month later, the captain called me to his stateroom. "Ensign Haynes, I have something I think might work for you."

"What's that, Captain?"

"Remember last fall when we talked about you riding a ship while we're still in the yards? I know the skipper on USS *Terry*. She's heading down to GITMO later this week. I spoke to him on Sunday. He welcomes you to ride her for four or five weeks of REFTRA, maybe all six weeks." REFTRA is "Refresher Training."

"No kidding, sir? That's incredible. I can't thank you—"

"Wait. Calm your ass down and listen. I am sending you to GITMO for your traveling pleasure in the tropics. REFTRA is not fun."

"Yes, sir, Captain, no, it's not."

"We're going to GITMO in early July. I want you to go down there now and soak up everything. Make copies of the drills and exercises the trainers put the *Terry* crew through. You're our advanced scout, gathering every ounce of intelligence you can. I want this ship to be off and running when we get there. Better yet, you'll help this ship get up to speed *before* we arrive in GITMO next summer. When you return, you will brief the engineers, weapons, and damage control teams on REFTRA. Understood?"

"Absolutely, sir. Thank you, Captain."

"I expect you to make this thing worth your while. There are all sorts of SWO qualifications you can work on while the ship is in training because the training staff won't be on your ass. *Terry* is a Knox-class frigate, just like us. Ask the skipper if you can move around to watch training evolutions in engineering, weapons, operations, and deck division. He'll approve your request when you make it. Maybe you can even drive the ship if he says it's okay. Move around, but don't get in the way."

"Aye, aye, sir. Thanks again, Captain."

"Go make those arrangements and get ready to travel to Cuba. Dismissed."

"Aye, aye, sir. You won't be sorry. I'm ready to go." I turned and headed straight to Yeoman Second Class Stuart in the administrative office. He would furnish my orders and travel money.

Two days later, a Navy cargo plane carrying me and three other sailors touched down at Leeward Point, GITMO Naval Air Station. I was informed that the fleet training group headquarters, Naval Station GITMO, was a twenty-minute ferry ride across Guantanamo Bay. The aircrewman tossed my seabag out the back door of the plane onto the tarmac below, yelling over the noise of the engines, "Welcome to GITMO, Ensign Haynes, land of lizards and landmines. Watch your head stepping down. Keep low and stay alert on the runway so no prop chops your head off. Good luck, sir."

The plane was airborne minutes later, heading back to the States. GITMO was fast-paced. I liked it right away. Hot, humid tropical air buffeted my face as I walked towards the NAS administration office, unzipping my windbreaker. It had been twenty wind-chilled degrees when I'd left New York that morning. After switching planes in Charleston, then taking on fuel and a new crew and more passengers at an Air Force base in central Florida, we finally landed in the crumbly, barren outpost in southeastern Cuba known as Guantanamo Bay. I had no idea *Terry* was in a world of trouble that afternoon.

I arrived aboard *Terry* excited, ready for REFTRA to begin. The OOD immediately directed me to the XO's stateroom, where I rapped twice on the door, loudly announcing, "Ensign Haynes reporting as ordered, sir. Permission to come aboard?"

The XO, Lieutenant Commander Max Bishop, glanced up from his desk before resuming his work. The three other officers in the space were anxiously pouring over an engineering schematic covered with red markings. The XO wore a two-day stubble, his eyes bloodshot. Taking a long drag on a cigarette clenched in his front teeth while he held the blueprint up, he drew a large red circle in the middle, jabbing at it with his forefinger. Through clenched teeth, he said, "This is what I want you to look at, gentlemen, right here." He continued, "If seawater or rain in *any* amount gets inside the Mack, things will get a whole lot worse before we can fix it. Rust, mold, contamination, all that shit." The other officers nodded, staring blankly down at the blueprint.

Taking a deep breath, the XO turned back to me and growled, "Now, who the hell are you again, and what do you want?" He leaned to his left, crushing out his cigarette, before straightening up to slurp a large mouthful of coffee from a coffee cup on his desk, "Bill, fill 'er up again, will you?"

The officer on the far side of the Exec reached over and grabbed a half-full coffee beaker, then refilled the XO's cup.

The XO looked up at me a second time, his scowl deepening. "Well, ensign? We're waiting."

"Uh, sir, I'm Ensign Haynes reporting from *Joseph Hewes*, as ordered. I'm here on temporary duty, sir."

The XO grimaced. "Terrific. And this one's only here, temporary duty," he muttered, running his hand through the few remaining strands of hair on his head. Waving me in, the XO gestured toward a chair in the corner. "Go ahead, sit down over there. Sit down, I said." He jabbed at air with the eraser end of his pencil. "Give me a minute."

I had just entered a hornet's nest of investigations, official reports, and damage repair activity. *Terry* was preparing to go to sea without the capability of generating her own propulsion or electrical power. Two boiler technicians had violated standard written boiler light-off procedures the previous evening, with disastrous results. Instead of using a lighted torch to ignite the fuel moving from the fuel manifold to the nozzles atomizing it into the furnace box area, they showed off to their shipmates by turning the fuel valves on to use the internal brickwork on the far side of the boiler firebox to light the boiler. In Navy lingo, the process was called, "Lighting off the back wall." It was illegal, a serious violation of standard Navy light-off procedures. The boilers were always lit by a flaming torch thrust inside the firebox through a small opening, then the fuel pump pushed fuel to the burner front where the torch would ignite the fuel as it exited the nozzles.

When the fuel didn't ignite after striking the firewall of the boiler, a large pool of fuel collected inside the firebox, at the bottom of the boiler. The two sailors outside the firebox discovered the brickwork was not hot enough to ignite the fuel directly from the brickwork. They thrust a lighted torch into the firebox to hurry things along, and the ensuing ignition of the fuel fumes hovering above the liquid DFM [diesel-fuel marine], caused the fuel inside the firebox to cook off and ignite. The explosion then caused catastrophic damage to the constricted housing of the forced draft blowers because the blast's energy was forced up through the blowers, basically large fans drawing oxygen into the boiler to keep the fuel ignited adequately. The explosion in the boiler firebox rendered the blowers inoperable. They needed to be replaced.

The entire sequence happened in the blink of an eye, the blast taking the path of least resistance up and out into the ship's combined mast and stacks, referred to as "the Mack." The explosion of the fumes from the fuel wrecked a vital section of the ship's engineering plant, knocking it out of commission. *Terry* violently rocked back and forth where she lay tied up to the pier, nearly causing her mooring lines to snap. Everyone aboard the ship and many personnel ashore felt or heard the blast. Some thought the ship was under attack.

The explosion ripped open the blowers along their welded seams like someone had opened them up with a giant can opener. Until the blowers were repaired, the boilers could not be lit off. The ship would have to be towed back to Charleston, a decision made one hour before I arrived aboard. *Terry* faced at least six months of repair on top of the twelve-month major overhaul period she had just completed. The new repair costs would be astronomical.

"Ensign Haynes, I'm sending you home tomorrow. There's nothing more for you to see or do on *Terry*. We're leaving, too," the XO told me, after rapidly briefing me on the situation. "Sorry." My heart dropped to my knees.

A lieutenant commander sitting next to the XO said, "Sir, this guy could do something else that wouldn't impact us at all."

"What are you talking about, Chuck?" the XO asked in exasperation.

"*Aylwin's* pulling in here in a few days' from Jamaica liberty. We could ask Ensign Haynes' XO if he can hang out here in GITMO and wait for *Aylwin* to arrive. Then, he can ride her through REFTRA. I mean, why take away this guy's chance to learn something, sir? He's come all the way down here from Brooklyn. Just sayin'..."

"Wait, lemme think... oh, all right. Alex, get an immediate message off to both *Aylwin* and *Joseph Hewes*. Tell them we need an answer pronto. That meet with your approval, Ensign Haynes?"

My eyes lit up. *Aylwin* was another Knox class like *Joseph Hewes*. "Sure, sir. That's great."

"Okay, go stow your gear in Boys Town. See you at dinner tonight."

I headed forward to find my sleeping quarters. Later, one of the ensigns took me down into the hole to show me where the boiler front was singed black from the flare-back. A slight bulge showed on the outside from where the explosion had pushed out against the boiler front. The two boiler technicians involved in the incident were facing charges of dereliction of duty and – because of the extent of damage – were most likely facing dishonorable discharges and a long stretch in Fort Leavenworth military prison. I never learned their fates.

We climbed up inside the Mack, the single vertical cylindrical metal post rising from the ship's main deck, holding the ship's radar gear and running lights in place. I absentmindedly put my hand along the split smokestack seams. I marveled at the extent of the damage, immediately sustaining a deep cut to my right index finger when I caught it on a razor-sharp edge. A sailor handed me a small paper towel, which I used to apply pressure on the wound, as I quickly made my way to sickbay, where a corpsman recommended wrapping it in gauze and white medical tape, telling me the injury required two, maybe three stitches. I told the corpsman to stitch it and forget it, the finger was fine. I wasn't going to risk being sent home because of my stupidity. He numbed the area of the wound with some white cream and quickly did his stitch work. I felt some pain but said nothing. I begged the ensign and the corpsman not to tell the XO, and they agreed to keep my injury a secret even though injuries like this were required by regulations to be officially documented when they happen on active duty. I silently handed ten dollars to the corpsman from behind my back. I kept my bandaged finger hidden at dinner that night.

Miraculously, no sailors were injured in the firebox accident down in the hole. I marveled at how a single act of stupidity could jeopardize the lives of nearly three hundred sailors. In the middle of the night, we received messages from *Aylwin* and *Joseph Hewes*, both agreeing to our proposal. I could ride the *Aylwin* during REFTRA.

The following day, in the wardroom, the XO handed me some papers over a cup of coffee, saying, "Okay, Ensign Haynes. Here are your orders to GITMO Naval Station. You'll be here for four days, waiting for *Aylwin* to pull in. The latest word is she'll be at Echo Pier on Friday afternoon at 1600 hours. Is this your first time in GITMO?"

"Affirmative, sir."

"You might want to go up to the border area, check out the marine patrols, and look at the minefields. Do that at a safe distance. Wear a helmet and a flak jacket. And no sail boating in the bay, either. One of the Fleet Training Group staff went fishing a month ago. He got drunk, passed out, and his sailboat went up into the interior bay. The Commies snatched him up, and we almost had a diplomatic crisis before they sent him back a day later. We see Russian, Cuban, and Chinese container ships going north into the interior part of Guantanamo Bay all the time.

If I were you, I'd visit the FTG staff and ask them for training check-off sheets to take home. Do you golf?"

"Yes, sir, when I can. I'm not very good."

"Well, if you get bored, the GITMO golf course is all sand and cactus, no grass, but the greens are oiled and rolled weekly. You can rent clubs cheaply. Don't let those fat, ugly Gila monsters running around there scare you, but some of the snakes are poisonous. Drink lots of water. You might want to check out the O-Club. It's got a decent pool and tennis courts, and the beer is cold and cheap. One last thing." The XO pointed his finger at me like I was a first grader.

"Yes, sir?"

"Just because you got yourself a little four-day vacation here in a tropical paradise, you damn well better be on the pier when *Aylwin* pulls into port. Call the Port Authority every twelve hours to determine her location. They know where all the ships bound for GITMO are from three days out and closer. Be ready to report aboard the minute she is pier side. Ships go to sea quickly here in GITMO, sometimes with no warning. They won't wait on you. Got it?" He glared at me.

"No sir. I mean, yes, sir."

"Good luck, Ensign Haynes. It's time for you to shove off now. 'Bye." He turned away from me to scan an updated weather report, which a sailor handed him straight from Radio Central.

"Thank you, sir. Good luck to you, sir." I never saw *Terry*'s commanding officer. He was probably too busy explaining the stupidity of his two engineering petty officers and the pending million-dollar repair bill to his superiors at Atlantic Fleet headquarters in Norfolk.

At dawn the next day, USS *Fox*, a U.S. Navy guided missile cruiser, dropped anchor in Guantanamo Bay, a short distance from *Terry*; the ship remained in cold iron status, unable to generate steam because its boilers were inoperable. *Terry*'s official displacement (the tonnage of the ship) was less than half of *Fox*'s eight thousand tons. One hour later two Navy tugs tied up to *Terry*'s – one at her port bow, the other at the frigate's starboard stern – and slowly maneuvered the frigate into a staging area one hundred yards directly astern *Fox*. The cruiser was tasked with towing *Terry* north to the United States.

I stood on a hillside balcony at the Guantanamo Bay Naval Station, watching the action through a set of Navy "Big Eyes," large binoculars used by lookouts reporting unknown contacts at sea and by signalmen reading semaphore flag signals and tactical flashing light messages when electronic transmissions were secured.

A chief warrant officer stood nearby. He was a short man with two eagles with wavy banners in their talons reading "U.S. NAVY" tattooed on his forearms. The warrant wore six or seven crisp rows of multicolored service ribbons over the left pocket of his uniform shirt with sharp military creases in all the right places. Only those chiefs or higher-ranked individuals with sustained superior performance, outstanding leadership abilities, and the potential to serve as commissioned officers were designated warrant officers.

He turned towards me. "This your first trip to GITMO?"

"Yes. Arrived from the Brooklyn Navy Yard yesterday. Slept aboard *Terry* last night. She's in bad shape," I said, pointing at the silent frigate in the harbor. "I'm Rod Haynes. Good to meet you, Warrant." I nodded at him.

"Pleasure. I'm Alan Burke," he nodded back. He pointed towards the frigate. "Soon as you get back to Brooklyn tell your wardroom buddies what those two dumb-ass snipes on *Terry* did to show off. It took 'em five minutes to ruin their skipper's career. She's looking at a minimum of six months or more in the yards, depending on how bad it is. Hope they think it was worth it." The warrant shook his head, looking out over the harbor.

"Why would anyone do that?" I wondered out loud, instantly feeling stupid.

"You ever drive drunk?"

I paused. "I guess I have. A few times."

"Well, just like you – and me – these two idiots wanted to show off, thinkin' that nothin' bad would happen. Cocky idiots. Now it's gonna cost their skipper his fourth stripe. He's one of the better commanders around. And now look."

"Tough business," I said, shaking my head. The ships continued maneuvering for a position with a third tug standing by the other two tugs tied up to *Terry* for backup.

"Tougher than most people ever know," he said, unbuttoning his shirt pocket, withdrawing a Pall Mall cigarette, and lighting it. "Remember what I said about telling your buddies, Ensign," he called out over his left shoulder as he walked back inside the building.

A gloomy sadness stirred inside, not unlike what someone feels at the funeral of someone they've loved their entire life. Walking through the ship the previous day, I saw heads down, no one slinging insults at each other, starkly contrasting with the relentless jabbering between sailors working regular workdays on *Hewes*. Whatever crew morale existed before the ship pulled into GITMO six days earlier had evaporated with that awful explosion down in the hole.

A few hours later, *Terry* embarked on her slow, mournful journey north through the Windward Passage towards Charleston. I checked into the BOQ before walking down Main Street, the tropical heat of the late afternoon beating down. GITMO's climate was predictably hot and humid throughout the spring and summer. The afternoon tropical rains sweeping over that part of Cuba worsened the high humidity. There weren't many trees offering shade. The landscape included sand, rocks, prickly shrubs, and cactus. Through the big-eye binoculars, I saw larger trees on the communist side, clustered on the rolling mountainsides looming over Guantanamo Bay to the north.

Each of the three times I was in GITMO while on active duty, I was constantly aware of my situation: I was a visitor in a foreign land, standing on disputed ground claimed by my government. Thousands of heavily armed, sworn enemies of the United States were twenty-five minutes from my position. The base must be always prepared to initiate evacuation procedures in the event of attack or swift-moving hurricanes. Personnel assigned to GITMO were in "forward deployed status" by the Navy, qualifying them for additional pay. Still, base personnel were allowed to have their dependents accompany them to GITMO, a risk of some kind.

Later that afternoon I returned to Fleet Training Group (FTG) headquarters to speak to my new friend, Warrant Officer Burke. He cheerfully helped me pull a large stack of training reference material and shipboard exercises from four filing cabinets, material I hoped would show my captain that my trip to GITMO was a wise investment. I hit the jackpot with Warrant Officer Burke. I stashed all the paperwork at the bottom of my seabag like it was Top Secret material. It wasn't classified at any level. After a quick shower, I walked to the officers' club for dinner and drinks, pleased with my deal-making.

The GITMO officers' club offered a spectacular view of the bay below, not including the inner harbor area where the warships tied up to the piers. Twenty minutes before sunset, I was looking across the water to Naval Air Station Leeward Point, where my plane had touched down the day before. The warm wind and soft colors of the Caribbean sunset splashed across the western sky reminded me of Rodger and Hammerstein's musical *South Pacific* scenes. I sat on an elevated deck area looking down at the dying daylight, marveling at how life kept throwing new things my way, mostly good these days. While *Terry* had suffered a terrible indignity and her captain's career was toast, thank God I wasn't there when it happened. My heart went out to USS *Terry*'s crew.

Darkness came on slowly. I momentarily forgot where I was, sitting on a lawn chair, lingering outside until the warm tropical blackness of the evening enveloped me. I sat reflecting on everything I'd seen in GITMO thus far. Then, I went inside to grab a beer.

I asked the bartender, "Say, barkeep, got a question for you."

"What's on your mind, bub?"

"Today, I saw three huge metal cattle trailers driving down Main Street, the kind used to ship livestock in. They seemed out of place here at GITMO."

The bartender laughed.

"What, did I say something stupid?"

"This is your first time here, ain't it? Those cattle cars are used for the enlisted club." I asked him to explain.

"Sometimes we have three or four ships in port at one time. When liberty call goes down, the enlisted crews head to the E-Club to drink. If it's payday, the base is flooded with cash. That means you got a bunch of young sailors whoopin' it up. They get rowdy and start swinging at each other, so the Shore Patrol throws everybody in the Club who has anything to do with the brawl straight into the cattle cars and drives them down to the piers. Some of those guys duke it out in the cattle car on the way. If things get terrible, FTG might toss the ship out of GITMO or anchor the ship in the harbor for six weeks. No liberty for no one. And no matter how many times the crews are warned not to fight at GITMO, it still happens, over and over again."

"Wow. Never heard of this." I was impressed.

"Welcome to the Fleet. Let me tell you another story. This one's *real* bad, but it happened."

"I'm listening."

"A destroyer pulls in here two months ago. Three officers off the ship were in here one night, and I served them their beers. One of these guys was struggling with his wife back home. He thinks she's talking to a lawyer about divorcing him. His buddies bought this guy drinks the whole night. He got pretty juiced up. The guy was crying and carrying on, all that shit. The next afternoon, he was on duty on the quarterdeck when the mail call came down. Then..." The bartender stopped.

"What?" I asked, sipping my beer. "Go on."

"Well, first, this officer opens a letter from home. Then he orders his petty officer of the watch to hand over his .45 and the bullet clip, so the kid does it. The officer slaps the clip into the gun, flips the safety off, points the gun at his temple, and pulls the trigger in seconds. The kid who gave him the gun is still scrambled eggs back at the mental ward at the Charleston Navy Hospital. Tough stuff."

I almost dropped my beer. "Is that *true*?"

"I just said it was. Too serious to joke around, you know. GITMO is a tough place for sailors, like being at sea. It's tough for those who come here for six weeks, too. It gets awfully hard, especially if things at home are bad. You got the pressure on the ship, the family separation, and all that BS. Ask anyone who's been here a coupla times."

"What's your name?" a guy sitting three chairs away interrupted us. He and another young man were sitting at the bar drinking tequila shots. I guessed them to be officers, but civilian contractors were also allowed in the officers' club.

"Rod Haynes. Flew down from Brooklyn on a C-3 yesterday."

"Brooklyn?" The second guy asked. "That's a long way to come."

"I'm the CIC Officer on *Joseph Hewes*. She's in overhaul. We're coming down here this summer. I'm the advanced scout, checking how REFTRA works."

"Uh-huh. This is Ray-Ray," the guy sitting closest to me said, pointing at his friend. "I'm Beetle. We're both off the JFK." USS *John F. Kennedy* was an eighty thousand-ton-plus aircraft carrier. Noting my smirk, he quickly added, "We're brown shoes. Like a beer?"

In the Navy vernacular, the term "brown shoe" referred to the brown shoes worn by officers in the air community. These two guys were pilots. I wore black shoes as a member of the surface warfare community. There was an intense inner-service rivalry between black and brown shoes dating back many generations. I did not fully appreciate this rivalry until later.

"Thanks. I believe I will have another. What're you guys doing here?"

"When the carriers do REFTRA they don't pull into port. This place can't handle three or four thousand squids. The port would have to dredge the channel big-time to squeeze JFK in here, plus they'd need forty cattle cars to handle the crew on liberty. We're both lieutenants. We fly Caroline back and forth between here and the JFK."

"Caroline?"

"Caroline's the name of the COD, the carrier onboard delivery platform. She's a small prop aircraft, a C-2, ferries personnel, and mail to the carrier and back. Didn't they teach you that at OCS?"

I shrugged my shoulders. Who could recall all those airframes? I didn't remember whether we discussed the carrier transport planes at OCS.

"'Course, Caroline's named after JFK's daughter. We usually do two runs or so a week. Currently, JFK is somewhere between Trinidad and South America, making donuts in the ocean."

"I've never been at sea. I mean on a navy warship." The two officers exchanged looks. The guy who called himself "Beetle" grinned.

"Where've you been doing your time, Rod?"

"After commissioning from OCS, they stashed me in the Philly shipyards for eight months before I went to Surface Warfare Basic in Newport. I reported to *Joseph Hewes* in Brooklyn last summer."

"We've got something you might want to consider," said Ray.

"What's that?"

"How'd you like to land on a bird farm?"

I sat straight up. "You mean fly out on Caroline and land on the JFK with you guys? Really?"

Beetle smiled and answered, "Why not? There's nothing like hooking the wire on a carrier and coming to a complete stop after flying 170 miles per hour a few split-seconds earlier. Your head almost goes straight through your asshole when we hit the wire. You'd like it." He drained his beer and ordered another round for all of us.

"But I got no orders. How can I—"

Ray interrupted, "You just leave that to us. We have connections."

"I don't know. If I'm not here Friday afternoon when *Aylwin* pulls in my ass is grass."

"We'll take care of you. Come see how the real Navy lives," Beetle said, almost taunting me. "Let's go take a swim in the pool." We went outside to the pool and had a few more beers as we floated around the water in inflated chairs. I'd worn my bathing suit under my jeans on the recommendation of the front desk clerk at the BOQ.

Ray asked me again, "What's it gonna be Rod? You got any hair on your balls? You with us?"

"I'm probably an idiot, but what the hell. How many times can a guy land on a carrier off the coast of South America? What time is the flight?"

"We are wheels up at 0800 but get to Leeward Point an hour early. Beetle and I will be there. And don't go blabbing about what you're doing. That's important." Ray emphasized.

"What about my orders?" I asked as I climbed out of the pool and toweled myself dry.

"I already said we'll take care of that. Just keep your mouth shut at the Air Station admin office. Act like it's Top Secret." The two flyboys looked at each other with a grin passing between them. My new friends stayed behind in the pool for a while, talking.

"See you tomorrow morning," I called out to them, heading out the door into the locker room to change and return to my room. What luck. I made a great connection tonight.

Figuring I needed a two-day supply of clothes, I grabbed a small knapsack and stuffed my gear in it before heading across the bay the following morning. The aqua-blue water was calm and warm. I looked back at Windward Point, then towards the FTG building, the rest of the main base, and the hills looming in the background. Tactically speaking, those peaks were a distinct advantage to Cuban forces overlooking the base below.

A Russian trawler steaming westward into Guantanamo Bay crossed directly in front of our ferry, rapidly gliding from our port to the starboard side, the prominent red flag with the yellow hammer and sickle on the vessel's smokestack asserting its presence as it slid by. There were large pockets of running rust throughout the weather decks. I recalled the lectures at OCS about how poorly most Russian ships – civilian and military – were maintained. Who would want to claim this rust bucket as their own? I thought they should be ashamed.

Two enlisted men, both seasoned boatswain mates, ran our miniature ferry from GITMO Naval Station to Leeward Point NAS. Although the sun had only been up less than two hours, it was insufferably hot. The water reflected the sun directly into our eyes. I reached for my prescription sunglasses, thankful I remembered to pack them.

At the landing at Leeward Point, I grabbed my backpack and jumped ashore, thanking the two sailors. Turning the ferry around, they saluted and immediately set off for Windward Point to pick up another group. I climbed the small hill to the administrative office and found Beetle and

Ray waiting for me just outside the entrance. Beetle held a piece of paper. "Hey, Rod, how ya doing? Here are your orders. Just give them to the yeoman petty officer inside the building. He'll stamp them and we can take off." Ray went on smiling as I made my way inside.

I'd never landed on an aircraft carrier. I had no clue what to do. I handed the processing petty officer my piece of paper, and he stamped it without looking up, quickly handing it back. The *Kennedy* battle group, consisting of the carrier and seven other Naval units in company over a fifty-mile span of water, was operating somewhere in the south Caribbean operating area, approximately ninety minutes flying time from Guantanamo Bay that morning. After a short run down the runway, we lifted off and veered off sharply to the south to join her.

During our transit to the carrier, the petty officer on the aircraft briefed me on emergency egress procedures, explaining that should the plane overshoot the arresting cable and land in the water, there was a small emergency escape hatch at the top of the cabin. He patiently went through an elaborate safety checklist of steps to take in the unlikely event of a water landing, assuming we didn't get run over by the ship if we ditched directly in front of her. I became confused after the first eight steps. Maybe landing on a carrier wasn't such a great idea. I concluded a water landing meant we were dead, period. The rest of the rescue protocols seemed beside the point. I was nervous now.

Beetle called back to me over the aircraft intercom from the cockpit, "Rod, c'mon up here and take a look at our home."

Unbuckling my seatbelt, I lurched forward to where the pilots were preparing to land on the carrier. The *Kennedy* lay directly ahead of us on the surface of the ocean. She looked small, churning through the water, leaving a frothy wake as she turned into the wind to prepare to launch some jets and then immediately land multiple aircraft, including ours. I saw all kinds of activity far below us as microscopic men scurried back and forth, holding fuel hoses, towing lines, and the chains and chocks used to secure aircraft to the flight deck.

"You're looking at a flight deck area of about four point seven acres," Ray shouted at me. "The ship displaces over eighty-five thousand tons, stands twenty-three stories from her keel to the top of her mast, and can go almost forty knots if necessary. She's more than three football fields long and almost a full football field across at her beam. JFK's got four propellers. They each weigh thirty-four tons. We'll have a crew complement of almost five thousand sailors when we deploy."

"Incredible. But the landing area looks like a postage stamp from up here!" I shouted at Beetle. "How do you—"

"You let us worry about that. Head back and buckle up. We'll put this bird down on our next pass."

"Okay, Beetle. Listen, I don't want to swim in the Caribbean today, so let's do it right the first time, okay?"

"Piece of cake. We'll be on the deck in a minute. Carrier landings are better than any ride at Disney World."

I sat back and buckled up.

The crewman next to me, Petty Officer First Class Jennings, leaned over and tugged my seatbelt and shoulder harness twice. My perspective was somewhat skewed because I was sitting with my back towards the cockpit, looking aft. All I had was a small window to look through. In a split second the plane's forward momentum would come to a screeching, abrupt halt, if all went well. My heart was pumping furiously.

Jones asked if I had any more questions. I answered, "What if I've changed my mind and want to go back to GITMO right now?" He laughed and looked away.

My stomach leaped into my throat as Beetle eased off the engine throttle, and we dropped out of the sky. Jennings, seated looking forward, grinned and offered a double thumbs up. I watched him brace for impact. We veered off very slightly to port, then corrected our heading to starboard, a blast of wind contesting our course adjustment. A flash of aircraft and sailors shot by our window in a blur. I was violently yanked forward, my heart all but leaping out of my chest as the plane's rear tail hook grabbed and held onto the arresting wire on the flight deck. It was frightening and fun all at once, just like what Beetle had discussed. I yelled, "Wooo! Let's do it again!" In seconds, the plane was taxiing off to one side, making way for the next landing. Jennings grabbed my hands, struggling with the seatbelt, yelling for me to stay strapped in until told otherwise.

Moments later, a sailor on the flight deck opened the passenger-side door and jumped inside the COD, where he knelt by my side.

He was wearing hearing protection, hollering, "Sir, I want you to follow my footsteps when we jump out. Put your feet *exactly* where my feet go. No wandering, no stopping, no questions, no nothing. You got that? We don't want your arm sucked up into an engine or your head whacked off by a propeller. Do exactly what I said, okay, sir?" Released from my seat, I shot him a double thumbs up.

An aircraft carrier's deck is dangerous: fuel hoses, ammunition being pulled by miniature carts, arresting cables running and skipping across the landing zone, and vehicles hauling planes that have just landed. Everything was orchestrated in complex ways, as planes landed and elevators moved up and down to remove some planes and bring other aircraft topside. Everyone I looked at was focused on doing their jobs.

I halted momentarily at the bottom of the plane's ladder to look around. I felt a push from behind. "Come on, get going," the sailor said. "Leave the pilots behind. They got aircraft checks to complete."

I was escorted to the ship's administrative offices, where I met the senior chief yeoman responsible for checking newly reporting personnel aboard JFK. He asked me for my orders, which I produced from my knapsack. He stared at them a long time before finally looking up and asking me, "Sir, can I ask where and how you got your hands on these orders?"

"Is there a problem, Senior Chief?" I asked.

"Well, sir, outside of whoever wrote these orders didn't know what they were doing, and I can't figure out who you are and what you are doing here I'd say there aren't any problems. Now, who are you, and how the hell did you get out here?"

"I'm Ensign Haynes. Well, Senior Chief, see, I met Beetle Lancaster and Ray-Ray Battenfield at the O-Club in GITMO last night and—"

"Oh, no, not again. Mr. Haynes, did those two jokers promise you a free plane ride out to JFK last night?"

"Ah, yes and no, Senior Chief. Is that a bad thing?"

"Well, God damn it, Ensign, if you don't got no official orders stating you belong out here, you're sure as shootin' right it ain't legal for you to be here. Didn't they teach you that at Annapolis or wherever you come from? What, you think we're TWA airlines or somethin'?"

My stomach was churning faster now. Opening and closing my mouth without speaking, I started backing toward the hatch to go find my two pilot friends.

"I'll just go get Lt. Lancaster, and he can explain what—"

The senior chief put his hand up. "Sir, don't you go nowhere. Stay put, right here. You can't go out on that flight deck. And I don't want to see neither of them two jokers. And you better not go blabbing to anyone else what you done." The senior chief sighed, looked at me for what seemed forever, and then shook his head. I thought I saw a little grin cross his face for a moment. Then, he grew serious.

He looked up and pointed his finger in my face, "Sir, I mean no disrespect here, but you did an idiotic thing today. If your plane splashed down in an emergency and we never found you 'cause you're sitting upside down drowned in five hundred fathoms of Caribbean blue water strapped into a plane for eternity, there's no official record of your coming out here. These orders are forgeries and *bad* forgeries. No one back at Naval Air Station GITMO knows you are here, exceptin' maybe some yeoman third class pinhead those pilots gave twenty dollars to so you could carry these shitty-forged orders with you. If you had died today, your dependents wouldn't get your life insurance benefits, and you might get a dishonorable discharge after you were dead. You think about that?"

"No, Senior Chief. Umm, I think I have one other problem."

"What's that?" He looked up at me as he scrounged inside his desk for something. He looked up at me, annoyed. "Sir, you gotta tell me everything. Right now. I can't fix what I don't know is broke."

"Well, see, I'm supposed to meet USS *Aylwin* in GITMO in three days, and if I'm not there on the pier when she pulls in, I'll be considered UA," I said as quietly as possible. No one else needed to know this.

"Sir, that is a problem, possibly a real big one. You know why?"

"Not exactly." I held my breath.

"Well, I'll tell you, then. I have over three thousand sailors and civilian technicians on this ship. We also have extremely limited space on the aircraft, leaving JFK outbound for GITMO or the states each day. There's a strict waiting list, and only a few of us assign the priority of who flies home when. That plane is usually packed to the gills with travelers who must get somewhere fast. A stupid decision by some boot ensign is not a priority over a sailor needing to get to a family funeral. The worst part of your problem is the XO of this ship, a full-bird captain, looks at this list daily. You better hope and pray he doesn't ask about you when your name comes across his desk. If he finds out, you'll be cooked meat. No foolin'."

My heart began to race, and my mouth completely dried up. The XO on *Terry* had warned me I was on my own if I did something to screw this up, and here I was five hundred miles from where I was supposed to be. Oh, God, would I go to jail? *Damn those two pilots!* I thought. *I'm going to hunt them down and throw them to the sharks.* How could I be so trusting? What would my captain back in Brooklyn say? *I'm dead. I am so stupid – so gullible. When the hell will I ever learn? Those damn pilots!* I almost cried.

"Sir, just stop. Calm down a minute. Here, take these meal tickets. They'll get you into the officer's mess. The mess cranks serve meals 'round the clock. I'll have Seaman Apprentice Aguilera take you down to your berthing area. I'm not sure how I will work this out yet." The senior chief ran his hand over his bald head and stared at me with clenched teeth.

Then, unexpectedly, he laughed out loud. "You new surface warfare types are such easy bait for those fucking pilots. You'll be lucky if you see those two guys again. And you don't want to see 'em. They're down in the squadron ready-room telling everyone how they hijacked an ensign blackshoe from Guantanamo Bay out to the carrier, and now you're trying to get home. You played right into their hands."

I left the senior chief as he shook his head. I felt ashamed, angry, and lost. Aguilera led me down a maze of passageways and metal ladders towards temporary officers' berthing. He told me the best way to find my way around was to "look for the black lettering on yellow field signs located in every compartment on the ship."

"Say, Seaman Apprentice Aguilera, is your senior chief pissed off at me?" I asked as he prepared to leave me alone. "Or is he just pulling my leg? I can't tell, exactly."

"Well, sir, the good thing is that you aren't the first ensign tricked into coming out to 'Big John.' I've seen it done a couple of times before, and I just got here six months back. The question is how many times the senior chief is gonna put up with this bullshit. I get the idea he'll try to help you get home. Just be nice to him. I wouldn't recommend bugging him too much. Leave him alone. He knows you got to get back to GITMO. Just don't bother him. He knows where to find you when he wants to."

"I'll be nice. When do you think I should see him again?"

"Give him a day or so to cool off. Come by tomorrow after I tell him you didn't mean to get suckered into coming here without authorization." The kid smiled and said, "Don't worry, sir, we'll get you out of here. Meanwhile, stay away from those pilots. They're trouble. One last thing, sir."

"Yeah?"

"You might want to look at the ship's bowling alley near the bow on the fourth deck if you're not doing anything else. I think it's somewhere near frame twenty-six or twenty-eight."

"Hey, thanks a lot, Aguilera. I'll see you guys late tomorrow." I jumped into the upper bunk bed. I was going to take a nap before heading out to find the bowling alley.

"Not a problem, sir. Bye." Aguilera quietly shut the stateroom hatch as he left.

Forty minutes later, I was roused from a deep sleep by a piercing blast over the ship's loudspeaker system, followed by a rapid, high-pitched announcement: "Now hear this, now hear this. This is a drill, this is a drill. General quarters, general quarters. All hands, man your battle stations. This is a drill, this is a drill, this is a drill." I stayed hidden in my stateroom for thirty minutes before the word passed, "Secure from General Quarters. Now set the normal underway watch." The time was now 1800 hours. I decided to grab a bite before heading out to watch night flight operations from the O-7 level. That evening, I ate beef, noodles, and green beans. I was impressed by all my food choices when filling my tray.

One of the most remarkable nights I ever spent in the United States Navy was my first night aboard USS *John F Kennedy*, watching the flight crews do their thing from high above the flight deck on one of the highest weather decks on the carrier. Slicing through the sea with a speed exceeding thirty knots, the carrier launched aircraft from one of four catapults powered by high-pressure steam. In between launches, planes returning home were trapped and secured. These traps were practice maneuvers before the ship deployed six months later, familiarizing pilots and landing personnel with the complex dance involved in landing planes.

Some landings were merely "touch and go" maneuvers, where the pilots came close enough to the deck to touch their wheels before roaring off into the night. The aircraft on final approach appeared from nowhere in a loud, roaring cacophony of noise and tire rubber slamming into the carrier's deck. The air crew had to move fast when removing the trapped plane from the wire because another plane was landing right behind it. In between traps, the steam-driven catapult flung outbound jet fighters into the evening sky. Occasionally, a helicopter settled down on deck or lifted off. Their mission was to remain at a nearby station in an emergency, like plucking a downed pilot from the water if he survived a crash.

During wartime, planes required quick refueling and rearming before being sent to the catapults for immediate takeoff. This operation resembled a remarkable ballet involving people, machines, fuel, and weapons – a spectacle I had seen on television countless times but never witnessed in person. The aircraft carrier served as the nerve center of the United States Navy's Maritime Strategy, which aimed for America and its allies to confront threats directly in Russia's heartland, as well as in the North Atlantic, the Pacific Oceans, and other locations around the world designated by President Reagan, our civilian Commander-in-Chief.

The following afternoon, I made my way back to the administrative office, where I made it a point to look up Seaman Apprentice Aguilera. "Hey, Aguilera, how are you doing today?"

"Sir, I wasn't expecting to see you—" Aguilera looked to escape, but I wasn't about to let him go.

"I know you weren't. Guess how I spent most of my day today?" I asked him sternly, trying not to smile.

"You weren't looking for a bowling alley, were you, sir?" he asked nervously.

I wasn't about to tell him I had fallen for the gag hook, line, and sinker. "Now why would I look for a bowling alley on an aircraft carrier, Aguilera? We both know that such a thing doesn't exist. That would be like looking for a bucket of steam, or running up and down the ship looking for a left-handed monkey wrench, wouldn't it?"

Senior Chief Shell suddenly appeared, walking through the hatch while waving me into his office. He poured me a cup of coffee as I sat down. "Now, Mr. Haynes, go easy on Aguilera. I didn't tell him to send you off looking for no stupid bowling alley, but that's just one of the things everybody does to new people. He was looking for a bowling alley a little while back, too. He didn't find one, neither. Besides, sir, I got excellent news for you today."

"What's that, Senior?" I asked, hoping against hope.

"I got your orders for you to fly out of here tomorrow afternoon, back to GITMO. The XO didn't catch on how you got here. You just had better make it there without ditching into the sea 'cause if that happens, I will get in *serious* trouble. And you'll be dead, so I can't pin it on you. All I got was orders to get you back to GITMO. There still ain't no official orders that got you here in the first place."

"Senior Chief, I... can I pay you something? I can't thank you, " I said, reaching for my wallet.

The Senior Chief raised both hands. "No. Stop. Let's call it even. And don't say anything more. Just take these orders and prepare to board Caroline when she launches tomorrow afternoon. The two pilots who brought you here yesterday won't be flying this time, and, as I mentioned, don't go looking for them either. One last thing, sir: don't believe them next time. They like to joke around, and this time they really pulled a fast one on you. That's the only reason I'm not letting you twist in the wind. You could have found yourself in a serious predicament. Do you understand, sir?"

"I understand, Senior Chief Shell. I learned a valuable lesson out here and I got lucky in the end. Thanks a lot."

"You're welcome. Good luck, sir. And please leave Aguilera alone. He's good people. He just got you to bite on one of the oldest aircraft carrier jokes around."

"Understood, Senior Chief. No problem. Good luck. Thanks again."

I waved goodbye to Aguilera, who was punching a typewriter inside the office, and he nodded back. The following afternoon, the COD flew back to NAS Guantanamo Bay. I didn't know the pilots were returning me to Cuba. As luck would have it, the ferry arrived back at the Naval Station pier two hours before the arrival of *Aylwin*. This time, I made my connection back to the Naval Station on time, without any drama.

Temporary Duty, USS *Aylwin, FF-1081, March 1982*

The Ghosts of Wallabout Bay

Standing watch in January on the East River at 0200 hours was grueling. It was brutally cold, made worse by the constant wind blasts blowing off the water. I was the Officer of the Deck, and Operations Specialist Second Class Carl Franz was my petty officer of the watch. We served four hours of duty together that frigid, memorable night.

"My God, this is freezing, Mr. Haynes," Petty Officer Franz complained, stamping his feet and pulling his reefer collar closer to his chin. "Sure do wish we were in Charleston."

"Me too, Franz, me too. It's worse here than in Philly. And I thought that winter watch duty sucked."

"Same difference to me, Philly or Brooklyn. I hope none of them ghosts show up." Franz answered grimly.

"Ghosts? What are you talking about?"

"Weatherspoon and me went to Fort Greene Park and saw the memorial to the POWs from the Revolutionary War. You know where it is?"

"Never heard of it."

"Fort Greene is four blocks east of here, near the Bed-Sty projects. There's a monument that the Daughters of the American Revolution put up about eighty years ago."

"So what about the ghosts?"

"Look straight out there," Franz said, nodding towards the Manhattan skyline. "A good chunk of the Brooklyn Navy Yard was once a stinky swamp called Wallabout Bay. Two hundred years ago it looked a lot different. See, right here is where the redcoats parked four or five old battlewagons that were decommissioned. They were junky wooden prisoner of war ships."

"That's amazing."

"Well, there were hundreds of American POWs on each ship. Rotten food. They had no heat, there were diseases like smallpox and typhoid and measles. It's believed each ship lost five prisoners or more every day."

"How do you know all this?"

"Like I said, we went to the park and looked at the memorial. It's only a five-minute ride from here. A few days later I went to the local library and asked a librarian about the colonial history of the Navy Yard. She pulled a few books off the shelf. I spent a Saturday afternoon reading them."

Our breaths billowed out before us in frosty clouds. "Wow, Franz," I said, rubbing my hands. "I didn't know anything about this."

"Yeah, so what happened was when the watches on the prison ships turned over, the replacement guards would open the hatches and yell down to the prisoners, 'Bring out the dead.' Volunteers would carry the bodies out to sand bars that used to be out there, along the shore of the East River and bury them. When they built the Navy yard, workers kept finding old bones. They tossed the bones in hogsheads and stored them. Then some veterans or whoever decided the dead should be honored. Long time later, the DAR collected enough money to build that memorial at Fort Greene."

"Ah, I get it. There's probably a bunch of ghosts or spirits all around us. That's wild."

"Yeah, and don't forget the other history of this place."

"What's that?"

"The Battle of Brooklyn."

"Remind me."

"So General Washington and his army were dug in not too far from right here, the trenches were facing east. 'Course this was all farmland or woods during the war."

"Right. Brooklyn Heights was part of that line. Is that the battle where Washington almost got annihilated, but he got away? Or one of those battles?"

"Yeah that's it." Franz cast his gaze across the bay. "See, where the Verrazano Bridge lands in Brooklyn, the redcoats landed a bunch of regulars from Staten Island. They marched west towards Washington's position. They had him cornered, with overwhelming numbers against him. So, the plan was for the redcoats to charge straight at Washington's position the next morning. But then, early in the morning of the planned attack, a thick fog came rolling down the East River. Washington collected all these small boats from the Lower East Side of Manhattan, the locals helped him. His army muffled their oars and rowed across the river to Manhattan. Back and forth all night. Even most of their horses got away. When the redcoats attacked a couple hours later, they found empty trenches."

"Then the two armies fought up Manhattan Island 'til Washington evacuated to the mainland to the north. Most everyone escaped."

Franz nodded. "That's the story, Mr. Haynes."

"Did you know about a mile upriver on the Brooklyn side is where the Navy built the USS *Monitor* that fought in the Battle of the Ironclads in Hampton Roads in the spring of 1862, against the CSS *Virginia*?" I asked.

"Nope," Franz said. "Lotta history here."

Brooklyn Navy Yard from World Trade Tower, 1982, Author Photo

"No doubt. How come you're so interested in American history?"

"I guess I never told you I got a degree in history," Franz answered without a hint of bragging.

"Good for you." I stared intently at my partner-watch stander. "Me, too."

"Yeah, I heard that. I went to junior college for two years. Then I took my next two years to get my bachelor's from Cal State-Chico."

I looked at him. "Why don't you—"

"Go to OCS, right?"

"Well, now that you mention it, why not?"

Franz's eyes were on the water again. "I was asked to take the test two years ago. I said, 'No.' I got just over a year to go on my contract, then two years reserves and I'm out."

"To do what on the outside?"

"To teach history, of course. I got some benefits I can use to get a master's in teaching, and I'll be good to go."

"I'm jealous of you," I said.

"How so, sir?"

"You're doing what I wanted to do at one time in my life."

"Still time, sir."

"I'm staring down three more years of active duty. Then we'll see. But I appreciate the history lesson tonight. You're very good."

"It's what I like to do," said Franz. "Not hard to do something you are passionate about, right?"

"I agree. Good for you, anyway, Petty Officer Franz."

"Thanks, Mr. Haynes. I'm excited about the future."

Extortion Letter

One morning after quarters, Chief Sanchez pulled me aside to compliment me. "Ya know what, Mr. Haynes? You might be gettin' the hang of things a little bit these days. I heard you nailed Seaman Moskovitz last night at the quarterdeck."

"I don't know that the operative word is, 'nailed,' but I did ruin his evening if that's what you mean. Three times this week at quarters I told the kid he was overdue for a haircut, *three* God-damn times. So, last night he tried to go ashore, and as Officer of the Deck I told him he wasn't leaving the Navy yard looking like Ozzy Osbourne. He threw a hissy fit in public, on the fucking quarterdeck, 'til I told him to knock it off, that he wasn't going on liberty without looking like a United States Navy sailor. I saw this morning that he still hasn't gotten a haircut. I can wait 'til the Fourth of July. Or Halloween. He stays onboard 'til he looks like a squared-away sailor. Tell him I said so."

"He whined about it today, to me."

"And?"

"Like you said, all it takes is going to the ship's barber and getting a navy haircut. Problem solved. I told him that, too. I give him two more days. Then he don't have a choice but to cut it. I'll do it with garden shears if I got to."

"Your call," I said. "Tell Moskovitz the XO better not see him."

"Yeah, I'll do that. Mr. Haynes, I need to talk to you about this paint job you mentioned to the division this morning."

"What about it, Chief?"

"I mean, you know how cold the thermometer says it is today? If you're painting navy warship bulkheads in cold weather, you damn well need to know, sir. It's forty degrees."

"Thanks for sharing, Chief. I'll make a note of it in my chit list book."

"Mr. Haynes don't be jokin' with me. See, you got the guys painting the O-1 level bulkheads with primer and then navy gray in forty-degree weather. And it's fixin' to go below freezing overnight."

"Once again, translation for the ensign, please."

"Mr. Haynes, you *can't* go paintin' navy gray on metal in 40-degree weather and expect it to stick. It's wasting manhours and it's wasting your paint. All you're doing is setting it up, so we do the fuckin' job twice. It's busy work with no purpose. See my point? The deck apes – 1st Division boatswain mates – are laughing at us. We look like idiots."

"Let me talk to Lt. McDonald. Hold off for twenty minutes. I'll get back to you."

"If you need me to go with you, I can tell him myself."

"No need. I get it. Besides, it's for me to explain to him, like you just explained to me. Just hold off on putting the guys to work for a bit."

I made a beeline to the wardroom where Ted McDonald reviewed the latest project timeline blueprints. He was bent over an open page, scribbling notes in his notebook. "Lt. McDonald?"

"Ensign Haynes?"

"Sir, can I speak to you for a minute?"

"Yes. I'm going to review these project timelines with the XO, so make it quick. What's on your mind?"

"Sir, about OI division painting the exterior bulkheads on the O-1 level. It's 40 degrees outside and the temperature is dropping."

"And Chief Sanchez says paint won't stick to metal in this weather."

"Uh, well, that's about right," I said. "How did…. See, the problem—"

"He spoke to me about this last night just before liberty call. I'll tell you what I told him. A senior captain from Surface Forces Atlantic is due here in the morning to get an overhaul progress report. The captain says he wants it done today, wherever we can 'spiff up' the weather decks. Pronto."

"Sir, I just think—"

"Listen, I get it. Your men paint the O-1 level today, and next weekend the paint is flaking off the bulkheads."

"So why—"

"Because I said so."

"Sir?"

"Rod, I don't have time for this, so I'll cut to the quick. The captain says to paint the bulkheads, we paint the bulkheads. If he says paint the anchor and it's lying in fifty fathoms of water, we paint it. Or at least we try to. There will be *no* back-and-forth discussions, no forming of committees, and no meetings of the minds. I don't want to hear Chief Sanchez kicking up a storm. I was given an order. Your job is to make it happen. Explanations don't come with this order. Sometimes we need to act without questions."

"Sir, I want—"

"No. You go tell Chief Sanchez to put the men to work. If you want to blame somebody, blame me."

"No, sir. I already gave the order at quarters. I'm responsible for my division."

"Alright then, get to it. I want to see you up there making sure they know you're watching them. They'll hate you for babysitting them. Go earn your pay."

"Aye, aye, sir."

As I opened the hatch to leave the wardroom, Lt. McDonald called over to me. "Ensign Haynes?" I turned towards the operations officer.

"Sir?"

"In your navy career you will receive more than a few orders you either don't understand, don't like, or, possibly, want to ignore. Bottom line is when you and I are told to do something by a superior officer, the only right answer is a cheery, 'Aye, aye,' and you do what you are ordered to do, to the very best of your ability. You don't have to like every order but carry it out anyway, no editorial comments. That's true if you are in combat or if you are in a shipyard doing a paint job. It's that simple. Why am I explaining this to a commissioned officer, anyway? Did they cover this at OCS or not?"

"They definitely covered it, more than one time. I understand, Lt. McDonald. I don't have any questions, sir."

"Okay, then. Get to it." The Ops Boss returned to reviewing his project document. I quickly left the wardroom to find Chief Sanchez. I found four of my men on the O-1 level smoking cigarettes. Chief Sanchez was ahead, picking at a section of the bulkhead with his pocketknife. I ensured he was out of the hearing range of his men.

"Look at this sir, it's rusty beneath the paint here. We need to take all this shit down to bare metal when the sun comes out and the temperature is right, give it a good layer of primer, and then make it haze gray before we can underway for Charleston."

"Put 'em to work, Chief. They need to be painting these bulkheads in five minutes. The morning is passing, we need to turn to, and get moving."

"What? I told Lt. McDonald—"

"Yeah, I know what you told him yesterday. Listen, you and I got to understand each other. If you go discussing division business with him and don't let me in, that's dirty pool."

"Dirty pool? How you figure?"

"I can't run a fucking division if my right-hand people are going around me without my knowing about it. Where does that put me? Out on a limb not knowing what the hell is going on. I wasn't let in on this deal, which makes me look like an idiot."

"Sir, I'm just trying—"

"Chief, listen. You're an experienced Navy seadog, and I mean that with all due respect. I have made a habit of listening to you very closely. Your advice is almost always right on the money. I will disagree at times, but that's normal. I can't lead this division if you go making side deals with the senior officers I'm supposed to be reporting to. They won't respect me. I lose face and I look weak."

"I told you—"

"You told me when I got here last July that I need to work with you and check with you if I have questions. That's exactly what I've been doing, Chief. But sometimes, like, right about now, you *have* to let me take the reins. You still get to decide who goes on liberty each afternoon. You still get to assign the jobs each morning. You still get to tell me if you don't agree or if there's something I need to know, or if I'm really stepping in it, but now I need to do a few more things on my own. The two of us got to work together, but there's only one division officer in OI division. That's me."

"This paint job is bullshit."

"Yeah, it's bullshit," I said. "Tell me, Chief. How much of everyday life inside and outside the Navy is bullshit? Maybe a whole lot? And who makes the bullshit orders happen?"

The chief glared at me, biting his lip.

"Tell the men to get the paint from 1st division to prep these bulkheads and paint them properly. You decide how much bitching you will accept from them. I don't care. Put them to work right now. The morning is wasting. And I'm not going anywhere. I'll be around, watching. Blame me if you wish."

Ensign extortion letter. Winter 1982

"I ain't blaming nobody. Aye, aye, sir," the chief muttered. He stood tall, rendered a half-hearted salute, and walked away unhappy. I saluted him back.

Two days later, I stood before the division, holding a piece of paper. I found it taped to my reefer jacket that morning. "All right gentlemen, looks like I'm dealing with some pirates in OI division. Somebody tell me about this ransom note." The men in ranks shifted their feet, looking side to side, trying not to smile.

"Ah, Mr. Haynes?" Petty Officer Davis slowly raised his hand.

"Petty Officer Davis?"

"I don't know who did that terrible thing there, but I think I know the demand."

"The demand is for a case of soda in exchange for my ensign bar someone stole off my reefer jacket the other day," I responded. "I understand that much."

"Seems about right, sir. This is like an exchange agreement. You pony up the soda. The ensign bar gets back to you. Win-win." Davis looked at me nodding slightly.

The grins among the men in ranks broadened. I looked over at Chief Sanchez. "Chief? You got any skin in this?"

He shrugged. "I don't know nothin', sir. Seems somebody's got you cornered. This is your deal. Count me out on this one."

I sighed. "Alright, Petty Officer Davis, what's it gonna be?"

Davis answered, "What's what gonna be, Mr. Haynes?"

"I'm asking what *type* of soda. The note doesn't specify what kind of soda is being demanded. I'm surprised these extortionists don't request beer, but I guess soda it is."

"Oh, well, that would be two six-packs of Sprite, two six-packs of Coke."

"Done." I looked over the division, saying, "If any of you guys know who the perpetrator is, or perpetrators are, tell him or them the case of soda will be on the ASROC launcher tonight at midnight, as demanded in the note. I expect my ensign bar to be returned by tomorrow morning. Win-win, right? Chief Sanchez is the intermediary, which means the bar gets back to me through him." The men broke out laughing. I tried, unsuccessfully, to stifle a smile but wasn't successful. Chief Sanchez remained at attention, staring straight ahead. I saw no emotion in his face. It was time to get to work. I barked, "OI division, let's turn to, commence ship's work. 'Ten, hut. Dismissed." The men came to attention, they saluted as one. I returned their salute. We began the workday.

Detective Work

The Fourth of July 1982 dawned hot and steamy in the Brooklyn Naval Yards. Six NATO warships had arrived in town that week to help celebrate New York's Harbor Festival. They were berthed at the navy pier on the Hudson River, on the west side of Manhattan. I'd been onboard *Hewes* for exactly 10 days.

I represented *Joseph Hewes* in a formal "friendship exchange" on a German destroyer wearing my white summer outfit from head to toe. I was alone, with most of the *Hewes*' crew on holiday leave. Two German junior officers traveled to Brooklyn to visit *Hewes* simultaneously. I figured I got the better of that deal. *Hewes* still lay in thousands of pieces inside a drydock, her exterior ground down to bare metal. The painstaking work of bringing her back to life had not yet begun.

US Navy visits German Destroyer, NYC, Fourth of July 1982

My hosts capped the tour off by inviting me to join them in the wardroom where I sampled cold Bavarian brew fresh from the tap. Drinking beer on a warship was a novel experience for me because the US Navy had banned alcohol on their vessels. I had heard that on rare occasions, while on extended deployment, the Navy gave crewmembers two cans of cold beer each at a ship-wide picnic in the middle of the ocean. European navies routinely served wine and beer to their crews. The two German junior officers assigned to escort me around spoke excellent English. They said the ship was heading to a Great Lakes cruise down the St. Lawrence Seaway to Chicago. American sailors loved what was little more than continuous parties and public adulation wherever the ships tied up in Great Lakes ports. "You've got an outstanding summer ahead," I assured them.

After finishing two beers, I bid farewell to my new friends. It was time for a walking tour of lower Manhattan. I began snaking my way southward toward the Battery, through the canyons of the city's financial district. I joined thousands of people on the street milling through the heavy, humid heat and grimy city air. Many streetwalkers nodded respectfully at me as I marched along. The Fourth of July was the best holiday to be in military uniform in New York. I couldn't help but relish all the attention I was getting.

A white Chevrolet station wagon appeared from nowhere, approaching where I stood at a red light. The driver leaned over to the passenger side, unrolled his window, and raised his head towards me.

"Hey, buddy, wanna lift downtown?" Startled, I looked down at him. "Nah, thanks. I'm sightseeing on foot. Appreciate the offer."

I started across the street, the car slowly following close behind. "Hey, seriously, jump in here a minute," the stranger said.

I stood still for a moment. I was in uniform. The chances of being mugged in broad daylight were low. I approached the car and leaned into the window. "What *is* your fucking malfunction, pal?" I said, then went on walking.

The driver put the car in park, opened his door, stepped out onto the street, and yelled loud enough to be heard blocks away, "Hey, Mack, I'm a cop." He waved his beer at me, gesturing for me to come back.

I stopped and turned around, incredulous. "You're a WHAT?"

Reaching into his coat, he pulled out his wallet and moved to the sidewalk. "C'mere, squid. Take a look." Flipping open his wallet and thrusting it towards me he said, "See? I'm the real deal."

I saw a large, gleaming badge in the hot sun. Passersby peered around my shoulder quizzically. "Here, let's see this," I said, grabbing the wallet. The badge was shiny metallic gold and felt heavy. It had dark, blue-colored inscriptions showing a badge number and "New York City PD" across the center. The lower part of the badge read "Detective" in plain block letters. I looked at him, then tossed his wallet back. "Are you for real?"

The man returned to the driver's side and sat inside the car. From the passenger window, he called over to me, "What, I'm kidnappin' a Navy officer? 'Course I'm 'for real.' Got a brother who's a jet mechanic on USS *Independence*. They're overseas right now. Have a beer on me to celebrate the Fourth. We'll drink to my brother. Oh, so you know, I'm a vet, too."

I hesitated, glanced around, yanked open the door and slid into the seat.

"I better not be in the headlines of the *New York Times* tomorrow morning. I can get in deep shit for this," I said, exhaling loudly.

The man threw back his head laughing, reaching behind his seat and pushing aside a red-plaid wool blanket covering a large white Styrofoam cooler. He offered his hand. "Not to worry, you're fine – name's Tommy DeAngelo. I work out of the Sixth Precinct, vice squad. You stationed on one of those navy ships over there?" He pointed back at the pier area, three blocks to the north.

"Nope. They're all foreign NATO units in town for the holiday. We're over in the Brooklyn Naval Yards for an eight-month overhaul. I'm Rod Haynes." I shook his hand. "Good to meet you. This is a first for me."

"How so?"

"You're a cop on duty cruising around in a vehicle with an open Budweiser Kinger in your hand giving a lift and a brew to a naval officer in uniform. What's wrong with this picture?" I cracked the Bud and drank deeply. "Ah, but that's good, real good," I said. "It's liquid hot out there. I know this isn't right, but it sure tastes good."

"Relax, this is New York," said Tommy. "Nothing like a cool one on duty on the Fourth of July in New York with a sailor, while you're on the clock, I always say." He laughed. "So, you're in the yards in Brooklyn. How are you liking the 'Big Apple'?" A routine voice-check-sounding official blared from the police radio unit attached to the dashboard. Tommy grabbed the mike, saying in a low voice, "Unit 478, Ten-Four." The radio went silent again.

"I know a bit about New York. We used to come down here. I'm from Rhode Island. My college roommate lived on the Upper East Side, so we got around when I visited him. I love New York, but it makes me feel small."

"Born and raised in Dallas," Tommy answered. "Don't miss it much."

"You're a long way from home, friend."

"Yeah. The ex-wife's family lives in Queens. She's a stewardess with American Airlines. I was a cop in 'Big D,' and New York is always looking for experienced police officers, so they took me on pretty quick after we came east to be near her folks. Six years later, my wife got sick of being married to a cop, so now she's trying to get married to an airline pilot. At least I don't have to pay alimony. Maybe she'll try life with a farmer or an auto mechanic next."

"Too bad."

"Best thing that ever happened to me. Let's head over to the Bowery, in the East Village. There's some hookers I need to check on." We drove due east on Houston Avenue.

I swallowed a mouthful of cold beer. "Are these hookers, uhm, friends of yours?"

Tommy grimaced, then shook his head. "Don't have too many street friends. Let's say I don't do any personal business with 'em, but sometimes they get good information they share on a 'professional' basis — sort of an unspoken arrangement. I check in with 'em occasionally to see what's going down. I don't bother the girls, much. You'll see."

We were heading east through SoHo, south of Washington Square, towards the Bowery. There were many cars in Manhattan that day, so we kept our beers low as we slowly made our way across town.

"So, tell me, Tommy, did you know Serpico?" I took another long swig of beer.

Tommy sighed. "You know that son-of-a-bitch caused us more headaches. Every time I meet somebody the first time and they hear I'm a cop that's the first God damn question I get asked. No, I never knew the guy. He was gone five or six years before my time. Some guys at the precinct knew him. I guess Pacino in that movie hurt NYPD, but there was less hostility at Serpico from the regulars than you think after it all came down. Some of us believe Frank Serpico was sticking to his principles. You can't fault a guy for that, you just can't. He just got his face shot off for not being crooked, along with those other assholes." Tommy was scowling as he finished his beer, crushed the can, and threw it into the back. "Hand me another, will you? I'll slow down, in a bit."

I asked, "Do you use that gun much?" I pointed at the weapon protruding out of his holster.

"Not if I can help it. It stays in its holster unless I get in a pinch. Book says you pull it out, you better be ready to use it."

"Ever shot someone?"

Tommy looked away before answering slowly, thoughtfully. "Few times, yeah. In April, I caught these three Puerto Ricans breaking into a furniture store uptown. It was midnight and I couldn't see them too good. One of them wouldn't stop coming at me. He was holding a bat, and I told him to stop and lie on the ground. He kept at me even when I told him three times to stop, so I shot him in the arm, just once. I only nicked the son of a bitch, no big deal." Tommy smiled as he recounted the scene. "My backup got there in four minutes. Pretty good bust, 'cause those guys had been at it for a long time, we found out later. Internal investigations cleared me two months after shooting the prick. Like I said, the rule is the gun stays in the holster unless I have to use it."

"Like your job?" I asked.

"It's a living, I s'ppose. Like yours?"

"I think so, but I'm new, so ask me a couple of years from now. We're going down to the Caribbean and then overseas to Europe in a year. Should be fun. Can't wait to go to sea. I think it's gonna be fun."

"Let me tell you something, man. I did one tour in 'Nam in '66 just as things got hot there. Came back stateside in early '68 when guys were coming home in boxes by the hundreds and the service was full of junkies. The smack in Vietnam was cheap, and it was everywhere. The Army was a good place to be if you were here or in Europe, but not if you got shipped to Southeast Asia. I grew up a lot. I'm lucky I got out without being whacko like some of my buddies are now, from that fuckin' war. The military ain't just pretty uniforms and fancy marching music, you know."

"Yeah. Somebody told me that, once." I deadpanned.

We drank our beers silently as we weaved towards the Bowery through heavy traffic and jaywalkers. The neighborhood we entered was rougher than anything I'd seen that day. We passed rows of abandoned buildings, piles of litter and glass bottles scattered on vacant lots between them. A series of liquor stores and pool halls lined the streets of the Bowery, including what Tommy referred to as cheap flop houses. This area resembled the parts of Brooklyn surrounding the Yards.

Tommy said, "This isn't a place to be whenever you have cash. Even when you're *broke*, this is no place for a sailor on liberty. Tell your buddies I said that. There's my 'Baby Cakes,' Charlene, over there." He pointed to a tall woman in a white miniskirt wearing black boots and a red halter top. She waved at us from across the street, standing on a corner with two other women. She slowly walked over towards us, swaying her broad hips. Charlene was a platinum blonde with huge breasts.

Tossing her head, she leaned into the driver's window, her rear end protruding provocatively out into the street. "Well, hello, hot stuff. Got a cigarette for your girlfriend?" She pressed her breasts together tightly. The resulting crevasse was deep. Her chest looked gorgeous.

"Hey, beautiful, here ya go. This here is Rod. He's a Navy officer. How's business?"

Tommy shook a Marlboro from a pack in his shirt pocket and fired up his lighter for the hooker. Her face was caked with heavy makeup. She wore bright red lipstick.

"Hey there, sailor boy. I'm Charlene." She looked back at Tommy. "Business is going good, real good. At this rate, I'll retire at forty. Or be dead." She stood up, looked up and down the street, her hand resting on the top of the car. Then she pulled her blouse down over her stomach, spilling over a belt tightly wrapped around her midsection. Charlene leaned into the vehicle again, her hand covering her mouth. "Jimmie ain't here," Charlene murmured. "Somethin's going on in the Bronx this afternoon, so he left us alone today. Didn't say nothin' more about it."

"What's going on up there, doll?"

"Like I tol' you ten times, Sweetie, I don't know nothin' about Jimmie's business. He walloped me the one time I asked him twice, so I don't do that no more. All I know is he's carryin' a big piece and a huge fuckin' wad of money today, maybe ten G's or more. I seen it this mornin' when he collected from us. Jimmie's comin' back here tonight. Sandy says the last shipment made Jimmie some serious bucks."

The detective searched the hooker's eyes for a long time. Nobody said a word for a while. Tommy finally asked, "How does she know how much Jimmie made, huh?" More silence.

Charlene pleaded, "Listen, Tommy, none of us are selling. Honest. Jimmie's connections in Harlem and other places, who are moving the stuff. We ain't using, neither."

"If you get caught dealing, baby doll, I can't help you. Was Anthony or Bobby in the car with him today?" Tommy again stared straight into her eyes.

The hooker sighed. "Yeah. Both were." She leaned further into the car and winked at me, chewing her gum with her mouth open. She pressed her breasts together again and leaned over some more to give me a second peek. I again stared directly down at the front of her blouse. Those things were real. And most beautiful.

I swallowed hard and stammered, "No, thanks. I'd like to, but I'm just riding around with Tommy. Appreciate the offer."

She frowned, shrugged, and glanced back at Tommy. "Did ya hear about Crystal?"

"Nope," said Tommy.

"Some customer gave her the clap real good. She's out of action for a bit. Jimmie got pissed off when he heard about it, so he slapped her a few times. He even made her give up next week's profit in advance when he found out. She doesn't make all her customers use rubbers."

"That's a shame. Listen, doll, you gotta be careful with Jimmie. I'm telling you straight: you get mixed up in pushin' junk, I can't help you. It ain't business as usual with coke or smack. I'm serious, Charlene. This is the last time I'll say it."

"Yeah, I know, you say the same thing every time I see you. I told you, Tommy, I'm off the stuff now. Can't afford it no more. I need to earn my money doin' my business. I already said none of us here are movin' any coke or smack. I got my kid to look out for. You know that."

"All right, see you in a week. You call me at that number if something big comes down, right? Tell the girls to stay off the street tomorrow afternoon for about two hours after dinnertime, okay?"

"Yeah, thanks. I'll spread the word."

"Hey, not too much. I don't want the place empty, right? We got to take a couple downtown. Looks bad if we don't."

Charlene sighed. "Okay, okay, Tommy. See you in a few days. 'Bye, sailor boy. You tell your friends to come see me, right?"

"Yeah. See you around, Charlene. Good to meet you," I replied.

Tommy pulled out of the parking lot and drove north towards midtown.

"Is Charlene a whore or a prostitute?" I wondered out loud.

"That's a funny question." Tommy laughed. "She's not working for free, for Christ's sake. Why do you ask?"

"Makes me wonder. She charges for her services, so that makes her a prostitute, but she's whoring her soul at the same time. So, in a way, she's a whore."

Tommy stared at me long and hard before laughing out loud. "Strange. You're a sailor and you're thinkin' these thoughts? Everybody's got to make a living. What, you think you're so superior?"

"Truthfully, I feel bad for her. It's a tough life on the streets, period. I was almost out on the streets in Seattle a while back, so I know."

"It is hard, you're right," Tommy agreed.

"I don't see how you can keep all of this straight," I told the detective.

Tommy asked, "Whaddya mean 'keep this straight'?"

"Well, you get information from Charlene about drugs, but let her be a hooker. Where do the rules start and end?"

"Ensign, this isn't rocket science. If someone wants to buy a prostitute, that's a lot different from pushing or buying cocaine or junk. You're talking about two separate things. One's a misdemeanor, the other is a felony. I let her do what she does so that I can move on to the more serious things. Civilians think everything works like on *Kojak*. It ain't that way in real life on the streets."

"I'm just saying this doesn't make total sense. Charlene could be in a bad spot if anybody gets wise to her talking to you. Drug dealers hate snitches if the movies are accurate. And if her pimp gets busted, she needs a new one. Right?" I cracked open another beer.

"I know that. I think about her safety. I don't stay long when I talk to her. She's trying to survive holding down a rotten job. We leave her and a couple of her friends alone so she can make a living. This is a dirty business. Some people get rich, and a lot more find trouble working the streets, whether it's sex or drugs or breaking into warehouses."

Tommy took a long pull on his beer, emptied it, and crushed the can in his fist before tossing it to the back seat. "And we just try to survive all the surrounding bullshit. Grab me another, will ya?"

I popped another Bud for him. We drove silently as Tommy reached over and turned up the radio to listen to classic country music on a local radio station.

"What's good about being a cop in New York?" I asked. "I mean, you've been doing it for ten years now."

"It's exciting, for one," Tommy said, a glint creeping into his eye. "You never get bored. Every day, you get something new. You try to do good even though sometimes somebody loses. Your buddies stick with you in the tough times. And you go through a lot of tough times, believe you me. Benefits are excellent. We get pensions. Sometimes you deal with injustice in a job where you're supposed to be on the side of justice. And, sometimes, the bad guys lose."

"You mean like in *Serpico* where everybody threatens him because they think he's ratting them out? Sorry, shouldn't have said that." The moment I said it, I wanted to take it back.

"No, not like that. Well, okay, maybe it *does* happen that way. Sometimes, I guess. Of course, there's crooked cops. Just like you got bad guys in your line of work. Wait till you meet some real asshole senior officer you want to crack in the mouth. It depends on what you want to see in others, I guess. The cop business isn't simple, like, 'this guy broke the law and that one didn't.' You gotta make some calls every fuckin' day and not every call is gonna be fair. Just like life, like Charlene and her pimp, and the drugs and everything else. It doesn't all come in a neat package with a bow. Like I said, this ain't *Dragnet*, pal."

We drove around for two more hours on the Fourth of July, north to Central Park and then downtown again. Tommy offered me a ride back to Brooklyn as evening fell, but I said no. He let me off at the station so I could catch a subway back to Flatbush Avenue. Tommy shook my hand. The station wagon lurched directly towards a fire hydrant, swerving around it at the last second. I watched as it screeched around a corner and vanished. I never made it to the Battery that Fourth of July. And I never saw Tommy or Charlene again.

Dad Comes to Brooklyn

During my visit to Rhode Island over the New Year holiday I asked Dad if he had ever seen a warship in a drydock under repair. He said no. Here was an excellent opportunity to visit me aboard *Joseph Hewes* while she was on the blocks. Dad was busy, he said, but he could make it to Brooklyn for two nights. He would stay with me in the officers' quarters.

He arrived in Brooklyn late Friday afternoon. We jumped in a taxi and headed out to Alfredo's, an Italian restaurant in Brooklyn Heights. It was a low-key neighborhood eatery. The food was excellent. At our corner table, one covered with a white tablecloth and a slow-burning candle, we ordered a bottle of red wine to accompany our entrees. Dad had his bourbon and water. I ordered a draft beer.

"What do you think of the ship, Dad?"

"It's hard to tell. She's in pieces right now. When are you due back in Charleston?"

"Late Spring. We're in Guantanamo Bay in July. Ugh."

"The drydock is a loud, dirty place," he said. "Chaotic."

"True, but at least the engineering and combat systems are opened up. I've been tracing steam lines and electrical wiring. I get lost in all the piping. How's business?"

"Same. Start and stop. We've got a few contracts going. I'm hoping a couple more will come through. It's not a steady, predictable business. Feast and famine, as they say."

"Well, become an artist full-time." I smiled as I said it.

Dad barked a loud laugh, then sipped his drink. "Now that's a thought. No, teaching at RISD is keeping food on the table and doing the restoration work is bringing in extra money."

Both Mom and Dad were graduates of the Rhode Island School of Design. Dad went on to earn his architecture degree there. "But Chick is a great help. I'm happy to have him." Chick McGowan was a senior draftsman in Dad's architecture firm. He was extremely talented and reliable. They always seemed to be on each other's wavelength.

"Good for him," I said.

"What made you say that?" Dad asked with raised eyebrows.

"What do you mean?"

"That tone. Why the sneer?" Dad was puzzled.

"I'm going to tell you something Dad," I said, sitting back. "I've wanted to share this with you but never found the right moment."

"Now is as good as any. What's on your mind?"

"I came back from OCS and spent a week at Mom's place. One afternoon I came to your office to have lunch with you. I was in uniform."

"We went to Geoff's for sandwiches. You had pastrami and a can of Sprite."

"Yes, that day. When I first came into the office you were on the far side of the room. I stepped inside the door and Chick hustled up to me and gave me a palm-up salute, like the British salute."

"I don't know where you're going with this, Rod, but this is the first I've heard of it."

"I know. It's hard to bring it up now, so long after it happened. So, I said, 'What the fuck is this, Chick?' He backed off and said it was a welcome back from boot camp salute. I told him I didn't think mocking the uniform was a good thing, so don't do that again. Then I found you. That's it."

"Rod, you've lost me. Chick popped a salute at you when you came into the office. Is that your point?"

"Not exactly. I accept without question that Chick was a draft dodge— I mean, conscientious objector during Vietnam."

"Rod, I think you need to—"

"You asked me to tell you what's on my mind. The uniform I wear isn't some kind of costume in a Three Stooges skit. It's not a joke, not an object to be made fun of."

"Did anyone say otherwise? Come on now—" He leaned back with open arms extended.

"Dad, since I've known Chick as a kid, I've seen him disrespect Mom. Not publicly, but he's never been nice to her. He's barely considerate, always gives her the cold shoulder, like she's not fit to be your wife. Always. I don't like it, especially given your relationship with him. How does it fit into this conversation? You tell Chick if he ever does what he did that day in mocking me or the uniform, I'm gonna pop him. I suspect he might pop me back, I'm not good at violence, I try to avoid it. But this shit ends. You tell him when I am in his presence he can keep any negative opinions about the uniform, the Navy, whatever, to himself."

"You're out of line, Rod. Relax. As for his treatment of your mother, I never saw anything negative."

"No, you didn't. You weren't looking for it. His opinion of Mom was and is something you didn't give a shit about. That was clear to anyone looking at it."

"Christ, what's with you tonight?"

"Dad, I've had this on my mind a long time. Chick's still being rude to Mom, and his mocking me or the uniform or whatever, that's where it ends."

Dad stared at me and sipped his drink twice. He looked puzzled and slightly annoyed.

"I don't want to fight with you or ruin this weekend or anything," I said. "You and I need a new understanding about certain things. One is that if Chick thinks a Navy uniform is funny, he is entitled to his opinion. He is *not* entitled to make fun of the service. For god's sake, you are a veteran. Why am I explaining this?"

"I don't think you need to, but you're entitled to your opinion. Let's drop this, Rod. I'll share your thoughts with Chick, in my way, but I will tell him you took his joke badly." Dad sighed a long sigh and looked away for more than a moment.

I leaned towards Dad, almost in his face. "Things have changed. I'm not the person I was a year ago. I don't know if it's for the good or better, But I've learned to say what's on my mind where before, I was reluctant to speak out."

"No, you were *never* reluctant to speak your mind, but I still think you could take it down a few notches."

"I meant I was leery of speaking to you about certain stuff before. I'm not anymore. The cannelloni here are out of this world. Let's grab a couple, and two cappuccinos."

"Okay."

"We're going to the East Village tonight."

"Oh? Where to?"

"Do you know the Village Vanguard?"

Dad threw his head back, laughing out loud. "Do I know the Vanguard? There are all sorts of popular recordings from that place; it's an institution. I think it's a great idea to go and take it in." The bill came.

"Dad, let me get this."

"What?"

"Do you know how long I've wanted to say that and have the money in my pocket to back it up? I'm done leaning on your wallet whenever we go out for dinner."

"Rod, it's not necessary."

"I didn't say it was necessary, Pop. I feel good just having the ability to do this now. All right?"

"Fine. Thank you." Dad looked on approvingly.

"Like I said, I'm not the starving student or road traveler with twenty dollars in my pocket anymore."

"No, but you aren't rich, either."

"True, but neither are you. I have a steady paycheck now and it feels good to be self-sufficient for the first time in a while. Probably for the first time, period."

We took a long taxi ride over to the Lower East Side. We walked down a flight of stairs from street level when we arrived at the Vanguard.

"Good grief, that's Jimmy Williams over there," Dad said when we entered.

"Who?" I pointed towards an available corner table.

"Williams is a jazz pianist I've seen several times before," Dad said. "This is unbelievable. What luck!" He followed close behind me, clutching my right shoulder for a moment.

We sat down and ordered drinks. Dad said, "Almost forgot to mention seeing you on television a few months ago. Your mother screamed; she couldn't believe it was you. I was visiting her at her apartment."

"Yeah, Miss Universe. It was on Broadway." I said hesitantly. One more sordid incident to talk about. Wonderful. "It was one of those 'Command Performance' things where the XO said, 'You guys go over there to that beauty pageant and do it and don't give me any guff. I expect to see you represent the United States Navy on national TV with pride.' So, I just went."

"You guys looked snazzy in those spiffy white uniforms of yours," Dad said approvingly. "You reminded me of your Grandfather Day. Was it fun?"

"Uh, not exactly, Pop." I took an extra-large swig of beer. "Remember me walking out to the front of the stage holding that stupid lion cub?"

"Yes, yes. I meant to ask about that. How strange..."

"Yeah, well, here's the deal on that. I was escorting Miss South Africa. She brought a present from her homeland to give to the Deputy Mayor of New York City." I took another mouthful of suds.

"The lion cub?" Dad asked.

"Yeah, that stupid lion cub. I pulled it out of its cage and walked on stage. Its claws were digging into my arms, through the uniform. I mean, those claws were digging deep. It hurt. Then, when everyone in the theater saw the cub, they started clapping, and the cub got frantic. The thing weighed about 45 pounds, clawing me like crazy. He wanted out of there."

"I don't remember that part."

"Good. Anyway, the applause startled the shit, or should I say, the piss out of him. The whole front of my service dress white jacket was drenched in lion piss."

"WHAT?" Dad leaned back and roared with laughter, shaking his head and covering his mouth with glee. Then he leaned towards me and clapped his two hands on my shoulders. "Of course. It's perfect. What is it with you and these weird situations you seem to attract?"

"I wish I knew, so I could steer clear of them. You probably didn't see me hold the fucking cub up to the Deputy Mayor for about two seconds and then I almost ran off stage. I was supposed to let the viewers at home get a good look and be impressed. Instead, I hustled back to its cage just out of sight off-stage and put him back in there. Then I took a cab back to Brooklyn smelling like a toilet. That was the end of my night."

"Rod, I keep telling you, you gotta write a book."

"I think the cub has been sent to the Bronx Zoo, but who knows? I'll put writing a book on my daily to-do list, Pop. Thanks for the advice." I shook my head and grimaced.

We spent the rest of the evening drinking beer and listening to fantastic music. The crowd and the cigarette smoke made the Vanguard feel claustrophobic, but we still enjoyed it. We headed back to Brooklyn around 11:30 pm.

"Nice neighborhood," Dad remarked as we exited the Brooklyn Bridge and entered the Bedford-Stuyvesant projects.

"I don't go outside the gates at night. Pretty scary here."

The following day, we took the subway to Central Park West, where we had lunch at the historic Tavern at the Green restaurant. Then we walked north to the Dakota. I pointed to the spot my friend Kyle and I had been standing twenty-four hours before John Lennon's assassination.

We stood together in silence. Then we walked another six or seven blocks to the Museum of Natural History and spent the afternoon wandering around. That evening we had tickets to watch the New York Knicks take on the Washington Bullets in a lackluster game at Madison Square Garden. Dad left for Rhode Island the following morning. It had been a good visit, all things considered.

Underway At Last

Joseph Hewes steamed south down the eastern seaboard at a leisurely ten knots. We left New York on a sparkling summer's day the previous morning. Most of the crew not on watch crowded the weather decks to watch the Statue of Liberty pass down our starboard side, with Governors Island off to port. Inbound traffic grew thicker as we steamed towards an inlet known as the Narrows, passing beneath the Verrazano Bridge. James and I stood up on the flybridge on the port side, watching a teeming summertime crowd at Coney Island through the Big Eye binoculars. Our first day at sea was relaxing, the focus being on the engineering plant and its operators. We hoped they could get us back to Charleston without incident.

USS Joseph Hewes, *FF-1078*

I stood my first two underway watches up on the bridge as junior officer of the deck under instruction. LTJG Sullivan spent the watch peppering me with questions about navigation, tactical maneuvering, shipboard emergency procedures, and how to let go the anchor in an emergency. The bridge team practiced sending tactical signals over the squawk box, the interior communication net, to the Combat Information Center below.

The following day, we were forty-five miles east of Cape May, New Jersey. The boatswain pipe had sounded throughout the ship at 0600 hours, calling the crew to their feet for another working day at sea. James and I slept blissfully through breakfast and officer's call, but our absence had not escaped the eye of the XO.

Just before 0900, the XO slammed open the door to Boys Town – the tiny stateroom where four of us ensigns berthed – and began shouting, "Ensign Haynes, Ensign Lee, on your feet!" Shaken from our slumbers, we leaped to attention next to our racks, dressed only in our boxer shorts.

"What time is it now, gentlemen?"

James glanced at his watch. "Sir, it is 0845."

"What the hell are you doing in your racks? You two think you have special sleep-in privileges?"

I responded, "No, sir. We just slept through officer's call. I apologize, XO."

The XO rubbed his jaw, his eyes flashing. "This is unacceptable. Where are your men right now?"

We answered in unison. "Yes, sir. We don't know, sir."

"I want to see you standing in your division spaces in five minutes. Move!"

James and I scrambled for our pants and shirts and ball caps. A crowd of enlisted men had gathered outside the space, listening to XO chew us into a pulp. Stalking from our stateroom, the XO pushed some sailors to one side, hollering, "Make a hole. Don't you men have work to do? If you don't, I'll give you some!"

The ship traffic on the eastern seaboard was heavy, but we encountered glassy seas for the entirety of our trip, which was unusual for that time of year. As we steamed south, the ship was put through a series of systems tests to check if the radar, weapon systems, engineering updates, and sonar systems were functioning according to design specifications. Before the Navy formally accepted ship delivery from the repair contractor, these checks had to be performed on all systems overhauled in Brooklyn. Millions of taxpayer dollars in ship repairs had to be appropriately accounted for. The test results were mixed.

The twelve civilian technicians riding the ship calibrated the systems and identified areas that still need "tweaking." The ship was due to set sail for Guantanamo Bay refresher training in five weeks. Between now and then, much training and material preparation was laid in place to ensure the ship was fully seaworthy and ready to perform her missions at sea.

I first saw Buoy 2-Charlie bobbing up and down alone in the Atlantic Ocean several miles east of Charleston, South Carolina. When sailors referred to 'making Buoy 2-Charlie,' it meant much more than arriving at just another navigation channel entrance into port. Rendezvousing with Buoy 2-Charlie confirmed our safe return home from sea. Just before the buoy passed down our starboard side, the conning officer ordered, "right standard rudder, steady course 270." The captain sat silently in his chair, monitoring the piloting team's activity on the bridge, feet planted on the console and a cigarette in hand. The boatswain mate of the watch kept a sharp eye out for a signal from the Old Man to refill his USS *Joseph Hewes* porcelain coffee cup. It looked like it had last been washed before the ship's repair period began.

Cooper River Bridge, Charleston, SC

The smell of rotting marshes and complex nutrients of the island shores mingling with the brackish waters surrounding Charleston on three sides wafted over the pilot house as Buoy 2-Charlie grew smaller and smaller astern of us. This odor was welcomed by sailors returning from sea, proof positive terra firma beckoned. Historic Fort Sumter lay in the foreground, with the city of Charleston looming up behind the spot where the American Civil War had begun in April 1861. I wasn't excited about seeing Charleston for the first time, even though my mother's father had been stationed there for a time during World War II. I was resigned to living in the cradle of the Confederacy, taking in the area's sights when I could. But I wasn't thrilled about it.

Pilots were available for warships arriving in Charleston Harbor, especially for units unfamiliar with local inland waters. *Hewes*' captain deferred to the pilots for close maneuvering once his ship arrived at the naval station, sometimes not even then. When many ships were in port, making the danger of collision more acute than usual, two tugs were tied up to *Joseph Hewes* (one on the bow, the other on the stern quarter, typically on opposite sides). The ship was then slowly shifted around into its assigned berth, most often tied up outboard a sister warship.

Just before noon, *Joseph Hewes* maneuvered into her final position pier side at Charleston Naval Station. All junior officers were ordered to the bridge to observe Lieutenant Commander Alexander direct the complex evolution of mooring the ship to the pier, requiring an intricate series of commands to the six stations on the ship where mooring lines held the ship in place. One critical factor was whether the wind was on-setting, helping push the ship towards the pier, or if the wind was off-setting, pushing her away from the pier. Frequently the wind was at an odd angle off the pier, making the mooring evolution more difficult.

When the ship was finally secured, a single whistle signaled to everyone that the *Joseph Hewes* was officially tied up at Charleston Naval Station. Some faint cheering was heard from inside the ship now that we had officially arrived home.

The captain clicked on the squawk box down to main control, "Engineering officer of the watch, this is the Captain. Secure the steam plant, we're home. Tell the snipes they did a good job on our trip from Brooklyn. Bravo Zulu." "Bravo Zulu" was radio shorthand for "well done!"

"This is Chief Nelson. Aye, Captain, thank you. Main control is securing the plant. When we get wrapped up down here, we will report the plant status to the Command Duty Officer. Out."

"Very well," The captain said, then turned and walked off the bridge, heading down below to greet his family in the wardroom.

Seconds later, a crane on the pier carried the brow over to our portside stern area. After the boatswain mates secured the brow to the ship, the visitors came streaming across the brow onto the quarterdeck. A small navy band standing half-way down the pier tried playing *Anchors Aweigh*, with limited success. They needed practice. We were finally home.

Navy JAG Visit

Two days later, the XO ordered the sixteen officers he read off a list to muster outside the captain's cabin immediately after the officers delivered "the word of the day" to their divisions.

James and I were on the list. I was extremely nervous. "James, what's this about?"

"Got me, man. Guess we'll know in fifteen minutes. See you up there."

"Yeah, no choice. Command performance. God damn it all." I briefed OI division before returning to the captain's cabin.

Destroyer Squadron Four's Commodore had sent two Navy Judge Advocate General (JAG) lieutenants to the ship that day. JAG officers were Navy lawyers. I could not imagine what was happening. One by one, fifteen *Joseph Hewes* officers (three others included the captain, XO, and supply officer) were brought into the captain's cabin and informed of their legal rights before being advised of the charges being brought against them. This all happened before they could make any statements in their defense.

I was the third officer brought in. Directed to sit down, I was advised that three-quarters of USS *Joseph Hewes*' wardroom was being charged with "misappropriation of Navy funds." "Ensign Haynes, you are among those being charged."

I stood straight up. "Say what? What the hell are you talking about?"

He looked up from an open folder, sternly replying, "Foul language is uncalled for. Please lower your voice, Ensign Haynes, and grab a seat. Were you not a resident at the Bachelors' Officers Quarters at the Brooklyn Navy base for approximately eight months?"

"Yes, I was. And so were those other guys out there. So what?"

"Along with those other fourteen officers on *Joseph Hewes*, were you not provided living quarters, meals, and a place to gather with your peers?"

"Yes, sir. And while you mention it, we had cold-running beer and a pool table. And a stereo system that played great rock music, clean rooms, and decent showers. But despite our best efforts, we didn't have any women residing with us."

"That is precisely what this investigation is all about."

"Sir?"

"Mr. Haynes, all of you submitted requests for additional subsistence funding while you in Brooklyn due to 'inadequate living conditions on base.' Do you recall filing that form?"

"Just a minute, Lieutenant. I signed a form when the supply officer handed it to me and said it was 'routine paperwork.' You make it sound like I initiated this whachacallit, which I did not."

"That will be considered when the squadron adjudicates this matter."

"What do you mean 'adjudicate'? This is ridiculous."

"Once again, Ensign Haynes, I must ask you to restrain yourself."

"*You* need to understand something here. None of us knew we were improperly collecting subsistence allowances up there. The guy you need to be talking to is Lieutenant Watson. I just said I didn't ask for this. None of us did. He told us it was within our rights. There was no conspiracy to rip anyone off. I'm not, none of us, are criminals. Write that down in your log."

"We are addressing that issue separately."

"So, what now? Am I staring down a six-year stint in Fort Leavenworth? What are you going to do to us?"

"That is the discretion of Commodore Miller at DESRON Four." Miller was in charge of all the ships in Destroyer Squadron Four. "Once all the necessary paperwork is complete, we will revisit the ship and brief you all about the next steps. Please sign here, and here." I scribbled my name twice on some legal documents.

"Sirs, don't take this wrong, but I say this is pure crap. If I had conspired to rip off the navy or understood what I was getting into before this came down, I would've steered clear of it. I just got commissioned two years ago. I'm not going to jail over this."

"We understand completely."

"Yeah, well, Jerry Watson is the guy to hang, if anybody is gonna swing for this. We were assured it was okay. We don't know all the disbursing and supply rules and regulations. It's Jerry's job to keep us on the straight and narrow with all that stuff."

"We intend to inform the Commodore of that fact. You are now excused."

"Yes, sir. I'm not feeling pleased just now."

"That is understandable."

I met James as I was leaving. I stopped him for a moment. "Hey, Rod, man. What's up?"

"You'll find out, James. Stand by for heavy rolls. You won't believe this one."

"Shit."

"Yeah, that's it, all right. Total bag of shit. See you in the wardroom after you're done?" I headed below.

"See you there." James knocked and entered the captain's cabin.

Ten days later, the sixteen officers were mustered into the wardroom to hear the verdict from the two JAG officers. We would have our paychecks docked in equal amounts over the next twelve months until all the subsistence allowances were paid back to the Navy. The matter was closed once the final payment was received. Our permanent records would not reflect this incident in any way. I wanted to ask Jerry Watson what was in store for him, but he was transferred off the ship the next day. I wondered if the captain or XO were formally charged. I never found out.

There was no further follow-up from the JAG officers after our interviews. The money was paid back as ordered. I never knew Lt. Watson's fate, but much later I discovered that Al Richards had found the irregularities and reported them directly to the squadron without first notifying Captain Beckham. That miscue by Al resulted in a lot of heat on Al from the captain. Al's failure to follow the immediate chain of command was a fundamental mistake no officer, however new, should make. He knew better, but he went around Captain Beckham anyway. It was a bad career move.

Charleston Naval Station

Early evenings in springtime Charleston were delightful before the heat and humidity of summer in the Low Country descended with a vengeance. The days grew longer, and soft shadows basked the piers in multiple light shades. The temperature was mild, and the chilly blasts in Brooklyn two weeks earlier were now a distant memory. There was a flurry of activity aboard the ship, with endless streams of contractors and civilian repair personnel investigating and ordering repairs for the problems identified during the ship's transit home from New York, the majority of which were in the engineering and weapon areas.

James, Al Richards, and I found a cheap apartment to rent west of the Ashley River. Each day we weren't on duty, we drove across the Charleston peninsula over a bridge spanning the Ashley River and then drove north a short distance into our complex.

Five days after our return, Destroyer Squadron (DESRON) Four sprang a surprise "Zulu-Five-Oscar" drill on the ship. Our security detail failed miserably in our response. Maintaining security on the naval station was a big deal even in those days. Everyone – civilian and sailor – was required to present his identification card and then formally request permission to leave or come aboard the ship. The OOD intercepted anyone trying to board or depart *Joseph Hewes* without permission.

A Zulu-Five-Oscar drill was essentially an attempt by one or two sailors from another ship to breach *Joseph Hewes'* security. Posing as terrorists, the intruders tried to reach the captain's cabin without being detected. If they made it, the host ship failed the drill. If the invader found the captain in his cabin, he would be "held hostage" until the CO picked up his phone and expressed dissatisfaction with his watch standers down on the quarterdeck. Sometimes those who had allowed the perpetrators aboard, including the roving security guards who wore .45 caliber pistols, were ordered to stand back-to-back watches as punishment. I figured commanding officers probably caught an earful from the commodore, their immediate superior, whenever their ship fared poorly during a Zulu-Five-Oscar drill.

Typically, a ship that failed a Zulu-Five-Oscar exacted revenge on the ship the intruders came from. Occasionally the DESRON had to intercede to stop the escalating "tit for tat" animosity between ships. Other times two ships might cooperate by tipping each other off when a security drill was coming down. No one lost in that arrangement, assuming the DESRON didn't catch wind of what was happening.

One afternoon James and I walked towards his car in the parking lot after liberty call went down. It had been a busy day, and we were both looking forward to relaxing in our apartment that evening. At the end of the pier, we saw three Shore Patrol officers with a German shepherd police dog in tow. One of them randomly tapped the trunk of a car and the dog nervously sniffed around the perimeter on one side, then across the front, to the far side of the vehicle. We watched the dog do this three times on three separate cars, quickly.

"They're looking for drugs," James murmured. "I hope you left your stash at home this morning."

"You're a real comedian, James," I replied. "You need to know my weed is in your glove compartment. Uh, oh. Too late. Look, now they're inspecting your car. It's all over for you, pal."

Walking towards James' car, we suddenly heard a commotion a few rows over. The dog was barking and madly scratching at the door of a red Mustang while the handler desperately tried to hold the animal in check. Two other members of the Shore Patrol approached the window on the driver's side and tapped on it twice with their nightsticks. As the window was rolled down, vast clouds of pungent pot smoke billowed out into the faces of the three MPs. The dog howled and lunged at the open window, snapping and snarling.

"This doesn't look good for the home team," I murmured to James.

"Nope," James agreed. "Those boys just bought themselves a heap of trouble. Bad scene, man."

Three men in civilian attire were led out of the car and made to empty their pockets on the car hood, then spread their legs before being handcuffed. An MP rapidly spoke into a hand-held radio as one of his partners held the dog back, and the third MP searched the car. Moments later, he emerged with a plastic bag containing a leafy green substance.

"Bingo! It's curtains for them," I said. "This show is over."

A small crowd of sailors gathered to watch from a distance. Five minutes later, a Shore Patrol wagon pulled up and ushered the three prisoners into the back. A tow truck appeared, hitched the Mustang to its back hook, and the car was on its way to an impound lot.

The next day, at officers' call, the XO announced that the navigator, damage control assistant, and communications officer aboard the USS *Bethel*, a sister ship in our squadron, had been placed under arrest for possession of a controlled substance: marijuana. The Shore Patrol had first brought the three officers back to their ship to speak with their commanding officer. The CO informed them that they had "exactly fifteen minutes to grab your gear and get your collective asses off my ship." They were promptly taken to the Naval Investigative Service (NIS) office for processing.

We knew all three officers from recent officers' club social gatherings. Two of them were recent graduates from the Naval Academy. The officers were likely facing bad conduct discharges. What was unclear was whether they would serve any jail time. We never learned their fate. *Joseph Hewes* left port for the Mediterranean when the matter went to trial.

"You know why this is going on, don't you?" James asked me at the apartment a few days following the arrest of the officers. "It's obvious."

"It's illegal to smoke pot in the military, so stick to booze if you must become addicted to intoxicating substances," I responded. "That's my motto, anyway."

"No, I'm serious here. Think about the crash on *Nimitz* last May. Remember? Looks like the Navy's putting their foot down like they said they would."

A Navy electronics warfare jet landing on the supercarrier *Nimitz* on May 25, 1981 had skidded off to one side as it touched down, causing havoc on the flight deck. The crash happened around midnight on the sixth attempt at landing by the EAB-6 Prowler. Seven sailors aboard the plane died when the plane went over the side and sank. Fourteen sailors were killed and forty-eight injured in the mishap. The official finding by the Navy was that pilot error was the cause. A new pilot who was not experienced in nighttime landing was in the cockpit. Still, the controversy over the accident was just getting started.

The repair costs for the accident, including aircraft repair, exceeded $100 million. Worse still, the toxicology reports on the dead sailors confirmed nine or ten of them had traces of marijuana or other illegal substances in their systems. Within weeks of the crash, random drug tests in Norfolk and San Diego, two major naval installations, revealed more than forty-five percent of the sailors tested had recently used marijuana, hashish, or other illicit drugs. The news about the accident made *Time* and *Newsweek* magazines. It was also splashed across the front pages of many major daily newspapers in America. The *Nimitz* incident was a major public relations disaster for the United States Navy. I recalled my close call with a urinalysis test when I signed my contract to go to OCS. I could have easily been caught and refused permission to stay in the Navy. I somehow avoided detection, never understanding how it happened. I was fortunate.

Three weeks later, the waterfront was buzzing with scuttlebutt about another grave incident aboard a destroyer in port. A Spruance-class destroyer was moored fifty yards forward of *Joseph Hewes*. The ship's disbursing officer and roughly one-quarter of a million dollars in cash were missing. NIS agents swarmed the Naval Station, looking for clues and investigating possible leads. Two days later, the missing officer had been found. He was dead, shot twice in the head, his body shoved into some deep void in the bowels of the ship. A few days later, further word came that $256,000 in cash had been confiscated from a deposit box in the Navy Federal Credit Union on base. A first-class petty officer aboard the ship was promptly arrested and charged with murder and robbing the ship's payroll. He had rented the deposit box at the credit union earlier that month. The victim left a young wife and two kids behind. The perpetrator was awarded a lifetime sentence in the Fort Leavenworth penitentiary for his terrible deed.

Chief Petty Officer's Initiation

Three weeks after returning to Charleston, the Navy's personnel command released the latest list of first-class petty officers selected for chief petty officer. The much-anticipated announcement included four designees aboard *Joseph Hewes*.

"Hey, Mister Haynes, I have been meaning to talk to you," Petty Officer First Class John Mullins, a machinist mate, told me late one afternoon as he was preparing to leave the ship.

"What's on your mind, Petty Officer Mullins?" I replied. "Hey, I heard you made chief. I'm glad for you. You earned it."

"Thank you, sir. Next week I got to go to the chief's initiation ceremony over the chief's club. Would you go and be my defense counsel?"

"What's that?"

"You just gotta go and watch me go through a ritual before I become a real chief. Nothing much. You'll be acting like a lawyer escort for me. It's fun."

"Never heard of it. All right, I'm in," I said without a second thought.

"Appreciate it, sir. It starts at 1300 hours next Tuesday."

"I'll be there."

Given my experience – both good and bad – with chiefs up to that point, I should have been cautious about dealing with them in any fashion outside of the professional relationship with my chief. For the short time I'd been around the Navy, I had learned a lot about the habits of chief petty officers. I needed to steer a wide berth around the chiefs whenever possible. I did not do it.

At OCS, Senior Chief Sherman ordered me to march in the sleet for three hours as punishment for being late to my first watch in the Navy. Afterward, I received more than my fair share of abuse from the other chiefs at OCS (the sleet march debacle had been front-page news for a while), but I never held anything against those chiefs. I found myself respecting most of them because of the real-life Navy stories they told and the practical wisdom they willingly shared in the classroom. Not all chiefs were golden, of course, but I knew several of them who proved their professionalism, leadership abilities, and willingness to teach. I was in debt to them. They are a special breed of sailor.

Of course, there were chiefs on what was known as "The ROAD Program," or, Retired On Active Duty. These chiefs spent their time in the goat locker (the chief's mess) drinking black coffee and telling sea stories, making their senior petty officers in their division oversee the daily work performed by the men. They were lazy sloths without pride in their exalted status within the military hierarchy. Most chiefs were not ROAD, but some were. Every ship had one or two or three of them. They were an embarrassment to their profession.

Five days after reporting to *Hewes* in the Brooklyn yards, the chiefs invited me over to their quarters on base to "play pool" after we had finished a softball game between the officers and chiefs. Chief Sanchez was in Norfolk in training. I hadn't been there twenty minutes when the boatswain mate chief – who had made insulting remarks to me the day I arrived on *Hewes* after I saluted him by mistake – produced a glass with two shots of Wild Turkey and two shots of buttermilk mixed in a short glass.

The chief sneered, "Mr. Haynes, you ain't fit to serve as an officer in this man's Navy if you can't down this in one gulp."

Six or seven chiefs looked on skeptically as I drained the glass.

The chief repeated this a second and third time in quick succession. I quickly dispatched the vile concoctions each time. On the third round, I immediately vomited the contents of my stomach all over the pool table before passing out on a couch. I was carried back to the bachelor officers' quarters by two chiefs and left unconscious on the doorsill where the XO found me a short time later. I heard later that week about the XO warning the chiefs that any future "socializing" with his junior officers in any way, shape, or form would be strictly monitored. If anything like what happened to me occurred again, there would be an unspecified "accounting" exacted from the chiefs. It appeared the XO felt my feeling miserable over the next two days was sufficient punishment for my stupidity.

I'd witnessed commendable actions by chiefs in my first year of service, like on a winter day in Brooklyn when a fuel barge caught fire in the middle of the East River and drifted towards the naval station. I was the senior officer in the group, uncertain how to handle things, so the senior chief stepped up and issued orders to the team to prepare them to fight the fire by telling me what to say to the men. The senior chief made it appear that I was directing the effort, but I followed his lead. I told the XO what happened once I returned to the ship. Captain Beckham knew I wasn't an on-scene hero at the fire, but he was pleased I was there to help and learn the ropes. He was right about the incident being educational for me in many ways. The East River tragedy was one of the most memorable incidents in my Navy career.

Most chiefs I knew were respected by both officers and enlisted. They were technically savvy senior enlisted sailors with ten to twenty years of experience under their belts. It was hard for a bluejacket to put anything over on a chief, who had seen just about everything in his or her career at sea. I was aware not every chief was dedicated to his job, that some were just marking time until retirement. Certain officers took similar paths, regrettably.

After his selection, a chief-designee was assigned a "sponsor" from the chief's mess, whose job it was to help the designee through the next three or four weeks of indoctrination leading up to finally wearing the uniform of a chief petty officer. The designee carried a "charge book" everywhere he went because any chief he encountered had the right to offer instruction or assign a task, provide guidance, or accuse the chief-designee of gross incompetence within the pages of the charge book. The book quickly became crammed with false accusations and other trumped-up "criminal charges." It was the perfect tool for making life miserable for the future chiefs before initiation day, and then the chiefs-to-be were required to bring their charge books to the initiation for review.

Initiation day finally arrived. The entire Naval station was abuzz with activity as chief designees reported to the chiefs' club. Beer flowed freely when we arrived there and took our designated positions. The defense counsels and designees were ordered inside a large rectangular enclosure of tables. The chiefs from the various commands on base sat on the outer perimeter of the tables to watch and comment on the action happening inside the tables. The charge books were opened and scrutinized as the ceremony began. The hazing tools used at the Kangaroo Court were disgusting. An individual might be ordered to pick up a pea lying on a piece of ice, with his bare buttocks. "Bombardier School" was where the designee was ordered to lie down on his back and look straight up while a chief cracked an egg and dumped its contents on the designee's face from a height of five feet, yelling, "Bombs away!"

The judge of the court repeatedly ordered a designee or his defense counsel (sometimes both) to drink from a glass of "truth serum," a blended concoction of raw fish, Tabasco sauce, Rocky Mountain oysters, asparagus, Jack Daniels whiskey, radishes, Ex-Lax, and any other combination of organic ingredients a human might typically consume, but indeed not a drink containing all those ingredients in one glass. Those who drank truth serum frequently vomited the ingredients on themselves to the delight of the chiefs looking on from a safe distance. The offending person was required to clean up the mess with his bare hands. The shouting and cursing grew louder as more beer was consumed by spectators and participants alike. The ceremony reminded me of some fraternity initiations I participated in during college, but the chiefs' initiation had a level of rawness that the fraternity ceremonies did not. I supposed a new chief felt the need to formally join the others, even if it meant enduring this degree of foolishness.

"One of you guys tell us a joke and it better be good," the judge roared to a group of designees. I stepped out of the light, hoping I wouldn't be selected.

"I know a good one," belched the chief-designee I had accompanied to the ceremony. He strutted up front without asking permission and stood unafraid directly before the judge.

"Who gave you permission to speak, asshole? That's twenty bucks to you. Give it here. Well, we don't have all day," the judge snapped. "Speak."

The designee immediately forked over two ten-dollar bills to a chief sitting next to the judge, the designated fine collector. The money would not be returned. It was appropriated to finance the cost of the proceedings.

"Okay. There was this ragged, old, retired destroyer chief who shuffled into a waterfront bar, reeking of whiskey and cigarettes. His hands were shaking bad as he reached over and snatched the 'Piano Player Wanted' sign from the window facing the street. The old buzzard walks over to the bar and hands it to the bartender. 'I'd like to apply for the job,' he says. The barkeep wasn't sure about this filthy sea dog with an obvious buzz on. But since it was a long time since the place had a piano player and business was falling off, the barkeep decided to give this guy a shot. The old chief staggers over to the piano, where several patrons hunched over their beers and sat watching. By the time the chief was into his third bar of music, every voice in the bar was silenced. He played a rhapsody of sound and music, unlike anything anyone had heard in the bar. This guy played so great that there wasn't a dry eye anywhere when he finally finished. The bartender calls the chief over, hands him a beer, and asks him, 'What was the name of that song you just played, anyway, chief?' The geezer responds, 'I call it, Drop Your Skivvies, Baby, We're Gonna Rock Tonight,' just before taking a long pull from his beer. The bartender and crowd yelled for more, so the chief played a knee-slapping, hand-clapping bit of ragtime that got the place jumping."

"Does this story have an end?" The judge interrupted. "I didn't ask for a sermon. Get on with it."

"Yes, Judge, I'm almost done."

"Finish it, then," the judge growled as he leaned on his arms and looked around in exaggerated boredom.

"Thank you, Judge. So, after he finishes playing his second round of tunes, the chief bows to loud applause and whistles from every corner of the bar. He stands up, excuses himself, and lurches to the head to take a leak. Five minutes later, he comes out, and everyone turns around and stares at him disgustingly. The bartender runs around from behind the bar, sidles up to him, and says, 'Look, Chief, the job is yours if you want it, but do you know your fly is open and your pecker is hanging out?' 'Know it?' the old chief responded while lurching backward. 'Hell, I wrote it.'"

A chorus of boos and verbal abuse erupted from the crowd. Amidst the laughter, the judge made his mind up. "That joke was terrible. You just wasted this tribunal's time. That's fifty dollars to you. I want the payment in quarters only."

"But, Judge, I don't have any quarters," the designee begged. "Here's two twenties and a ten. Go ahead, please take it. How 'bout an extra five?"

"I said fifty dollars in quarters. You're a chief, damn it, leastways you *think* you are. Do what you got to do to get the job done. Be back here in ten minutes with the exact change, like I said, or you're in contempt of this court. And you know what that means. I don't want to see any paper money. You got nine minutes and forty-seven seconds now."

The designee turned to me. I shrugged, handing him a fifty-dollar bill. My "client" turned and ran around the room begging quarters from the audience but could only gather four dollars and change. Some chiefs threw quarters at him, but most told him to "get lost." Minutes later, the judge assessed him an additional twenty dollars for not producing fifty dollars in quarters as ordered. I agreed to pay the seventy dollars to the treasurer, including trying to sneak a few pieces of foreign currency, including Bermuda dollars from our recent trip there, inside the pile of

American dollars I handed over to the treasurer. My ruse was immediately discovered. The judge ordered me to drink a glass of truth serum and apologize to the gathering for my impertinence and stupidity in impersonating an ensign. I gagged down a half-glass of the serum, then I vomited. I was instructed to apologize again to the crowd before cleaning up my mess with a Dixie cup and bare hands.

The abuse continued for another ninety minutes. The agenda was topped off when the new chiefs were directed to take showers and don their new khaki uniforms to receive their anchor devices as brand-new chiefs. The traditional creed was read formally at chief initiations, accompanied by several other solemn admonishments, before the designees were finally declared chiefs. I looked around and saw more than a few old chiefs wiping their eyes as the ceremony ended and everyone lined up to shake hands with the new chiefs.

I was granted a rare glimpse into the inner workings of one of the most critical groups of Navy personnel anywhere in the military: the senior enlisted personnel who had worked hard and long enough to earn the right to be called "chief." I still consider it a privilege to have been there, even though I left the chief's club at the Charleston Naval Base a hundred dollars poorer. I heard somewhere that chief initiations of the kind I participated in back at the Charleston Naval Station are now history by order of the Navy. I don't know if the changes are necessarily a good thing.

Old Slave Market

The Spoleto Festival was an annual arts festival that combined music, theatre, crafts, and local food and was offered at different venues around Charleston. One of the most popular tourist attractions was the venerable Magnolia Plantation, situated north of town alongside the Ashley River, the body of water serving as the western boundary of the city proper. Magnolia's history dates to the 1670s when the Drayton family first owned it. It occupied a large, valuable tract of land, offering one of the most extensive public gardens anywhere in the state and serving as a wedding site and numerous other social functions.

Magnolia Plantation was a "working exhibit." People in period costumes operated the place. Hosts in antebellum attire welcomed guests and offered tours inside the big house. Other employees worked in the fields and gardens, the blacksmith shop, and many other venues open to the public. In its heyday, the fifty-year period before the Civil War, the heart of the economy in Charleston, and at Magnolia Plantation, was slave labor. The antebellum South was the fourth-largest economy in the world on the eve of the Civil War. South Carolina was the first state to secede from the Union, in December 1860. Early attempts by the U.S. Navy to capture Charleston using naval firepower during the Civil War failed miserably due to the Rebel batteries surrounding Charleston Harbor, creating a gauntlet of cannon fire that no ship could survive. Joining many other Southern cities, Charleston subsequently suffered tremendous physical and psychological damage before the city fell to U.S. General William T. Sherman's army shortly before the war ended in April 1865. Before capturing Charleston as the war came to an end, Sherman's forces had, the locals claimed, burnt most of the capital city of Columbia, South Carolina, to the ground to avenge South Carolina's leadership role in creating the Confederacy, South Carolinians would remember the destruction of Columbia for generations to come.

One afternoon after work, James and I headed downtown for a drink before returning to our apartment for the evening, on the west side of the Ashley River. We stood before a popular drinking establishment three

Old Slave Market, downtown Charleston, SC

blocks north of the Old Slave Mart. Once a place where slaves were auctioned off like cattle, the Market was now a major tourist attraction with eclectic shops and fancy eateries down in the slave pens where slaves were kept confined like cattle before being sold upstairs, a chilling testament to the Old South's heritage. James and I never spoke about the Market, but as a youngster, I'd seen pictures of it in my Civil War picture books, which I had read for years. I recognized it the first time I drove by.

"C'mon, James, after you," I said to my best friend aboard ship, holding the front door open for him.

A large white man with a red crew shirt and a two-day stubble appeared from nowhere, blocking our path with his left hand, saying, "Just hold on there, fellas. Y'all carrying IDs?" His eyes were locked on James. I estimated he weighed two hundred seventy-five pounds, his belly protruding from the bottom of his shirt. He stared at James, impatiently saying, "Well?" His eyes narrowed.

James looked at the bouncer and calmly replied, "I'm sorry I'm not carrying my military ID tonight. My wallet with my license is back aboard the ship. My friend drove us here." This was a rare misstep by James, as officers were expected to always carry their military IDs. I was more than a little surprised.

Stepping between my friend and our antagonist, I glanced over at James, then looked up at the bouncer, saying, "I'm the one who drove tonight. Here's my license. James left his wallet back on the ship. All right?"

The bouncer snatched the license from my hand, looking it up and down like we were entering a high-security complex. He returned it pinched between his two fingers, mumbling, "Okay, you're in, but not your friend. I want some ID from *him*." His protruding index finger almost struck James in his chest as he jabbed it at him.

"I already told you—" James began.

"What the hell is wrong with you?" I shot back. "We're both twenty-four-year-old commissioned naval officers. We want to drink a beer and grab a bite to eat. Let me speak to your manager."

"He ain't here. I want some ID from this guy," the bouncer pointed at James again. "No ID, no entry."

"But I saw you let those two guys in before us without carding them. They're younger than we are," I argued. "They're barely twenty."

James tapped me on my shoulder. "Let's go, Rod." He began to walk away.

I followed James, then I spun around and said in a loud tone, pointing directly at the bouncer, "Hey, hillbilly freak. We're leaving. Tell your manager I'm spreading the word about this dump back at the naval station."

James grabbed my arm and said, "Rod, that's enough. C'mon."

I shook him off. "Leave me alone, James."

As we walked from the restaurant, I yelled back at the bouncer: "Hey, you. Yeah, you, Jethro. The war's over. You guys lost." The bouncer ran outside, but we quickly moved down the sidewalk on the opposite side of the street.

James grabbed my arm and dragged me further away. "Knock it off. What were you trying to prove back there?"

I didn't say anything. We returned to the car, driving south through the city towards the Battery, the lower part of Charleston overlooking the harbor where the town's citizens gathered to watch the attack on Fort Sumter in April 1861. I was still seething as I popped a George Thorogood tape into the tape machine in my car. "Bad to the Bone" began banging out of all eight car speakers.

"For God's sake, it's 1982," I muttered.

"I've lived in the South my whole life," James replied quietly. "Don't lecture me about race."

The car passed over a series of cobblestone streets. I was driving too fast, the RX-7 bottomed out twice. I slowed down to avoid damaging the undercarriage.

"James, why didn't you say something? I was your witness. I woulda stuck with you."

This was one of the few times I saw James lose his temper. "I don't need someone trying to right the world's wrongs for me. You think Captain Beckham would go out of his way to support some gallant gesture you think you're making?"

"The captain would back us."

"Yeah, right. I didn't tell you the CO called me an 'Oreo' a few weeks behind me. Talbot overheard him say it at breakfast."

Petty Officer Talbot was a black cook who worked in the wardroom. He was privy to all sorts of officer conversations, which quickly made their way back to the crew.

"What's an 'Oreo'?"

James looked at me and laughed softly. "You never heard of 'black on the outside, white on the inside'? Please." Then he looked out of the car window, blinking a few times in anger.

I said, "Look, back there at the bar, I was just—"

"I know what you were 'just.' Do you think you're helping me? 'Just' don't bother, all right? One other thing."

"What?" I looked sideways at James.

"This, 'the war is over,' is bullshit. You Yankees make me laugh. There, I said what I didn't want to say."

"Of course, racism isn't just a problem here in the south. It's just as bad up north," I answered.

"No. It can be *worse* up north. Down here you never wonder how some white folks feel about you. Up north it's different. You don't know the ones who are your friends and others who aren't. They hide it until—" James stared out the window.

The Battery was just ahead of us now. I quietly asked my friend, "Why can't I have a serious talk about race with a non-white person? Every time I try it, I piss someone off."

When I first met James, I told him about having a black roommate at the prep school I attended in the early seventies and how rocky our relationship became in a very short time. It bothered me that I could not talk about the racial issues on campus and the bussing controversy in Boston with my roommate. He would immediately become angry any time the topic was brought up.

"Rod, listen. The race issue in the military or even civilian society is extremely complex. You think you understand my point of view, but you don't. Trust me, you don't want to walk around in my skin. You'd freak out in minutes."

We were silent for a few minutes, as we approached the Battery and stopped to look out at Fort Sumter off in the early evening fog hanging low over the water. The stone fortress almost seemed to hover eerily in the air, the mist obscuring its base. Numerous small craft were out on the water, their lights blinking intermittently as night fell. We absorbed the serene scene around us. Maybe this is what the Charleston Travel Bureau means when they call the city "charming" or "quaint." It couldn't be the people. It was wrong of me to think in such a broad way about an entire city. I did. I didn't like the place.

I spoke up again. "That's because you never share your views about race with me. We all generalize about people."

"I'll share when I feel like sharing. I don't know what to say about your view on prejudice, Rod. But the whole discussion usually quickly goes off the rails, leaving everyone angry or confused."

James fell silent again. Any thought of drinking in town was now out of the question. I drove north, away from the Battery, thinking about another situation back in Brooklyn about two months earlier. I had meant to talk to James about it, but I have never had the right opportunity.

"You remember that reunion of the World War II veterans at the Waldorf-Astoria in New York in February, the one where you decided not to go to at the last minute?"

"You came back to the officer quarters completely blotto and passed out on the couch in the lounge in your service dress blues." James smiled, thinking about it. "Wasn't very smart of you as the brand-new officer. XO got super mad about that one."

"Please listen, will you?" We were now driving across the Ashley River Bridge towards our apartment. I shared the story about the veterans laughing about throwing their new shipmate, who was black, off the stern moments after he reported aboard ship. The sailor – clutching his seabag – was left treading water while his shipmates stood around up on the main deck, looking down at him, laughing, pounding each other on their backs.

James looked over at me. "What did you say when they shared that story?"

"Not a damn thing. You know what? I had my chance. I didn't do it because I feared being the odd man out. I still think about it. I wonder if everyone would have cheered seeing you if you had walked in with me that night. I doubt it."

James sighed a long sigh before answering. "Rod, I don't need anyone protecting me. I can take care of myself. Understand? I'm my own man. Let it be that way."

"Fine. I don't have to worry. I'm white. I wonder how I'd do if I weren't."

"You mean if you weren't white?"

"Yeah, that's what I mean."

"Don't even think about it." James smiled thinly as we drove into the apartment parking lot. "Be thankful for what you are. Don't dwell on what you are *not*."

General Quarters

We were standing the mid-watch on a moonlit night in the Caribbean, steaming due south alone, engaged in what the navy called "independent steaming." The seas were calm, and the ship was quiet as it settled into an after-hours routine. That meant most of the crew was grabbing some much-needed shuteye. Only the ship's current watch teams were on their feet. The time was 0130.

I was the conning officer responsible for issuing rudder orders and speed adjustments to the Lee helmsman, who operated the engine order telegraph. The conning officer was often the same individual as the Junior Officer of the Deck on watch, who worked directly under the supervision of the OOD. The bridge equipment technology dated back to the middle of the 1960s. It was not state-of-the-art.

That night, the deck's officer was Lt. Rick Sliney, USS *Joseph Hewes*'s chief engineer. Rick, a prior enlisted submariner who was commissioned through Navy ROTC, earning an electrical engineering degree. Lt. Sliney was the best tactician on board and, aside from Captain Beckham, the most skilled ship handler on the *Hewes*.

We stood on the starboard bridge wing, discussing sports and our REFTRA plans. Lt. Sliney said, "Hey, I heard a good one about a tin can out of Norfolk two weeks ago. An old shipmate called me about it just before we left port."

"Cool. Spill it," I said.

"A destroyer pulled into Liverpool after a North Atlantic cruise for refueling and two days of R&R before heading across the Big Pond for home. No big deal."

"Ship's name?"

"I honestly don't know, and it doesn't matter. They pull into Norfolk and tie up to the pier, and all the wives and girlfriends come aboard. Everything is fine. Later that afternoon, roving security is down in Electrical Central. Suddenly, they see this young lady crouching behind a switchboard. No civilians are supposed to be in the hole, so they grab her, bring her topside to the quarterdeck, and report her to the OOD."

"Who, or *what*, was she?"

"I'll tell you if you stop interrupting. The OOD called the command duty officer and reported that roving security had found an intruder in the engineering spaces. The CDO escorts her to the wardroom to talk to her. The girl's got a heavy Cockney accent. The CDO finally finds out she's a prostitute the boiler techs smuggled aboard the ship just before setting sail for home from Liverpool. She serviced some of the crew across the Atlantic. Once the ship arrived stateside, she was given a bonus and a plane ticket home to England, which was business class. Word is, she serviced thirty or forty sailors across the pond. She got her money on time when the ship arrived home. Can you believe it?"

"Did that happen, or is it some stupid sea story?"

"I have no doubt it happened, especially with snipes involved. Whenever you think you've seen it all in this navy, something else happens. Nothing surprises me anymore. This is one more example of engineering ingenuity, anyway."

A deck seaman stepped out on the bridge wing and said, "Lt. Sliney, sonar is trying to call you on the squawk box. It's urgent, sir."

Sliney quickly stepped inside the pilot house. "Sonar, this is Lieutenant Sliney. Got something for me?"

"Bridge, sonar. We have a possible sub-surface contact bearing 235 degrees true. Confidence level low." Sonar detected a "whiff" of an acoustical signature from a possible submarine on *Joseph Hewes*' hull-mounted sonar. The sonar was in passive–listening only mode.

"Sonar, this is the OOD. What type of sub? Soviet?"

"Well, sir, according to the latest intel reports, there's one Tango- and one Whiskey-class submarine recently operating around eastern Cuban waters. Like I said, we only got a quick sniff of a trace, sir. Nothing confirmed." Tango- and Whiskey-class submarines were both Russian.

"Understood. Keep me posted with any, and I mean *any*, updates."

"Aye, aye, sir."

Lieutenant Sliney whispered to me, "Sorry, Rod. I need to take control of the ship. I have nothing against you." He announced to the bridge team, "This is Lieutenant Sliney. I have the deck *and* the con. Right standard rudder, steady on course 235. Seaman Dorsey, indicate turns for seven knots."

"Sir, my rudder is right standard, coming to course 235."

"Very well."

"Sir, indicating turns for seven knots."

"Very well. Quartermaster of the watch, I want detailed entries on everything we do. Write it down in that deck log. Stay alert. I want to see more than just speed and direction changes. *Everything.* Start writing. Understand me?"

"Aye, aye, sir," answered Quartermaster Second Class Garbowski.

Sliney walked over to the brass voice tube that dropped straight into the captain's cabin one deck beneath the bridge. "Captain? Captain? Are you awake?" There was a muffled grunt of acknowledgment. "Sir, this is Lieutenant Sliney. Sonar reports POSSUB Confidence Level Three. We're seventy-seven miles northeast of Cuba, heading south with calm seas off the starboard quarter tonight. We have no surface or air radar contacts within thirty miles. Recommend going to GQ now, sir."

"Wait," Captain Beckham said. "Don't go to GQ until the XO knows what we're doing. Give him a heads up. He had a long day yesterday. He's completely knocked out. I don't want him panicking with the GQ alarm. Ask him to meet me on the bridge in five minutes."

"Aye, Captain. Boats, hold off sounding GQ. Send your messenger to the XO's stateroom, tell him to call me."

Moments later a phone rang. Lieutenant Sliney grabbed it. "Lt. Sliney speaking. XO? Yes, sir, the captain says to meet him up here in two minutes. We've got a POSSUB, Confidence Level Three. Aye, aye, sir." He turned and said, "Boats, sound general quarters." POSSUB meant the contact was a Possible Submarine.

The boatswain mate of the watch pulled the general quarters switch, and the alarm blared throughout the ship, immediately followed by his voice report, "General Quarters. General Quarters. Now man your battle stations. General Quarters, General Quarters..."

"Sonar, OOD," said Sliney. "Combat Sonar will respond to my directives until the Tactical Action Officer reports manned and ready. Standby to go active on the SQS-26. We want a medium pulse at first. Acknowledge."

"Sonar, aye. Medium pulse. Standing by, sir."

"Andy, are you good to go right now?"

Andy Carson was the ASW – anti-submarine warfare officer. "Yes, sir, Lieutenant," he said. "Just tell me when to bang it out. We're ready whenever you say, sir."

"Roger. Combat this is the bridge. Establish a sub-surface plot immediately. Right now, all we have is a possible contact down bearing

235. It is now four minutes old. Ensign Hanslett, make it happen. Start a tactical log now. Acknowledge."

"Yes, sir. Maintain CIC watch officer's log on all tactical signals and maneuvers. Understood."

I stood off to one side, watching the action unfold, wanting to assist Lt. Sliney, but this was not the time to interrupt him.

"Main control, bridge. Make preps to light off Bravo boiler. You will *not* proceed until you are ordered to light off the second boiler by me. Make *preparations* only to light off at this point. Acknowledge."

"Main control, aye. Preparing to light off Bravo boiler. Do not light off unless directed by the OOD."

The captain abruptly appeared on the bridge in his bathrobe and ball cap. Following tradition, all watch standers announced in unison, "Captain's on the bridge."

Captain Beckham calmly walked over and climbed into his chair. "Lt. Sliney, make your report." He lit a cigarette, motioning for the boatswain mate of the watch to fill his coffee cup.

Sliney approached the captain and saluted. He then detailed the *Hewes'* speed, course, and combat readiness.

The captain listened intently. When Sliney finished, he said, "Very well. Tell Combat to check the secure circuit. I want to raise COMNAVSURFLANT." (Commander Surface Forces, Atlantic.) "I want this to be an immediate message, *not* flash traffic." Flash message traffic was reserved for critical traffic, such as a nuclear attack. "Make sure Radio Central knows *not* to send flash. Ask radio to check on our closest assets in the area right now. I want to know if there is a friendly oil tanker near us. What's our fuel state again?"

"We're at sixty-four percent capacity, Captain," said Sliney. "We're scheduled to take on fuel in GITMO tomorrow."

"Very well," The captain said as the executive officer arrived on the bridge. "XO, have the communications officer come up here. Let's send an immediate message to GITMO, Key West Naval Station, and Norfolk. I want the precedence to be immediate."

The XO responded, "Aye, sir."

"Lieutenant Sliney?"

"Yes, Captain?"

"Stand by to go active on the sonar. Let's see if we can drive the SOB right back to Castro tonight. Give him a splitting headache. He probably just got lost, and we'll just startle the shit out of him. Shouldn't be a big deal."

"Yes, sir. Sonar, this is the officer of the deck. Stand by to activate SQS-26."

"Sonar, aye. Standing by."

"Lieutenant Sliney, how long have we been at GQ?"

"Nine going on ten, Captain."

"What's the holdup with your snipes down there?"

"Sir, it's the repair lockers," said Sliney. "Only two of the three have reported manned and ready." Knox-class frigates had three repair lockers, essentially compact damage control stations, on the ship's second deck. The repair lockers were spread out from one another, so if one was wiped out in an emergency, the other two lockers could take control of damage control functions on the ship. Typically, 15 sailors from the engineering department divisions manned the repair teams in each of the three repair lockers. However, sailors from other divisions were regularly rotated through the teams to ensure sufficient backup was available throughout the ship. Damage Control Central was where the ship engineer directed the repair locker teams at General Quarters. DC Central also had direct communications with the OOD on the bridge, with the engineer speaking directly to the OOD to keep him advised of the damage control response teams' progress below decks.

"Well, damn it, get *on* it. I don't like this walkin' through molasses bullshit."

"Yes sir. Main control, bridge. Is the Main Propulsion Assistant with you right now?"

"Affirmative, sir. He is listening."

"MPA, listen, you get down to repair one and kick some ass. We needed those guys ready to respond by now. This is unsatisfactory. After we stand down, I want you to report the reasons for this delay directly to me."

"Yes, sir. On my way."

A voice came over the internal communications circuit. "Sonar, this is the TAO Lieutenant Commander McDonald in Combat. Do you hold any underwater contact at this time?"

"Negative, sir. Nothing. Wondering if we should go active now?"

"No. Captain, request permission to go active on SQS-26."

"No, not yet. We just settled on course 235. No rush."

"Roger."

Seven more minutes passed before word came back from main control: "OOD, this is the MPA speaking. Repair One is manned and ready now. I will have a full report for you once we stand down from GQ."

"This is the OOD. Very well. I want you up here on the bridge after we secure from GQ."

"Yes, sir. Understood."

The captain looked at Lt. Sliney and said, "Tell the TAO I want three 1000 millisecond pulses just to let the bastard know we're nearby. Then secure the sonar." The Tactical Action Officer (TAO) was a senior officer directing the ship's weapons and sensor actions (radars and sonars) from CIC. Most often on Knox-class frigates, the TAO at General Quarters was the ship's Operations Officer.

"Aye, Captain. TAO, this is the OOD. I relay from the captain, activate sonar for three 1000 millisecond pulses, then secure sonar. Acknowledge."

"This is the TAO. Execute three 1000 millisecond pulses, then secure sonar. Stand by for transmission, then we will secure sonar." Thirty seconds later three extremely loud pings were heard.

The captain approached the 1-MC and grabbed it to speak to his crew: "Good morning, *Joseph Hewes*, this is the Captain. It is now 0200 hours. Twenty minutes ago, Sonar detected a possible passive subsurface contact to starboard as we steamed south towards GITMO. The confidence level was not high. Based on recent intelligence reports, we might have encountered an old, creaky Soviet sub on patrol somewhere between Cuba and where we are now, in the western section of Windward Passage, but we can't be sure. We don't have any surface assets in the immediate vicinity to help us out. It's just us against him right now, and frankly, I'm not too worried about it, even if it is a sub. It does not appear we are under any threat. I wanted to test this ship's reaction to a real-time scenario tonight. Most of the crew performed acceptably. But the repair locker teams took almost twenty minutes to report 'manned and ready.' *Joseph Hewes* wins or loses our battles together, as one team. If one group isn't making it happen, we all lose. We will be in GITMO for the next six weeks. We won't go home until the refresher training team says we are ready to perform our duties in the fleet. I repeat, this crew will work together as a *team*. Everything we do from this moment forward is the real deal. We will keep going back to general quarters for as many times as it takes to get it right. Then we'll do it again. That is all."

The captain turned to Lt. Sliney and said, "Rick, you get with all three repair leaders in DC Central this morning and whatever you need to get fixed, get it *done*. I want to hear from you this afternoon that they understand *exactly* what we expect from them every time we go to GQ. XO, tell the master chief of the command to report to my stateroom in ten minutes. I want you to join us, alright?"

"Understood, Captain. Yes, sir, Captain," both the XO and chief engineer replied in unison.

Joseph Hewes never did regain contact with whatever was out there that evening in Windward Passage. We eventually stood down from General Quarters, and the crew went back to their racks and slept for another four hours before reveille sounded. We had three GQ drills in the daylight hours following the long night at GQ. All three repair lockers reported "manned and ready" well within the allocated time limits every time *Joseph Hewes* went to GQ in GITMO and for the remainder of the time I steamed with her.

GITMO Revisited

Moments after the ship tied up to Pier Charlie at GITMO, seventeen of the REFTRA (Refresher training) team trainers trooped across the brow to meet with the officers and chiefs in the wardroom. They explained the training schedule and laid down the ground rules for refresher training. We all came out of that meeting depressed. I knew what was coming. The meeting pressured me and my men; the whole ship was now one big training center for the next six weeks. Every single sailor onboard was required to play a role in defending *Hewes* against attack. Cooks were manning fire hoses. Electronic technicians were litter carriers (litters carried wounded sailors to sick bay). Below decks, Boatswain Mates hauled ammunition shells fed to the gun crew manning the five inch 54 caliber gun on the ship's bow. Every sailor had a specific assignment during General Quarters. Upon hearing the GQ siren on the ship's intercom, called the 1-MC, he must immediately report to his assigned station.

Seafarers must be prepared to safely maneuver their ships in all kinds of weather conditions, both night and day, in and around port, and at sea. When *Joseph Hewes* set out for the local operating area off the eastern coast of Cuba the following day, all the bridge windows were covered by brown paper and masking tape, requiring the navigation team to demonstrate their proficiency in maneuvering in restricted visibility in restricted waters (not open ocean). Only the commanding officer could stand on the bridge wing to monitor the ship's transit out of the harbor. He was there to ensure the ship's safe navigation. He had the inherent authority to stop the drill at any moment, if necessary.

During this low-visibility exercise, *Joseph Hewes* had to plot her fixes solely by electronic navigation. The surface radar would, "shoot ranges" to land masses, measuring the distance from the bridge to a specific section of shoreline by radar sweeps. A radar operator called out the distance, an arc was then cut on the navigational chart by the quartermaster, and hopefully a second arc cut from another range on the opposite side of the ship would immediately follow the first range. The two arcs were swung together to show the ship's location, or at least where the ship had been moments earlier.

We scored forty-five percent after *Joseph Hewes'* low-visibility exercise, significantly below average for a ship's first time out. The primary cause was poor communication between the two navigation teams and inefficient execution of rudder and speed orders. The captain said being in an unfamiliar setting under the watchful eyes of GITMO trainers was no excuse. We must be ready to transit tight navigation channels and unknown ports anytime.

Joseph Hewes underwent mass and engineering casualty control drills in the following days. We also regularly fired the five-inch, fifty-four caliber gun on the bow, practiced first aid, putting the ship at general quarters, conducting man-overboard drills, and engaging a mock combined Soviet threat from the air, surface, and sub-surface sectors. Sometimes the FTG trainers announced an air aerosol chemical attack was imminent, saying that intelligence reported an enemy aircraft spraying a chemical agent was approaching us. That meant all circulating air, including air conditioning, must be shut down throughout the ship. The discomfort inside the ship, which was buttoned entirely up (all hatches closed) for General Quarters, rose exponentially as the fresh air remained secured. Two REFTRA trainers with fake injuries stumbled into CIC. One had imitation blood spurting from a plastic half-missing arm, the other a bloody, gaping neck wound. We were expected to administer first aid and fight the war simultaneously. The situation seemed quite real to us.

One hot afternoon at sea, the ship's chemical-biological attack alarm sounded while we were at general quarters. Every sailor had a rubber gas mask strapped to his leg when he went to GQ, like in wartime. Moments after the alarm sounded, the mask had to be immediately donned and kept in place until the "all clear" signal was given. The trainers complicated matters by announcing one Soviet cruiser and two Soviet destroyer escorts were thirteen miles away and closing fast with their fire-control radars activated (a sign of hostile intent). We had to prepare to fire our bow-mounted gun to fend off the attack, wearing our gas masks. Once again, the bridge and CIC teams could not pinpoint our location in the ocean, which was a critical first step before working out an accurate firing solution. Our problems were compounded by communicators wearing gas masks on both ends of the phones in CIC and on the bridge, as a result, the sound quality was horrible.

Suddenly, the hatch at the top of the ladder leading to the bridge was thrown open and the captain appeared. His arms were flailing wildly, and although he was shouting at us, we could make out only snippets through his mask.

"You incompetent sons of bitches had better...dirty, no good... bust you down to Seaman Recruit, Ensign Haynes... god damn surface plots had better... fucking... very last time I ever... dicking off down here...." The condensation inside the captain's mask was slowly causing it to steam up, his bright red face slowly disappearing.

I tried to control myself but started laughing – twelve inches from the captain's face. This set him off far worse than when he first arrived in CIC. He started screaming and pounding the dead reckoning tracer with his fist to the point where I was afraid he would break the thick glass covering on top. The five junior enlisted sailors around the DRT laughed as they watched me choking down laughter in front of the captain. Seconds later, he spun around on his heels, stomped back up the ladder towards the bridge, and at the top stair, just before he stepped onto the bridge, he ripped off his gas mask and, flinging it downward into CIC, we watched the mask spin crazily towards us before landing on a radar scope as the captain screamed, "Assholes!" The hatch slammed shut, the sound reverberating throughout our space.

I was certain I was in serious trouble; it felt like a scene from a movie. The captain shouted at us with the authority of a king punishing his subjects while laughter echoed in the Combat Information Center. I told my operations specialist to quiet down, and the laughter quickly stopped. Our battle-problem grade was low because CIC and the bridge team couldn't agree on our location. We passed with flying colors when we repeated the drill three days later. The captain never mentioned the incident again, and it didn't appear on my fitness reports. While I knew my behavior was unbecoming of an officer, the entire operation was a mess. We acted like clowns in a three-ring circus and were not proud of it.

Over the next few weeks in GITMO, there were the usual incidents involving drunken *Joseph Hewes* sailors brought back to the ship in cattle cars, resulting in several sailors being put in hacks for the duration of the training. Meanwhile, slowly but surely, there were glimmers of the ship coming together as we endured long days of training at sea and fighting numerous pretend fires and floods in the engineering spaces. One afternoon, the junior officers took turns trying to anchor the ship in a small, designated area in the outer harbor. "Dropping the hook" was a delicate process requiring a good seaman's eye, excellent timing, and a feel for the strong currents and confusing action of the ocean waves in and around the island of Cuba. The protocol called for dropping the hook while the ship was backing down. Forward movement during such an evolution could result in the anchor chain damaging the sonar dome beneath the ship's bow.

The most aggravating thing at GITMO was the progress reports the Fleet Training Group sent back to our Destroyer Squadron in Charleston. I told James it was as if FTG expected us to arrive there fully trained. We were initially given lousy grades on our exercises for weeks on end and generally made to feel that there wasn't a more pathetic warship in the entire Atlantic Fleet. I knew the captain and the XO were under pressure to whip the crew into shape. I didn't accept that this was the military way of doing things, but it was. Demanding the impossible was the norm in the United States Navy.

We received sad news from Norfolk several weeks before we finished up at GITMO. There was a sister ship home-ported there. Three days before she was deployed for six months to the Mediterranean, a major fire broke out in her main engineering space. Somebody had torched a flammable liquid in and around the gears and other critical operating parts. It was determined a crewmember had sabotaged her to avoid deployment. The damage was in the millions. As a result, the ship was facing another four-to-six-month repair period. The accused, one of the junior-most members of the engineering crew, was caught. He was likely looking at a good stretch behind bars at Fort Leavenworth. We discussed the incident at the evening meal. The news shook everyone. How was it possible for *any* sailor to harm their ship and, by extension, their shipmates? Further, a second frigate had to be identified and prepared for a six-month overseas deployment within a few days to replace the stricken frigate. The stress on that replacement ship's crew and their families would be tremendous.

Throughout our training in GITMO, the repair locker teams slowly but steadily improved their response time to emergency drills. Slowly, the young boiler technicians and machinist mates in the engineering spaces began reacting more quickly in casualty control drills.

Two weeks after our arrival, we had our fill of GITMO, but the crew worked hard. We made steady progress in every department aboard the ship. Slowly, the grades improved, and our confidence grew. Communication between the bridge and CIC and between the bridge and main control improved noticeably. And the scathing reports back home to Charleston became more moderate in tone, eventually changing into glowing reports by the tail end of our training.

FTG trainers always emerged as heroes in molding what had once been a sorry vessel without personality into a smooth-functioning war machine manned by a motivated, skillful crew by the time REFTRA ended. We told each other that probably happened every time a ship rolled through the place, although we had heard of units thrown out of GITMO, told to return to homeport and not come back until they were truly ready to do some hard training. Those ships caught hell from their squadron commanders back in homeport.

Tragedy at Cable Beach

The shocking news about Al Richards' drowning at Cable Beach on the GITMO naval base hit everyone on *Joseph Hewes* hard, especially me. Two days after the accident, the crew stood in military formation high on a bluff overlooking the inlet where Al died singing "Eternal Father Strong to Save," the Navy hymn traditionally sung at Navy memorial services. It was late afternoon on a perfect summer's day on the island, the shadows lengthening and the soft colors of red, orange, and pink splashed across the sky as evening slowly came on. We stood in formation, dressed in our service dress white uniforms, paying tribute to our departed shipmate. It felt like a high school drama production, but it was all too real.

Captain Beckham solemnly read Psalm 23. He then nodded for me to begin. I cleared my throat twice. "This is a sorrowful day for *Joseph Hewes*. I met Al not long after I arrived aboard. He was popular, not just because he was responsible for distributing money on payday. I remember when the ship was on the blocks in Brooklyn. When the Emergency Response team put out a major fire on that fuel barge floating out of control down the East River, Al was the OOD on the quarterdeck..."

I told how my good friend embraced life. Al Richards was born and raised in Reading, PA. He was twenty-seven years old, balding, and slightly overweight but still athletic. Al's crooked grin revealed a chipped front tooth when he smiled, which was often. Days after we first met, I noticed his headstrong tendencies. Al was a consummate risk-taker. He liked living on the edge.

I didn't tell the story about Al's non-stop payroll saga in Brooklyn at his memorial service. I avoided highlighting the legal mess about our housing allotment that had followed in Charleston after our return home, but it was very much on my mind that day in GITMO. As *Joseph Hewes*' disbursing officer, Al routinely handled large sums of money, particularly around payday. Once, we were alone in his office on the second deck, and Al asked me to go with him to a bank in a bad section of Brooklyn to collect $300,000 in cash to be disbursed to the crew later that day.

"You're nuts, Al," I said. "Give me one reason why I should go."

"Why not? You need an adventure. Think how cool it would be holding all that money. And you get to carry a gun," Al grinned. "You know, like Dirty Harry."

"Are you saying we will carry $300,000 cash in broad daylight through Bedford-Stuyvesant? Why not have one of your men go with you?"

"I can do that. But I'm asking you first." Al drew his navy .45 caliber pistol from its holster, slapped a bullet clip into the pistol stock, grinned, and released the safety. Then he patted the barrel of the gun and, looking down the shaft of the weapon, said in an exaggerated growl, "Seaman Daniels will go with me if you won't. Look, I'm a badass, Rod. No one can screw with me. I'll blow them away." He pointed to an imaginary target. "BLAM."

"You just violated Navy regs by loading that thing. Stop waving it around my face. The safety is off, God damn it. What's the matter with you?"

"So, you coming?"

"I already told you no. I don't like the thought of two people in military uniforms driving through the worst part of town in broad daylight in a marked Navy vehicle holding three hundred grand. Why don't you get the money delivered here?"

"Not allowed. It's required that I sign for the cash personally in the bank. They're not a pizza delivery service, for crying out loud. Besides, I like carrying all that bread around."

Al infuriated me when he drew the .45 from its holster. This was the second time in ten days I'd witnessed a junior naval officer acting recklessly with a firearm. Just the day before, I'd told Al about a friend from Officer Candidate School, Ted Ryker. His ship, an oiler, was sitting in the drydock next to ours. I'd learned he was stationed on her, so I walked over to greet him after lunch one day.

It turned out Ted was the OOD that afternoon. He greeted my arrival on the quarterdeck by aiming a pistol directly at my chest, playfully saying, "Just hold it right there, Ensign Haynes. We don't like your kind. Quarterdeck, prepare to repel enemy boarders."

I considered punching Ted then and there, but I instead turned around and stalked off the ship without a word. Ryker leaned over the railing, yelling, "Hey, Rod. C'mon, man. It isn't loaded, for crying out loud. C'mon. Don't be a loser. Hey, Rod." His voice echoed around the shipyard. I wasn't having it. I reported the incident to the XO. He called Ryker's XO and reported him. I was glad.

Al was disappointed that I did not accompany him to the bank. Two hours later, I looked for him and was happy to see him return safe and sound. Every payday in Brooklyn, I anxiously waited for Al's safe return from his bank run, like a father waiting for his teenager to return home from a late date. I never went with Al, no matter how many times he invited me to go along, which was often.

Nothing terrible happened to Al in Brooklyn, but he kept on doing risky things. Ten officers drank beer at a tavern in Brooklyn Heights until early morning one night. Al suddenly stood up and announced he would walk back to the shipyard alone through Bedford-Stuyvesant, between the bar we were sitting in and home. We urged Al to hang around, reminding him the Navy van would soon be arriving to take us back. But he waved us off, laughing, heading out the door alone. He made it home that night. The next day Al told me he jogged through the projects, adding, "It was a little scary, but I made it. Nobody screws with me. It's thrilling to do that shit."

Al owned a 500cc Suzuki motorcycle. He liked to ride it at ninety miles per hour through the streets of Manhattan at midnight in the rain. One time I told him the nonsense he put everyone through reminded me of pop singer Billy Joel's song "You May Be Right" – especially the part where Joel sang about "riding motorcycles in the rain," and "walking through Bedford-Sty alone." The song fit Al to a tee, and he knew it, grinning sheepishly and looking away as I lectured him like an overbearing parent.

Al waved me off. "You just gotta learn to live life to the max, Rod. Honestly, you do. Don't be such a 'fraidy cat."

When we first returned to Charleston from Brooklyn, Al had been the one to uncover the irregularity in the ship's disbursement history, where most of the wardroom had accepted per diem at the same time they were living in plush officers' quarters in the yards.

On the day of his death, an eyewitness at the scene of the tragedy said Al entered the water alongside two shipmates who were both experienced divers. It was his first time handling scuba equipment. The two sailors quickly submerged and swam out ahead as Al trudged into the surf in his rented scuba gear. Seconds later, a powerful wave knocked him over where he stood. In the tangle of his equipment, Al became disoriented. He panicked, inhaling a mouthful of the Atlantic Ocean. Al quickly drowned, the equipment holding him underwater for too long. It happened quickly.

Two *Hewes* sailors watching from shore ran into the water and dragged him ashore to administer CPR. It was too late. Al was gone before the ambulance arrived on the scene. Everyone was staggered when the ambulance crew pronounced Al dead. They methodically zipped him into a body bag, hoisting him into the back of the rig. One witness later said it was like watching an episode of a detective show on TV.

That afternoon, I was sightseeing with James Lee on the other side of the base. We found out about Al when we ran into Ensign Bryce Bartlett sitting in the wardroom, travel orders in hand, staring blankly at the bulkhead. The captain had just ordered Bartlett to act as the ship's representative and escort Al's body back to Pennsylvania to present it to his parents. Bartlett had been aboard ship for less than a month, a brand-new ensign from OCS. My responsibility was to deliver Al's personal effects, including his new Honda Accord and any of his household goods in our apartment, back to his parents' once we returned to homeport. The XO ordered me to leave for Reading a few days after our return to Charleston.

The morning of Al's memorial service, I knocked on the XO's stateroom door while pushing it open, finding the space unoccupied. Standing in the doorway, my eyes immediately settled on a photo lying in an open folder on the XO's chair. I gasped and backed out the door, stepping on the XO's feet. I turned around and faced him, stuttering, "XO, I, uh, I, I... was just looking for you to firm up the plans for the memorial service this afternoon. I didn't, I mean, I shouldn't have... oh my god, look at that."

"What's the matter with you? That's sensitive material. You can't just stroll in here." He frowned at me, but he wasn't agitated.

"I know, sir. XO, I didn't open that folder or touch *anything* in here. I didn't know, I didn't go near it, I, I... is *that* Al?"

The XO exhaled, shook his head slightly, threw himself in his chair, and sighed, "Slow down, Rod. You know who it is. This is his autopsy report. Get in here. Sit down."

He gestured for me to grab a chair as he lit a cigarette. He took his ship cap off, running his hand through the few strands of hair on the top of his head. I waved off his offer of a cigarette. I had stopped smoking cold turkey a week before.

"Look," the XO continued, "we all know you were his best friend. I shouldn't have left this file out. It's my fault. Go ahead and get a last peek at Al. Don't get bent out of shape, and don't go flapping your gums around the ship. That's an order." The Exec looked straight at me.

"I understand, sir," I said quietly.

Taking the folder from the exec's hand, I stared at the naked figure stretched out on a shiny metal gurney in the photo from the coroner's office. The angle of the shot was from the side, at waist level. Al's head was turned towards the camera. He looked directly at me, his eyes seemingly locking on mine, which they weren't. There was no life, no recognition in Al's eyes. They were open, staring blankly, clouded over. His tongue hung out of his mouth, confirming his last moments had been a struggle. He'd fought hard to live but didn't make it. His face wore a surprised, sort of hurt expression. The stillness of the body was so unlike the rowdy character I had known over the past year. How had it come down to this? I felt the urge to vomit before tears formed in my eyes. I cried briefly, wiping my face and hoping the XO wasn't looking. He glanced away from me for a moment, slightly shaking his head. He remained silent.

The XO finally said, "Look, Rod. You won't forget this horrible situation, but you have your division to look out for. The captain and I expect you and James to keep your priorities straight. The men will check you out closely over the next few weeks to see how you handle this. I expect you to step up and do your job like the captain knows you can. Things happen fast around here. No time for slacking off."

"Yes, sir." I left to finalize Al's memorial service. I could not stop shaking.

The crew stood on the bluff, watching the sun drift into the Atlantic Ocean, throwing off a final shimmering splash of multi-colored and fleeting light. I finished my eulogy. The cruel irony of the sea claiming one of us while the ship was in hostile waters in Cuba was not lost on anyone; it was a terrible reminder of the relentless power and danger the ocean posed to anyone, even if firm, dry ground was a few feet away.

I concluded my remarks. "I didn't always agree with Al. He was stubborn, and he liked pushing the envelope. Some of you understand that. But I liked him, and I know he loved the Navy. He was a good officer. We'll all miss him a lot. I ask all of you to keep Al in your prayers. His family, too. Al was our shipmate. We cannot forget him. I never will."

Nearly six weeks after we arrived in GITMO, Fleet Training Group finally pronounced the ship ready to rejoin the Atlantic Fleet. We were going home. Our REFTRA performance, while not considered superior, was graded "Above Average" by the training team. We could accept not being average. The captain praised the crew for our hard work and "never say die" attitude. Despite Al's loss, the crew was in high spirits as we steamed northward towards Charleston. I felt very sad.

A year later, I found a photo I'd forgotten I'd taken of Al as he conned the ship through the challenging channels in GITMO harbor two days before he died. I debated sending Al's picture to his parents, knowing they were still agonizing over losing him. I asked James what to do. Pausing, James finally said it was appropriate to send the photo to them. "You might regret it someday if you don't go ahead and send it. You're doing it out of respect for Al and his parents, too," James said thoughtfully. I agreed. In the end, I sent the picture to Al's parents with a short note. His folks immediately returned a letter indicating my gesture was well received in Reading.

Stormy Weather

My most frightening experience as a naval officer on active duty happened in October 1982. *Joseph Hewes* was ordered to conduct "Soviet box operations" in the Bermuda operating area. The ship steamed alone from Charleston to an area three to five hundred miles north-northeast of Bermuda to conduct passive searches for Soviet ballistic submarines for three to five weeks. In the 1980s, the area was a hot spot for Soviet ballistic submarines moving at two to four knots along pre-designated tracks, waiting for the signal from Moscow to launch their missiles at U.S. cities. The term "box operations" refers to our searching within a specific area of a vast body of water marked on navigation charts.

As we steamed towards the operating area, the navigator reported local weather reports were not promising. It was late October. The North Atlantic Ocean east of the Outer Banks of the North Carolina coast was treacherous even in summer months. Seas were building ominously. The forecast was for hurricane-level winds to move right through the area where we would conduct our searches. The captain ordered the ship to prepare for heavy weather at sea. When sailors referenced the "skin of the ship," they meant the part of the ship separating the elements outside from the internal spaces. In nautical terms, the superstructure's exterior was the ship's skin.

I instructed OI division to remove everything that could be removed from the weather decks inside the ship and lash down items that could not be relocated. All hatches outside the ship's skin were battened down to prevent water intrusion. I joined the crew in conducting a walk-down, identifying all potential missile hazards – loose objects randomly flying about – inside the ship's skin as she began taking heavy rolls. In our cramped stateroom, we grabbed loose items, tossing them in our footlockers and securing the hatches.

Down below in the galley, the mess cranks were stockpiling sandwiches, anticipating being unable to serve hot food in heavy weather. We arranged to top off the ship's fuel tanks from a nearby British military supply ship – the fully loaded fuel voids in the lowest region of the vessel maximizing our ballast. Meetings in the wardroom discussed optimum ship handling procedures in rough seas. The captain soberly explained his expectations. Additional members were added to all teams. That meant there would be less time between watch standing and less time to sleep. Watches would be port and starboard, four hours on, four hours off. You slept when you could. Safety was paramount.

The bad weather came upon *Hewes* quickly, a common phenomenon at sea. The barometer – under constant monitoring by the quartermasters on the bridge – continued falling rapidly, confirming an extremely low-pressure system was now in the operating area we had just entered, bringing lousy weather. Angry seas continued building, with swirling winds from no discernible direction for the first few days buffeting the ship at every angle, causing the superstructure to shake and rattle noisily. Planning a single-directional navigation track to ride out the storm was impossible. Visibility dropped and the clarity of the radar screens worsened as the seas rose to deflect surface radar waves in all directions. Many crewmen became sick. The foul smell of puke only prompted more sailors to vomit, sometimes up on the bridge where they stood their watches.

We had not expected a hurricane with winds exceeding eighty knots. A stream of weather reports warned Atlantic Fleet units that the tropical storm rapidly moving up the Gulf Stream from the Caribbean showed every sign of being extremely dangerous. There was no place to hide. If we were in port somewhere, the risk of damage by being tied up to a pier in high winds presented separate challenges. We had to ride the storm out underway at sea.

The SQS-26 hull-mounted sonar rhythmically slammed into the waves as the ship climbed up one series of waves and fell back down. Hearing the ship creak and groan and feeling the irregular wobbling of the vessel as the waves pounded against her repeatedly was nerve-wracking.

With all the chaotic forces acting on the ship, our bodies continually adjusted to the ship's confusing movements. It was physically exhausting. One structural enhancement on the ship's bow was a series of metal plates (or "strakes") rising above the main deck towards the sky. These "hurricane bows," which replaced the standard spun-metal lifelines originally in place there, were recently installed in Brooklyn. They were designed to direct the wave action towards the ship outward, rather than – before the strakes' installation – allowing the waves to slam straight down on the bow, creating tremendous stresses on the forward-third section of the ship. Theoretically, the ship was less prone to burying the forward portion of the vessel into the frothing sea because of the modifications in the hurricane bow. The additional weight added overall ship stability, but our operational efficiency in terms of fuel consumption was reduced.

The sea state intensified yet again, with whitecaps on the crests of the waves becoming more pronounced, and the period of the waves – the distance between each successive wave – elongated. The valleys and peaks in the waves became even more exaggerated, causing the ship to pitch upwards and downwards with greater force. The skies darkened at midday, and it looked and felt like twilight. The visibility was reduced to one mile, then only a couple hundred yards. All hands were restricted from the weather decks until further notice: no one was permitted outside the ship's skin for *any* reason. The captain told the crew going over the side meant they weren't coming home to Charleston. It was impossible to retrieve shipmates who went overboard in such dangerous conditions.

In the afternoon of the first day, the captain ordered all hands not on watch to remain in their racks until further notice. Crewmembers were sustaining bruises and cuts from being tossed around while on their feet, with reports of sailors stumbling down ladders because of the unpredictable action of the ship transiting rough seas. One sailor broke his ankle.

We kept a constant eye on the inclinometer on the bridge, indicating the number of degrees the ship was rolling to port and starboard, off its centerline. We approached forty-degree rolls. I was now terrified as the ship approached the extreme point of the roll, but a veteran sailor assured me, "This is *nothing* compared to other storms I've ridden through. But it's scary enough for me."

A huge concern was the ship's overall stability. As our fuel was consumed, the question of how to ballast down the ship when fuel tanks emptied was the responsibility of the chief engineer and his subordinate enlisted leaders. It was more critical than usual, given the present sea state. Fortunately, having 'topped off' our fuel tanks two days earlier gave the ship additional stability for the captain to work with for a few days.

I stood watch as junior officer of the deck four hours on, four hours off, throughout the storm, but this time I did not have conning responsibilities, issuing course directions and speed orders. The commanding officer was on the bridge for eighteen to twenty hours for each of the three days the storm raged, personally conning the ship, adjusting the ship's heading, adding a few turns to the screw, or taking them off, depending on how the ship interacted with the wave sequences. The pounding of the sonar dome continued, but the captain's skills in adjusting our course and speed helped maintain the dome's integrity. I studied the captain from a distance, even off-watch when I should have been attending to divisional responsibilities. He cut an impressive figure in the pilothouse, calm and steady, though I noted on the worst day of the storm he consumed almost five packs of cigarettes. Seeing how comfortable the man was in handling a small destroyer with 285 sailors and 20 officers embarked in this high-risk environment was reassuring. If he was worried by the maelstrom doing its best to pound his ship into submission, he didn't show it.

Hewes continued shuddering and screeching as she pitched and rolled her way through the angry seas, with the watch teams on the bridge admiring Captain Beckham's ship handling. His verbal orders to both the helm and the helmsman were minor adjustments to the course and speed of *Hewes*, but there was no question that his calculations were minimizing the impact of the weather and wave action against the ship. It was a most impressive display of seamanship in terrible conditions.

The galley was shut down after the mess cooks reported it too hazardous to work around a hot stove. Sandwiches were served around the clock for three days. The air in all the ship's spaces became increasingly stale. Sailors slipped and fell on the pools of vomit unseen in the dimly lit passageways below decks. With the ship's constant motion and extended time on watch, sailors became sleepy and lethargic. Coffee was made and quickly consumed in tremendous quantities. I never heard any complaints about its quality.

On the morning of the third day, conditions improved dramatically. The seas were still confused – there was still swirling wind out there – but the storm was dying. Conditions were such that we could soon resume our sub-hunting mission in earnest. The captain went below to grab a few much-needed winks.

Hewes tactical towed array sonar (TACTAS) was lowered into the water through a set of hinged doors located a few feet above the waterline at the very back of the ship. The TACTAS eventually sank deep into a selected "acoustic layer" at sea, listening for screw sound "signatures" from Soviet Yankee or Delta-class ballistic submarines – hopefully without being detected. It was a passive detection device consisting of a series of hydrophones, or listening devices, within a sealed flexible tube that paid out from the ship's stern.

Hewes' anti-submarine rockets, ASROCS, were torpedoes with rockets attached on the end. They extended the range of torpedoes ordinarily fired off either side of the ship. The decision to activate ship's sonar in combat only gave us minutes to localize and kill the submarine before the sub found us and blew us out of the water. But all that was during wartime. Our gravest concern was not being killed by a Soviet submarine when the possibility of being sunk by an early winter Atlantic storm at sea seemed too real a few hours earlier.

Hewes played a stealthy, complex cat-and-mouse game with Soviet submarines by remaining undetected while slowly moving in to better pick up the "scent" of our underwater prey. If the ship increased speed, the signature of her screw would become more pronounced, more identifiable, more susceptible to attack. The likelihood of the American "silent service" (submarine force) being with us was high. Still, we held little intelligence about where and how our subs were operating other than sometimes being advised that American submarines "might be in the vicinity." I sometimes wondered why we did not coordinate our searches with American submarines, but I knew the submarines' most effective weapon was their stealth and operational autonomy. Why should a sub risk detection by communicating with a noisy tin can like *Hewes* and risk revealing her location? If war came, we hoped our attack subs would prowl nearby, making a massive difference in the odds of our surviving enemy threats from below the sea's surface.

Should *Hewes* detect an enemy submarine during our mission, we would request Navy P-3 Orion fixed-wing aircraft assistance from either Bermuda Naval Air Station or Norfolk. P-3s came well-stocked with individual passive (and active) sonobuoys which, when dropped in patterns in the ocean, could triangulate a sub's position by collecting multiple bearings of a single source of sound. We could not move too fast when intercepting the submarine because our cavitation – the air bubbles created by the spinning propellers – would alert the enemy of our presence. On three separate occasions, we detected mild hints of enemy submarine activity, but no confirmation we had our prey cornered.

Hunting submarines was as much an art form as it was science. Successfully prosecuting submarines required the cooperation of the entire crew. Any missteps could ruin weeks of preparation and effort. If an enemy contact was alerted, they could employ many evasive tactics to quickly disappear into the vast depths and reaches of the Atlantic Ocean. The Pacific Ocean, the largest ocean on earth, afforded submariners substantially more escape options.

Bermuda Liberty

We looked forward to a well-deserved liberty port call in Bermuda after a trying five-week stretch in the North Atlantic. Bermuda was quaint and attractive, with stone walls lining country roads and various English-style pubs and small, expensive restaurants dotting the landscape. James Lee and I spent the first night in port sitting in an English pub, smoking costly but decidedly stale Havana cigars and drinking British lager. Twenty or thirty crew members found the same pub, we all drank to the ship's health. We shut the place down at midnight.

The following afternoon we encountered Captain Beckham and the XO in another pub. We dutifully paid our respects and moved past their table on our way out. The XO stood up, saying he needed a quick word with me. We stood in the foyer for a moment.

XO said, "I guess you three jokers had your fun at the golf course yesterday, didn't you?" He said this calmly, almost smiling, but a tone in his voice suggested the incident had better be the last one for us in Bermuda.

How did the XO learn about our adventures at the Blue Heron golf course? We hoped no one would find out. After sampling a few local ales in the clubhouse pub, Frank Davis, James, and I rented some golf clubs, strolled out onto the course, and began flailing away with our drivers and three woods. We were hammering balls two fairways to the left or right, slicing and hooking, causing shouts of surprise and anger from the other golfers around us. The fairways on the course were much narrower than back home because the land was such a premium on the island. We did not make ourselves welcome on the golf course.

Thirty minutes into our round, the pro shop finally sent their golf course manager out to hunt us down. He caught up with us on the fourth tee and politely but firmly instructed us to put the golf clubs in the back of his golf cart and follow him back to the pub for a free round of ales. Our golfing outing was over. Refunding the green fees was out of the question, so don't ask, he said tightly. We quickly downed our drinks and left.

"Sorry, XO. We got a little too excited golfing the other day," I replied. "Won't happen again, I promise."

He grunted something about "good ambassadors" before retreating to his beer at the bar.

We returned to the ship a few hours later. Around 0300 hours, Chief Sanchez knocked on my stateroom door and stumbled inside, saying, "Excuse me, sir. Mr. Haynes? Sorry to wake you. It's important."

I lifted my head and snorted, "Morning, Chief. What time is it, anyway?"

"Well, sir, the sun will be up in two or three hours."

"Come on now. This better be important."

"Well, sir, it's Seaman Franks."

"What about Franks?"

"He's down at the local constable's office behind bars."

"Wonderful. What's his story?"

"Well, sir, the security team inside the governor's mansion grounds found Franks climbing the flagpole out in front of the circular driveway. See, the flagpole is located inside the gated perimeter of the compound. Franks first jumped the fence to get in, then he tried jumping it again to escape, but security grabbed him anyways. Some of our sailors were having a few beers at a pub when they ran into some locals. There was this bet between those three idiots and these town folk and—"

"Let the kid rot in jail 'til morning. It'll teach him a lesson. Good night, Chief." I turned back to my rack.

"Wait. No, sir, we can't do that." Chief Sanchez gently held my arm for a moment. "Franks is one of our own, Mr. Haynes. We can't just let him stay there and make it worse. He's our shipmate, sir. We never leave one behind. I just got back from talking to the guy running the jail. He'll spring Franks tonight for three hundred U.S., no more legal hassles."

"What? That's robbery! It's called extortion. How much have you collected so far?"

"The division come up with $140. I kicked in another $50. That leaves us $110 short."

"Is this bail refundable?"

"Sir, please. You know better than that. It's cash-and-carry. We got to get Franks back to the ship. And skedaddle back to Charley-town day after tomorrow, I mean *tomorrow*. Whatever day, we single up all lines and go home."

"All right, here's what we'll do." I stood up to put on my shirt. "I'll get LTJG Heinz and write him a post-dated check for next payday. That guy's always floating in money. He'll front me the cash. I'll meet you at the quarterdeck in five minutes. Go on, get moving, Chief."

"Aye, sir. See you down below." Chief Sanchez disappeared.

I woke Tony, who was the ship's new disbursing officer. He said to grab $110 from his wallet before falling back asleep. I met Chief Sanchez on the quarterdeck where, in a stroke of luck, James Lee was standing duty as officer of the deck. James said the captain and XO had retired for the evening, so taking the staff car for a quick spin wasn't a problem — even though junior officers were technically not allowed to drive it. We hustled down the brow and, jumping into the vehicle, screeched off down the pier to spring Franks. We arrived at the jail, paid the fine, and Franks was released to our custody. On our drive back, the chief called the young man every name in the book, some I'd never heard before. Franks said he didn't mean anything by doing what he did. Then he nodded off.

The following evening all the officers not on duty gathered at a posh restaurant in Hamilton to say goodbye to Commander Bill Gaffney, our XO. He'd won the respect of almost every crew member aboard. Like most XOs, he was a strict disciplinarian. He ran a tight ship. But his sailors considered him fair. He was an approachable leader who made the crew work hard. He was probably the best XO I knew during my ten years in the Navy. Commander Gaffney eventually commanded USS *McCandless*, another Knox-class frigate out of Norfolk. The XO would be detaching *Hewes* after making Charleston in a few days. I would not miss him, but I appreciated his style. He was a classic officer.

After the meal was over, we repeatedly toasted the XO. The captain offered a moving speech about how he had depended on the XO and how much he would be missed. The XO then requested to speak to each member of the wardroom privately in a room down the P-way. I was the eighth or ninth officer to open the door and enter the room. The XO grabbed me and threw me into an indoor pool, where all the officers who had entered the room before me were standing in their clothes in four feet of water, beer bottles in hand, courtesy of the XO. This continued until every officer attending the farewell dinner, except the captain, was tossed in the pool by the XO. Commander Gaffney had his fun. We drove back to the ship in the van, it took three roundtrips to transport all of us, soaking wet and chilled to the bone.

On payday, Chief Sanchez approached me at quarters, envelope in hand. "Here you go, sir. $110. It's all there. Go ahead, count it."

I waved him off. "No, Chief. I won't take the kid's pay even though he deserves to be broke for that stupid stunt. But if you tell any of the men, I did this, I'll write you up. And Franks, too. I'm not a bail bondsman for OI division, so don't bother to give me the 'we always take care of our own' lecture again. Next time, whoever's in trouble swings from the nearest yardarm. Period. You tell the men no more nonsense on liberty. That's all, Chief." My stern demeanor didn't fool my top subordinate in OI division.

We both knew Franks and his wife had a new baby. He couldn't afford to drop that kind of money. When sober, he was one of the better sailors in our division.

The chief stared at me momentarily before breaking into a wide smile. He shoved the envelope back into his shirt pocket. He leaned into me and clapped me on the shoulder. In a subdued voice, he said, "Know what, sir? After all, there might be some hope for you in this man's navy." He winked, saluted, and then ambled back toward the OI division.

A Navy Chief Weeps

USS *Joseph Hewes* singled up all lines in Bermuda to commence our trip back to Charleston for Thanksgiving. Transit time would be just over two days back to Buoy Two-Charlie. *Hewes* was sailing home, proud of our just-completed mission. COMNAVSURFLANT sent a message to the ship, which the captain read aloud over the 1-MC. A three-star admiral lauded, "Your extraordinary professionalism and gritty performance in adverse weather conditions, an effort that brings great credit upon your ship and is in keeping with the highest traditions of the U.S. Navy. Well done, *Joseph Hewes*." I told James I wished we got a confirmed "practice kill" on a Soviet boomer, but it didn't happen, at least I didn't hear of it.

On the first day out from Bermuda, we encountered calm seas with intermittent rain squalls. A series of small waterspouts swirled around us. Sometimes – particularly over in the South Pacific – they could be dangerous, but the ones we saw were harmless. Overall, the weather was better than predicted. We were making good time, and the mood aboard the ship was positive.

The following day, right after breakfast, the executive officer's voice came over the 1-MC, ordering the entire crew not standing watch to assemble on the flight deck.

The wind had noticeably picked up an hour before. A stiff, pelting rain was slicing across the deck at a severe angle. In ten minutes, over one hundred and twenty crewmembers formed a circle, waiting for the arrival of the executive officer and Master Chief Al Decker. When the XO walked out on deck, his head was down. He was moving quickly.

I leaned over to James Lee and said, "Do you think he's still pissed at us about the golf course shit? I *said* I was sorry."

James glared back at me. "Will you shut up this one time? This could be serious."

The XO looked up and hollered over the storm's roar, "Gents, I'm gonna cut to the chase. Yesterday, this ship received a Bravo Zulu from COMNAVSURFLANT about the great job the crew has done these past two weeks. It made the captain feel proud. It made me proud. Let me tell you what just happened. Early this morning, First Class Hospital

Corpsman Lester opened the sick bay cage and discovered the safe with prescription drugs inside was cut open. Some son-of-a-bitch on this ship decided to open Repair Locker Five, steal the acetylene torch, and then cut open Doc's safe. Narcotic drugs – the kind we use in medical emergencies to help our sailors in pain – were stolen. We believe the torch was tossed over the side. One or more people are taking it upon themselves to steal a vital piece of damage control equipment, use it for all the wrong reasons, and then toss it over the side." He paused for emphasis, the bitter wind rattling the crewmen. "All for drugs! That means we have a single emergency torch onboard for the rest of the trip home. There is no backup. Master Chief and I have talked about this just now. Bottom line is everyone standing here will pass the word to every swinging dick on watch that until that person – or persons – who did this steps forward, *Joseph Hewes* will not be entering Charleston for Thanksgiving!"

The XO was now screaming over the wind and rain, clutching his hat, veins bulging from his neck. This was far beyond any anger I had ever seen expressed by any naval officer. I thought of Shakespeare's *King Lear* raging in the storm scene from my college English class. I turned around and looked at Senior Chief Machinist Mate Al Saltzman, a large, burly man and one of the most respected chiefs on the ship. Tears were rolling down his cheeks. Whether it was triggered by shame, anger, or disgust, it caused other crewmembers on the flight deck to tear up. I felt pure, white-hot anger. I didn't feel like crying at all.

The XO continued, "This is unacceptable." He stamped his foot. "I want those names, and I want them this morning. *Somebody* knows who did this despicable act, and if I find out anybody knew and didn't talk to Master Chief or me, that person will be considered guilty of accessory. This is the *worst kind* of selfishness. It is everything this ship does not stand for! I want those names. I want them now. If I don't get those names, we're not pulling into Charleston. Master Chief, dismiss the crew."

Master Chief Decker asked, "XO, do you mind if I speak to the crew after you leave?"

The XO replied, "Suit yourself, Master Chief. I'm done." The XO stalked away as the crew all came to attention. It was the last time Commander Gaffney addressed the crew before transferring a week later.

The Master Chief spoke briefly, "If any of you think this is gonna go away once we make Buoy Two-Charlie, understand this ain't an idle threat. Like the XO said, we want those names, and we want them today.

All chiefs muster in the chief's mess with me in ten minutes. That's all. Dismissed."

I distinctly remember no one leaving the flight deck for a minute or so after the master chief left, even with the wind and rain picking up. It felt like everyone there was struck by a giant sledgehammer – first, the congratulatory message from the admiral, then this terrible incident. I felt the emotional ups and downs of this trip gave the crew whiplash.

The guilty sailors turned themselves in to the command master chief four hours later. We did not know their names until our return to Charleston. Before any families were allowed to board the ship, an engineman and a boatswain's mate were led off the ship in handcuffs by NIS agents. The accused sailors were never seen again on *Hewes*.

New Job

The day before *Joseph Hewes* pulled into Charleston, I was summoned to the captain's cabin, where I found Lt. McDonald, Lt. Sliney, the XO, and the captain seated around a table. The captain waved me in, saying, "Grab a seat there, Rod."

I sat down in a chair against a bulkhead, worried. I nervously asked the captain if I was in trouble for something I did. He laughed, asking if there was anything I felt guilty about. I'd recently earned my SWO pin so I should be on top of the world. The captain got straight to the point, motioning for Sliney to speak.

Lt. Sliney said, "We think you did a good job on this trip and in GITMO last summer. And you just earned your surface warfare qualification. Look, Rod, before we deploy next spring, I proposed to the captain to move some officer personnel around and get them used to their new assignments."

"Am I being removed from my job in CIC?" I asked anxiously.

Lt. McDonald said, "'Removed' is the wrong word. You are being promoted to Main Propulsion Assistant."

I looked at the captain, then Lt. Sliney, then back at Lt. McDonald. "Eric, you can't be serious. I've finally adjusted to CIC and my men. They're starting to understand me. My chief and I are finally in agreement. Now you want to break us up? Who will take my place in CIC?"

"Lt. Reed," Lt. Sliney replied.

"Oh no, sir. Please. You can't do that, Rick. No offense, but when OI division learns I'm gone and Alan is replacing me, you'll have a mutiny." I stopped and looked directly at the captain. "Uh, sorry sir, I didn't mean that literally. My guys are okay. But, my god, you're talking about Alan Reed running OI division. The men are going to hit the roof. Not to say bad things about Alan, Captain, I just...."

Captain Beckham nodded his head, saying, "Slow down, Rod. Alan had a tough job getting the plant through those boiler light-off examinations in Brooklyn, but the boiler techs and machinist mates did well in GITMO after we left New York. He isn't popular, but his men understand he knows his stuff backward and forwards down in the holes. Alan cuts them no slack. Now we're back in the fleet and the lion's share of the work up for the deployment is done. B and M divisions need a break from Lt. Reed. They need a leader who will inspire them, not beat them around their heads and shoulders. I want them *wanting* to come to work. They need encouragement and positive feedback for a while. You can do this job. You *will* do this job."

Lt. McDonald added, "Chief Sanchez won't be happy. He told me a few days ago you're doing all right. And the change will be hard on OI division, but I think it won't hurt for them to have more discipline. I told the captain I would gladly take Alan in the Operations Department. Chief Sanchez has been through these things before in his career. He's been around a long time."

I turned to the captain and asked, "But sir, when do I go to Main Propulsion Assistant school in Newport? That's a sixteen-week course. I don't see when—"

"Rod, that's another thing. You aren't going to go to school. You'll learn as you go."

I was at a loss. "Sir, please. You're throwing a guy with dual History and English degrees down in the hole. The last time I was down there alone those God damn snipes locked me in the de-aerating feed tank—"

"We talked about that, too. They did that to test you. You were new aboard, and an easy target." The captain smiled thinly. "You'll get them to work for you like you did OI division. And you'll be down in the hole alongside the men. They'll help you learn if you let them. It's the best way: hands-on. Lt. Sliney believes you are the officer who can get this engineering plant through the deployment next summer, with his chiefs' backing. You rely on your chiefs."

"Sir, when is it effective?" I asked. "Does Alan know yet?"

"No. We're telling him in ten minutes. After we pull into port, we'll simultaneously meet with the snipes and OI division in different spaces. Rick will introduce you and Eric will present Alan to the OI division. We'll do it next week. I don't want *any* talk about this until then. And I mean, there is no talk about any of this. Don't go blabbing about this to James Lee, or anyone else. Is that understood? I want this to be quick and seamless. No long farewells, none of that. Clean and quick. That's it."

"Aye, aye, sir. Understood. Well, sir, I never—"

"Listen to me. We're *not* punishing you or Alan. You had over a year's experience in CIC, including this mission in the North Atlantic.

Now you'll be the main propulsion assistant. These are both excellent jobs for division officers and doing them both during your first sea tour will give you a big boost on your record. You earned your SWO pin in just over a year. You have future potential if you don't get too close to the men, which still concerns me, I'll admit. The snipes are not like operations sailors. You need to be firmer with them. You have three excellent chiefs down there and two that are passable. They'll help you if you let them and I believe you will. So, it's agreed, gentlemen? Rod becomes the MPA in the middle of next week." Everyone nodded.

The captain stuck his hand out, "Congratulations, Rod. You'll do fine down in the hole. Just keep your wits about you and stay away from dark spaces down there, right?"

I frowned. "Yes, sir, Captain. Thank you." I stood up to leave.

Rick Sliney looked up and said, "I want to meet you in thirty minutes in my stateroom to review transition plans. It's going to happen quickly. Like the captain said – no drawn-out goodbyes. We'll tell Alan you'll have a day to review paperwork, training records, evaluations, and outstanding maintenance items. Probably next Tuesday or Wednesday is when we'll make it official."

"Yes, sir. See you shortly." I left the space in bewilderment. The change came out of nowhere, and I was worried I would not survive this test.

Thanksgiving, 1982

Amy Aquino and I met for the first time at a Thanksgiving dinner in 1982, a week after *Hewes* returned from our North Atlantic stormy weather cruise. Amy, a confident and morally strong financial clerk at Charleston Naval Weapons Station, was going through a tough divorce. Despite her sense of humor, she was emotionally distressed due to her husband's repeated betrayals. We met for the first time at my chief's holiday dinner, an unexpected setup.

Within weeks, we were inseparable. Amy attended my holiday functions with the wardroom officers, I went to her holiday office parties. I quickly learned about Filipino culture – the food, the importance of family, and the Philippines' role in American history as an ally during the Second World War. Early in the twentieth century, American troops had acted shamelessly in the Philippines, putting down a desperate independence movement on the heels of their liberation from Spanish colonial rule when the U.S. won the Spanish-American War. I soon moved my belongings over to Amy's place in North Charleston. The daily commute to the ship was only fifteen minutes. Amy was nearly thirteen years older than me, with a mature outlook on life and a way of viewing things I had never experienced before. Every woman I'd previously dated was nowhere near as worldly and emotionally mature as my new girlfriend. Amy had a sobriety and seriousness I took comfort in and admired. Her reverence for the Bible was resolute, mine was not. I attended church with Amy every Sunday to accommodate her, not out of any deep-seated faith.

Amy was her father's favorite, she said. She had spent several years in Thailand with him, where he worked as a contractor, after having served in the American government in Vietnam during the war. She lived in Bahrain when her husband was stationed there in forward-deployed status in the Persian Gulf. A college-educated global traveler and a native of a developing nation, Amy had a decidedly more conservative bent politically than I, but I found wisdom and comfort in her views on life. Her counsel was sound, and her maturity was an anchor for me when I needed such stability.

Thanksgiving, 1982

I found in Amy the maturity, self-assurance, and religious piety I had always sensed were lacking in me. There were additional other admirable character traits in Amy, most importantly honesty and forthrightness. I wanted to emulate these qualities, but I knew that changes required serious effort. When we first met, she made it clear she was "not in the market for a man," military or otherwise. Her separation from her husband almost exactly a year earlier had been heart-wrenching.

Not only had Amy firmly declined all dating invitations at work, but she also kept herself busy making plans to spend the rest of her life as a single woman living quietly and attending church, while rapidly paying off the properties she and her former husband had purchased a few years earlier. I was the last thing Amy was looking for when we met at a dinner in 1982.

I sensed her affection for me quickly became more intense than my feelings towards her. As I now see it, there were two fundamental reasons for my not fully reciprocating her love for me in return, which I only fully grasped years later. I was still an immature young man living a life of non-commitment and self-absorption. The thought of marrying and dedicating my future to one woman seemed absurd when I first met Amy because I was still largely living the life of a teenager. I liked to drive sports cars, drink beer, and chase women. After our relationship quickly evolved into something more serious, I continued acting recklessly in not taking any sexual precautions with Amy, just as I had done for years with my other girlfriends, both casual and serious. It was a sign of my juvenile perspective on women in general, as well as a casual indifference to my own welfare. 1982 was on the eve of the devastating AIDS epidemic that would soon radically alter social scenes around the world. The free-love, casual sexual escapades without any strings-attached behavior I had indulged in since the age of eighteen were a poor backdrop for how I continued to conduct myself with the opposite sex. I was reckless.

Six weeks into our relationship, Amy announced she was pregnant. I was stunned, but I shouldn't have been. Amy was thirty-nine. She had no idea that she could have a baby. An abortion was out of the question, she told me. Amy was equally adamant that marriage was out of the question. She intended to raise the child and continue to work as a financial analyst for the federal government. I immediately agreed to financially support the child until he came of age. Acknowledging paternity was essential for Amy to receive benefits from the Navy. I fully cooperated, despite

Thanksgiving, 1982

the outdated bureaucracy of the State of South Carolina, which has built-in biases and administrative obstacles for babies born out of wedlock. This experience only deepened my strong disdain for the Cradle of the Confederacy. Charleston, with its superficial Southern charm, did not live up to the image it presented to outsiders. The myth of the Old South's refined culture never impressed me, it was merely a façade.

A year later, Amy and I decided to marry. We were going to raise a child together, after all.

Med Cruise 1983

Joseph Hewes began final preparations for our 1983 deployment to the Mediterranean in late March. Each day, trucks delivered food, spare parts, navigational charts of the Mediterranean waters, and helicopter parts to the ship. Groups of *Hewes* sailors were stowing supplies deep inside the ship, seemingly nonstop.

We took on ammunition at the Charleston Naval Weapons Station, forty-five minutes further north on the Cooper River. Deployment fever hit the crew and their families at home. Tensions escalated between husbands and wives as the six-month separation time drew closer. The crew had their family checklists to work through at home before deployment, covering everything from car tune-ups to compiling lists of housing maintenance contacts for their wives to call for repairs. During these final weeks, *Joseph Hewes*' sailors reported having sharp exchanges with their wives and kids. Counselors at the U.S. Navy Family Service Center said these combative interactions were, "normal." I didn't think so, but I had never prepared to be away from home for six months.

All crew members were required to visit the base dentist for a final checkup. Every sailor – officer and enlisted – was required to sign their Servicemen's Group Life Insurance form, which had a face value of $50,000, ensuring that the proper beneficiaries were listed. All junior enlisted personnel had a seabag inspection by their chief petty officers to confirm they carried all the required uniforms and gear mandated by Navy regulations. If necessary, chiefs held pay from their men – technically illegal but a widespread practice – until the men produced a full seabag.

On the day a ship left on deployment, most veteran sailors kept their families at home to avoid any public scenes on the pier. *Joseph Hewes* set sail for the Med in mid-April, a few days before a car bomb attack at the U.S. embassy in Beirut. That attack was a hint of things to come.

Conditions in the mid-Atlantic Ocean in early spring were unpredictable. Winter gales and angry seas were subsiding as ocean temperatures slowly rose, but the weather was a significant concern for ship commanding officers when we set out for the Mediterranean. We were in the company of a destroyer whose skipper was our senior, requiring *Hewes* to follow the other captain's steaming formation orders. We would join the USS *Eisenhower* carrier battle group (CVBG) hundreds of miles out at sea at a specific rendezvous point, where our two-unit navigational track would converge with the track of the eight-ship CVBG.

We enjoyed a perfect sunny day with glassy seas on the third day out from Charleston. We were scheduled to conduct a burial at sea in the mid-Atlantic. The deceased was a navy chief from World War II. Before the ceremony, I walked up to the helicopter hangar, where two boatswain mates were preparing the coffin to send him off to Davy Jones's Locker. The corpse was sheathed in multiple layers of white linen inside a flimsy wooden coffin. I leaned over to look inside and was astounded to see an automobile flywheel and axle lying next to the wrapped corpse.

"Hey, Boats," I said. "What's with the car parts?"

"Ever see that training film about burials at sea, Mr. Haynes?" another sailor named Baker asked.

"Oh, yeah. Now that you mention it, I do remember that film." At OCS, one of the training films everyone had to see was an actual burial ceremony at sea. As cameras rolled, Bible passages were read, a summary of the person's military career was offered, taps were sounded, and the order was given to commit the body to the sea. Two sailors solemnly lifted one end of the board that held the coffin, and it slid downwards toward the water below as planned. When the coffin struck the water, it began bobbing around like a cork amidst the waves. No one had cut the customary holes in the bottom portion of the coffin, which would have hastened its sinking. Crewmembers immediately started pointing and murmuring. A burst of laughter was heard off-screen.

Two quick-thinking Marines grabbed their rifles, and removed the ceremonial blank cartridges, slamming live rounds snatched from their ammo belts into the chambers. Seconds later the film showed the two Marines firing at the bobbing coffin off the stern of the ship. Several bullets struck the coffin, sending splinters flying. When a large hole was finally punctured in one end of the coffin, it rapidly took on water, standing straight before sliding beneath the surface.

When the film ended at OCS, we were incredulous. Burials at sea were supposed to be solemn, professionally-executed ceremonies. We had been warned not to laugh by our instructors, but when everyone roared with laughter as the film credits rolled at the end, the instructor left the room. Our burial at sea on *Hewes* went off without a hitch. It was quick and dignified, and the coffin cooperated by immediately sinking below the waves upon impact with the water.

Two days passed and the weather conditions and sea state remained calm. The next morning CIC reported inbound aircraft broad off the port bow, rocketing in low off the water. The signalmen reported they were F-14 fighter jets flying patrol off Ike. We conducted an exercise by pretending the jets were inbound supersonic ship-to-ship surface missiles. We tracked them with our Vulcan Phalanx Gatling gun mounted on the stern, which could fire 3,000 rounds of depleted uranium slugs per minute. Seconds after the signalmen sighted the jets on the horizon, they were upon us, a loud sonic boom cracking overhead as they sped by. Later, at lunch, the captain, looking stern, told his officers, "We needed to pick up those missiles at 120 miles out, or more, to give us time to react. What if they were Soviet anti-ship missiles? For the next six months we're playing for keeps, gentlemen." Everyone soberly nodded, silently finishing their red Jell-O dessert.

We picked up the eight-unit battle group on our radar scopes, closing in from the northwest a few hours later. Our two ships reported in and were quickly assigned a sector under the command of the battle group commander. The weather cooperated for most of our transit across the Big Pond, but when we were due north of the Azores, a weather system appeared out of nowhere, causing the seas to rise suddenly, with clouds blotting out the sun for three days straight. Conditions worsened to the point where the carrier group commander ordered that no personnel on any ships in the battle group were allowed outside on the weather decks "for any purpose whatsoever," including watchstanders.

Two days before we reached Gibraltar, the primary tactical net suddenly crackled with the sad news that a young sailor had just died on one of the missile-guided destroyers in our group. The young man, who had been aboard for less than a month, had disobeyed orders to remain inside the ship's skin. A gigantic wave crashed over the port side of the bow, picking him up and flinging him against the fifty-four-caliber gun mount instantly killing him. An hour later, the senior chaplain from *Eisenhower* conducted an impromptu memorial service among all the ships in the battle group on one of the primary radio circuits. We broadcast the proceedings on the intercom throughout the ship. It was concluded by a lengthy prayer for the soul of our newly departed shipmate. The sad accident wasn't the only thing on our minds as we approached the Mediterranean.

The news from Beirut was grim. Violence was surging everywhere, both in the city and the surrounding hills – known as the Chouf Mountains – overlooking the downtown. In response to repeated violent provocations from factions inside Lebanon who kept retreating inside the Lebanese border to escape Israeli counterattacks, Israel had invaded southern Lebanon in the summer of 1982, driving to the southern outskirts of Beirut. As part of the negotiated "truce" brokered by American Ambassador Philip Habib, a contingent of U.S. Marines had come ashore on the south side of the city, near Beirut International Airport. *Joseph Hewes* would witness the results of American diplomatic efforts in Lebanon firsthand in the coming months.

Straits of Gibraltar

Joseph Hewes steamed due east towards the straits of Gibraltar, about 30 miles east of the entrance to the Mediterranean Sea. I conned the ship during one of the most memorable experiences of our 1983 cruise. Checking the chart on the navigation channel, I noticed Gibraltar stood fifty miles inside the Med. It did not separate the Atlantic and Mediterranean Oceans, as I thought it did. We arrived at the straits at midnight, encountering thirty or forty radar contacts within a ten-mile radius of our position, all hovering around. Some ships were anchored, but most moved either westward towards the Atlantic Ocean or eastward into the Med. I experienced a few tricky hours on watch, made easier by the calming presence of the commanding officer.

At one point the captain put his arm on my shoulder, saying, "You're doing fine, Rod. Have Danny establish bearing drifts on all contacts inside three thousand yards. Don't order a rudder change without checking your bridge wing to ensure what's happening out there. Maintain eight to ten knots. Remember, we have two extra lookouts until the Rock is safely behind us. Stay alert."

I respectfully nodded to the captain, constantly moving from one bridge wing to the other to monitor the multiple navigational lights blinking around us. A ship that was CBDR (constant bearing, decreasing range) to *Joseph Hewes* was a serious threat. It meant that a collision was inevitable unless both units made an abrupt course change.

During a brief lull in the action, a veteran Navy chief from the weapons department stood on the bridge wing, tossed his cigarette over the side, and, turning to me, asked, "Well, Mr. Haynes, how many of the crew do you think are leaving their wedding rings on the Rock tonight?" A smile flitted across the captain's face.

In a whisper, I waved the chief over and asked what he meant.

"You never heard of the Navy legend about married sailors entering the Med, leaving their rings on the Rock of Gibraltar, and picking them up on the way home? That's so the married crew can have a good time on liberty while they're here. It's just one of those Navy sea stories, Mr. Haynes."

"New one for me. What about you, chief? You leaving your ring on the rock?"

"Nah, this is my fifth Med cruise. There's not too much I haven't seen or done around this part of the world. I'll keep my ring on my finger this time. I'm on my third marriage." He disappeared back down the ladder.

Our first port of call in the Med was Cannes, France. *Joseph Hewes* anchored out one mile offshore within a protective inlet where the city of Cannes loomed up before us. Its annual film festival was in full swing when we arrived there. Our visit to Cannes included day trips to the tiny principality of Monaco and the French seaside resort town of Nice. It was easy to see how the beautiful women could tempt our sailors, who were found all around the Mediterranean basin. It was a brilliant spring day in Cannes. I sat on the beach admiring my ship from the shoreline. This was seeing the world at its best.

RH, Cannes, France, April 1983, Joseph Hewes *in the background*

In Cannes, a shipmate from the wardroom and I took a bus that drove us for two hours into the Alps to Grasse, a major hub for perfume production. While there, we ran into the owner of a restaurant in the town center. He welcomed us to his eatery, where he prepared a variety of dishes and served three different wines to complement the meal. My French was barely passable. He shared stories about meeting American paratroopers passing through the village in 1944 when he was just five years old, developing a special fondness for American tourists and GIs from that day onward. In various villages and towns, small plaques narrated tales of bravery exhibited by French resistance fighters or American soldiers as the Germans were gradually pushed back toward Berlin. The day we spent in Grasse was a highlight of the cruise. I posed as Napoleon Bonaparte for the camera when I asked Mike to take my picture.

It was time to join other NATO forces in Beirut in the eastern Mediterranean.

RH, French Alps

Beirut

At the time of *Joseph Hewes'* deployment to Beirut, Middle East Scholar Amos Perlmutter referred to Lebanon as "more or less a country wracked by warfare, civil strife, assassination, and mass murder, fratricide, corruption, incivility, and violence, especially over the past decade but antedating them." In the late 1950s, President Eisenhower had ordered 4,000 U.S. Marines into the city. Civil disturbances were calmed by the presence of American troops and the Marines wound up leaving Beirut with minimal casualties. They would not be so lucky this time around.

In the summer of 1982, fed up with the constant rocket attacks, bombings of buses, and other hostile acts emanating from Lebanon, Israel had invaded the country, her forces driving to the outskirts of Beirut. Palestinian Liberation Organization forces under Yassar Arafat were driven back into Beirut before the U.S. ambassador Habib arranged a ceasefire, permitting Arafat and his fighters to depart Lebanon. A multi-national peacekeeping force was part of the arrangement. French, Italian, and American troops would be dispatched to "provide appropriate safety guarantees." Still, it was specifically spelled out at the time that "the American forces will not engage in combat." The intent of placing American troops in Beirut was to buttress a fatally weakened Lebanese army engaged in violence with local Palestinian, Druze, and Muslim militias.

By spring 1983, Beirut was fully engulfed in conflict, with many different factions destroying the city and her people. Syria, which bordered Lebanon to the east, had long considered Lebanon a surrogate state inexorably tied to them by history and geography, meaning that in their eyes, Lebanon was Syrian territory in all but name. Syrian agents backing the terrorist group Hezbollah were said to be in Beirut. Simultaneously, a lengthy list of religious and tribal factions inside Lebanon had resorted to violence. Renewed fighting between Druze and Maronite militias in the Chouf mountain area overlooking Beirut all portended disaster for Lebanon. The entire region was on edge.

In a widely publicized act of mass murder, Christian Phalange troops massacred nearly 2,000 Palestinian civilians in the Sabra and Shatila refugee camps in September 1982 while Israeli soldiers stood by without protecting the Palestinians. That month President Reagan had appeared on national television, referring to the U.S. involvement in Lebanon as, "a moral imperative, not a matter of preference... we also have an irreversible commitment to the survival and territorial integrity of friendly states... a stable and revived Lebanon is essential to all our hopes for peace in the region." What was not mentioned was Reagan's motivation to checkmate Soviet support of Syria – which amounted to over $2 billion in military hardware and 8,000 advisors – after Israel crippled Syria's armed forces in the early stages of the Lebanese conflict.

American foreign policymaking in the Middle East was hampered by a lack of policy consensus among President Reagan's senior advisors: Secretary of State George Shultz, Secretary of Defense Caspar Weinberger, and National Security Advisor Robert MacFarlane each had the president's support, but they rarely agreed on what would work best in the Middle East.

On April 18, 1983, a car bomb exploded at the U.S. embassy in Beirut, killing seventeen foreign service and military personnel, along with over forty Lebanese employees and citizens. A truck packed with explosives was the weapon of choice by the terrorists. Weeks later, Israel agreed to end their occupation of southern Lebanon if Syria agreed to pull its troops out of the country at the same time. Syrian President Hafez al-Assad refused to agree. The Israeli forces stayed put.

In July 1983, *Joseph Hewes* was a member of the peacekeeping force in a warzone where hostilities between Israel, Syria, the Palestinian Liberation Organization, and various tribal and religious factions in and around Beirut could be seen. Beirut, once known as the "Paris of the Eastern Mediterranean," was now a smoldering wreck, a shadow of its former self. *Hewes* was assigned to a carrier battle group led by the 85,000-ton carrier *Eisenhower*, nicknamed Ike, and a dozen American naval units in her company, including cruisers, destroyers, supply ships, and amphibious landing ships carrying U.S. Marines and their equipment.

While crossing the Atlantic in April, we learned about the American embassy bombing while the rest of the city was being reduced to rubble. After liberty port calls in Cannes and Gaeta, Italy, *Hewes* was ordered to assume a "ready-for-fire" position on the gun line in Beirut. That meant that if the Marines stationed near Beirut International Airport along a fragile buffer zone suddenly required ship-to-shore bombardment assistance, we were expected to deliver the ordinance on the targets designated by the gunnery spotters on shore. Marine helicopter gunships hovering in the area supported the troops below.

Joseph Hewes carried a single five-inch, fifty-four-caliber gun on her bow, with a maximum effective range of nine to eleven miles. Our duty in Beirut consisted of steaming back and forth at six to eight knots along a racetrack-shaped navigation track.

Soviet Kresta II cruiser, west of Beirut, Summer 1983

While in Beirut, a rusting Soviet cruiser routinely approached the ship as we steamed out of sight, away from the gunline, to refuel from a British tanker shuttling fuel back and forth from Cyprus to the warships on patrol. The Soviets maintained a respectable distance. This was their way of demonstrating their inherent right to transit international waters, reminding us of their regular presence in Middle East politics. Typically, Soviet warships remained twenty or more miles outside the war zone, never approaching the peacekeeping operating area where four or five American warships were patrolling together. They fished our trash out of the Med, which the cooks would hurl over the stern every evening as the sun was setting. We made sure no classified material made its way into those green plastic bags, telling each other it was a futile exercise for the bad guys.

One day, in response to a dare by a shipmate, a signalman up on *Joseph Hewes*' flybridge dropped his pants, bent over, and aimed his hairy rear end at the cruiser where his counterpart was peering through their "Big Eyes" binoculars at the signalman. It broke the monotony of the moment. Our captain found it amusing. The Soviets did not reciprocate.

When *Joseph Hewes* arrived in Beirut, we listened to conversations between the military leaders ashore and the senior leadership back in Washington. Issues such as whether troops should carry their weapons while on patrol around Beirut International Airport and daily reports on

RH, Officer of the Deck, Beirut gunline, August 1983

what was happening near the marine barracks at the airport were regularly discussed on secure shipboard communication circuits.

On the morning of the ship's arrival in Beirut, I was Officer of the Deck. Word was passed over the 1-MC to commence another workday at sea. The captain appeared on the bridge five minutes later.

I turned and saluted Captain Beckham, "Morning, Captain. All conditions normal."

The captain nodded his greeting. "Lieutenant Haynes. Boats, where's my cup of coffee?"

The boatswain mate of the watch immediately stepped up. "Here you go, Captain. Just made a fresh batch, sir."

The captain cupped his ceramic *Joseph Hewes* mug in his hands. "Thank you. Lt. Haynes, make your report."

"Aye, sir. The ship has assumed station nine miles due west of Beirut. Two other naval units are within visual contact, *Harlan County* and *Portland*. We have seventy-eight percent fuel capacity. We only have routine message traffic, nothing hot, sir. There may be a mail transfer from *Portland* this morning, but that is not confirmed, yet."

"Very well. What about my gun mount?"

"Sir?"

"I said, what about my gun mount?"

"I'm sorry, Captain. I don't follow."

"Lt. Haynes, our mission here in Beirut is to respond to any call-for-fire. We are now on station. I want to know if our gun mount is manned and ready for call-for-fire."

"Uh, uh, that's a negative, sir. It's my fault, Captain. I can—"

The captain twisted to his left in the chair he was sitting in to face the boatswain mate of the watch. "Boats, I want to see the weapons officer on the bridge immediately. Make it happen."

"Aye, Captain." The sailor snatched the 1-MC from its hook. "Weapons officer please contact the bridge. Weapons officer please contact the bridge." An interior phone immediately rang. The boatswain mate picked it up on the third ring. "Petty Officer Reed, speaking. Aye, Weps. The captain is here on the bridge. He says he wishes to see you up here immediately. Thank you, sir." Reed walked over to the captain and saluted.

"Sir, Weapons Officer says he is on his way right now."

"Very well. Thank you." The captain would not look at me.

Lieutenant Hill suddenly hustled through the port side hatchway and walked over to the captain, who jumped from his chair and motioned for the lieutenant to follow him out to the starboard bridge wing.

The quartermaster of the watch said, "Uh, oh. Here it comes—"

"Shut up, Grande." I snapped. Grande opened and closed his mouth, then silently resumed his watch position.

The captain's voice, which was growing louder, drifted into the pilot house, "... do you mean 'just getting manned up now'? I don't see a body within twenty-five feet of the gun mount. You had better get the second division moving, Lieutenant. I want a manned and ready report in five minutes. You understand? What kind of hotel are you running in Weapons Department?"

Seven minutes passed. Lieutenant Hill reappeared beside the captain's chair, saluting the commanding officer. "Gun mount and MK 56 fire director reports manned and ready for call for fire, Captain."

The captain returned the salute, muttering something unintelligible. Lieutenant Hill's face flushed red a second time. "Yes, sir. I understand. Manned and ready the moment we hit the gun line. Won't happen again." Wilson ducked out the starboard bridge wing.

"Lieutenant Haynes?" The captain waved me over.

"Yes, Captain?"

"Call down to CIC. Tell them I want radio checks done with the beach at least once per watch. Stagger the timing when we conduct the checks. We want to be sure our radio nets are up and working. Every time we do a radio check, I want it in entered in the ship's log. I think I read something in the message traffic last night about routinely talking to the other nearby units. Call down to radio and research that message to get the particulars. Put what you find in the OOD turnover log. Is that clear?"

"Aye, sir."

"I'm going to grab a bite. XO will be up here in about thirty minutes. Stay sharp. Call me if anything comes across any radio circuit. I mean anything. Understood?"

"I understand, Captain."

"Good. Make it so." The captain stalked off the bridge.

"Captain's departed the bridge," Petty Officer Reed announced.

Every day we saw puffs of smoke and parts of buildings in downtown Beirut exploding from constant artillery attacks. At night the firefights ashore were much more spectacular and frightening. The first night in Beirut, James Lee and I watched extended triangular firefights between the guerillas in the Chouf Mountains, the Lebanese forces closer to the city, and the Israeli army south of Beirut. As orange, white, and red flares, tracers, and blasts pockmarked the landscape around Beirut International Airport, we reminded ourselves that the U.S. Marines were hunkered down somewhere in the middle of that fighting. They were peacemakers in a situation where open warfare was raging.

Ten miles away, human beings were being annihilated while we watched from the relative safety of a warship underway at sea. I tried focusing on my men and my work to keep my mind off what was happening on the beach. One afternoon USS *New Jersey* joined our group. The old WW-II battlewagon was massive. Her sixteen-inch guns could hurl shells the size of Volkswagen Beetles over 23 miles. The sun was setting when I asked a sailor to take my picture with the City of Beirut smoldering in the background, and *New Jersey* lurking nearby, waiting to add to the carnage when ordered to act

Gunline, Beirut, Lebanon, Summer 1983

Party Beneath the Streets

It was late July. We entered Haifa late one evening. When we were tied up to the pier, I slept for a few hours. At dawn, I was awakened by a muffled explosion, followed by a pause and then another blast. I hurriedly dressed and quickly went to the quarterdeck where James Lee stood on watch as OOD.

"Hey, James. What's with those noises?"

"Morning. You mean the ones in the harbor?"

"Guess so. I was sound asleep. Then these blasts started happening."

"Standard procedure. Two Israeli naval officers stopped by an hour ago. They explained it is standard procedure to ride around Haifa Harbor and randomly toss percussion grenades into the water."

"Huh?"

"Yeah. They said that PLO frogmen have been captured in Israeli ports, attaching explosives to ships below the waterline here in port. This is one way of discouraging them."

"Wow. That's a new one."

"Yeah. Buckle up, man. This is real-world stuff. I called the XO down here so they could brief him on what was going on."

Two days after arriving in Haifa in the early morning, six officers and I met on the pier and jumped into the Mercedes taxi we had hired for the day. Our descent to the ancient Jewish fortress of Masada through the crumbly, dry, searing desert was the first of several remarkable experiences that day. Watching tents occupied by nomads in the middle of the desert flash by as we sped toward the Dead Sea, I asked our driver-guide why anyone would want to live under such difficult conditions.

"Oh, sir, these are the ways of life here in the desert, which have been practiced for many centuries. Their camels, goats, and the desert give them what they needed to survive. It's the way it is," the driver explained. "There has been very little change for these people in the past thousand years."

Left unsaid was the fate of the Palestinians who were living on the West Bank and the Gaza Strip. Their feud with Israel also originated in history, but the Jewish state was little more than thirty-five years old, and new tensions had arisen from ancient grudges. The driver, who was Arab, shrugged and said there would never be an entirely satisfactory solution to the Mideast conflicts for as long as man lived on earth. It was hopeless.

"I had an interesting experience in Haifa last night," I quietly told the driver.

"Yes, sir?"

"A friend and I had plans to visit one of the five-star restaurants across town, so we called a taxicab to the pier. When we told the driver, an Arab guy, where we wanted to go, he immediately stopped the car, saying that was impossible because Arabs were not permitted in that part of town. The authorities would arrest him if he were found there."

"What do you think about that, sir?"

"Pretty shocking. America had civil rights protests in cities nationwide not too long ago. Last night made me think about those times. Americans don't hear much about the Arab side of things in the media back home."

"Do you see why I said these things will never change? We ask you not to believe everything the Israelis tell the world about us. They tend to tell their side of the story and hope the world forgets about us. The world does not care."

Later that night, we agreed to top off a splendid day of touring the Holy Land by grabbing a bite and a brief visit to a local watering hole. An Israeli soldier we'd met in the old city section of Jerusalem directed us to an address fifteen minutes away for a nightcap.

We soon arrived at a shuttered shop window on a vacant street. It was too quiet for our liking. I told James, "I don't think we heard the guy correctly. This can't be the place. This is spooky."

Just then, a voice came from a speaker attached to an elevator in the passageway. "What do you want?"

Looking up I watched a remote camera swivel around to size us up. I answered, "Ah, we're American naval officers. We heard we could get a few drinks before heading back to our ship in Haifa, but it looks like—"

"Wait, wait just a minute. Don't move. We're sending the elevator up for you."

We looked at each other quizzically. The elevator door suddenly opened, and we hesitated for a moment before stepping inside. Noiselessly, the door shut, and the elevator descended two levels.

Dave DeJesus looked over at James and me and said, "Nice knowing you guys. Who would have thought my career would end in an elevator in Jerusalem?"

Everyone laughed.

The doors suddenly slid open. We emerged into a large, boisterous crowd lined up on either side of our path, leading to a bar at the back of the room. The entire crowd was yelling and applauding; everyone in the place was looking at us.

"James, we're celebrities," I yelled over my shoulder. "We just entered the movie *Saturday Night Fever*. Holy shit!" I pointed straight up at a glittering, rotating silver ball casting speckled light around the space. The music was blasting – positive energy pulsated from the crowd of approximately 150 partygoers. Making our way towards the bar, the partiers shook our hands and slapped our backs.

James nodded ahead. "Here comes somebody who can tell us what this is all about."

A balding middle-aged man approached us with his hand outstretched, yelling above the loud talk and music blaring from three large speakers just ten feet away. "Welcome, welcome, my friends. My name is Mortimer DeKime."

I cupped my hand and yelled into his ear, "Hi, Mr. DeKime. I'm Rod Haynes. My buddies and I are off USS *Joseph Hewes*. Just pulled in from gun line duty off Beirut a few days ago. Can you tell me—"

"Sure, sure. I own this place. It's a private club, not everybody knows about. Word gets around town pretty quickly, so we're building up a clientele. You fellas care for a drink?"

"That's the idea. Beers all around, please."

"My pleasure." Mortimer held up his two hands, signaling seven, pointing at a bottle of Heineken on the bar. He turned around to see me reaching for my wallet and he grabbed my arm. "That's enough of that, lieutenant. Your money is no good here."

"That's nice of you, but we can't—"

"Lieutenant, look around you. No one will let any of you spend your money tonight. Make it easy on us. Don't let's argue, okay?"

"If you say so, Mortimer. Thank you. Your accent: where in New York are you from?" I asked, yelling into his ear.

Mortimer smiled broadly. "Born and raised in Brooklyn, off Flatbush Avenue. We sold our dry cleaning business eight years ago and moved here to be with my two brothers and Estelle – that's my wife. She's got a sister and three brothers here, too. See her behind the bar serving those beers? Wave hello. That's my baby brother, Jacob, over there on the barstool."

I lifted my hand in her direction and smiled. She waved back. Jacob joined her in greeting us. Mortimer handed the Heinekens back to me through the throng at the bar. I passed them along to my shipmates lined up behind me. They were all talking to the crowd. Everyone kept hugging them, shaking their hands, and acting as if we had just returned home from a long deployment. We dispersed to different places to talk more with our newfound friends.

Before our arrival, I reminded everyone of the 0200 curfew, so we had to leave Jerusalem no later than thirty minutes past midnight to drive the seventy-five miles back to the ship. That left us two hours to party. We all agreed to gather at the entrance just after midnight to count heads and ensure no one was AWOL.

Mortimer continued introducing me to family and friends, who kept asking detailed questions about our duty in Lebanon. I explained I was not permitted to discuss ship's information. It was strictly classified information, not to be disclosed to anyone. Several had family serving in the Israeli forces fighting in southern Lebanon, Mortimer whispered moments later. One man sadly told me his son had recently returned home with a severe head wound. He would be incapacitated for life.

It was a furious party, dizzying. I told Mortimer about our day and all that we had seen. Even though I was not religious, I told him I had felt a genuine sense of history and spirituality in Israel. Mortimer asked me if I had any thoughts of living here sometime in the future. I hesitated, thinking carefully. We must be mindful not to offend our hosts. But I wanted to be honest in my answer, to share my concerns about how the Israelis treated their Arab citizens despite the bombings and rocket attacks the Israelis constantly faced. I held back, remembering my role as an ambassador of goodwill for America, and answered that I didn't see how I could live in Israel, but I was impressed by all that I had experienced. He seemed satisfied with my answer. We headed back to the ship ninety minutes later.

Left Behind

Our taxi approached the gates of the Haifa Port Authority ten minutes before liberty expired. The security guards' flashlights roused us from our slumbers. After producing our military IDs, we were quickly waved through the gate.

"Hey, Dex, where are we parked?" I asked our damage control officer, LTJG Dexter Rogers.

"Maybe Pier Charlie?" He sat up, mumbling. "Anybody know?"

James Lee spoke up. "Yeah, Pier Charlie. Half-way down on the right." I nodded at the driver, who drove in that direction.

Five minutes later, we were standing at an empty berth on Pier Charlie.

"Hey, James, you said *Hewes* was parked here. What the hell is going on?" Dexter asked.

"We were right here." James scratched his head. "Maybe we moved today?"

We all started talking at once. "Great, just great. Ten minutes to liberty expiring and we can't find the ship. We're screwed now."

James said, "We must find the administration building and the ship, pronto."

A voice emerged from the shadows: "Are you officers attached to USS *Hewes*?" A tall, lanky Israeli naval attaché stepped from a parked car. His epaulet on his left shoulder indicated he was an embassy liaison staff member. He held a large, sealed envelope.

"My name is Aaron Weir. I am an Israeli liaison with the American embassy in Tel Aviv. Please gather around me for a moment." We all stared at each other.

Peter Berkowitz, the senior officer among us, said, "We're all from *Joseph Hewes*' wardroom. We don't understand—"

"I realize that this is confusing," Weir interrupted. "Your ship has left port."

"Holy shit! Did you say it 'left port'?" I asked. We gaped at each other.

Weir nodded. "At 1100 hours today, Libyan forces crossed into Chad and attacked a series of military outposts and small villages. Chad's ground forces will counter-attack in the next few hours. All operational American Sixth Fleet units are on high alert and have been sent to sea. USS *Joseph Hewes* departed Haifa at 1530 this afternoon."

We shook our heads, saying nothing. This wasn't good.

"We're in deep trouble now. Just wait 'til the XO gets a hold of us," I eventually murmured to James.

Weir looked at me. "Oh, no, no. You see, gentlemen, just before *Hewes* took in all lines, they tossed seven seabags onto the pier, one for each of you. Your executive officer also left each of you $150 in American dollars. Here are instructions for the senior officer in this envelope."

Berkowitz stepped forward, "I'll take that."

"Here you are. We reserved rooms for all of you at the Hilton in Tel Aviv. Half of you can ride with me in my car. We have your seabags. The others can ride in a taxi. Is this satisfactory?"

Peter answered, "Okay, guys, I'll keep the envelope and cash. Everyone gets their allotment after we stow our gear in our rooms. We'll meet in the lounge to debrief. Any questions?"

Chuck Baker asked, "Peter, how can the ship function with only two-thirds of the wardroom? And what will the XO do to us when we return to the ship?"

Peter replied, "You heard Mr. Weir. First, nobody's in trouble. This came down without warning. We're not the only American warship in the Med missing some of its crew tonight. We must catch up with her. Nobody knows where we're headed next."

Weir spoke one last time: "Actually, gentlemen, you will find that your XO ordered you to stay in Tel Aviv for at least three days. He wants you to wait for further instructions through your embassy there. If you will, you'll excuse me for saying so. I think the key is staying together and being ready to respond to orders quickly and promptly. In the meantime, I suggest you settle into the Hilton and wait for further instructions."

"We can do that, I think," I responded. "Is the hotel bar open past midnight?"

Peter smiled. "Rod, knock it off. This is serious. Let's get moving."

We all jumped into the vehicles and took off for Tel Aviv. We were excited about the new adventure we had just stumbled into but worried about not being at our assigned posts if *Hewes* entered combat while we were ashore. We checked into the hotel. At our meeting in the lounge, we agreed to gather at 0900 hours the following day for a head check and to plan our next move. James and I then had an early morning dinner before retiring to our rooms, leaving the other officers in the hotel bar.

Morning came, and the first of a flurry of messages from the XO arrived at the embassy's front desk, directing us to stay put in Tel Aviv until further notice. Bobby McNeil, our electronics repair officer, piped up, saying there was only one reasonable thing left for us to do. He was going on a beer run and then retire to the pool up on the roof of the hotel to take in a few rays and read a book. Three of us chipped in for two cases of brew and agreed to meet at the pool.

Bobby arrived poolside with the beer iced down in a cooler. He tossed a frosty can to each of us. "Well, the sun hasn't dipped below the yard arm, but there are always exceptions to the rule. Drink up, gentlemen."

Lying in our lounge chairs in the hot midday sun, I leaned across James and said, "Hey, Peter. You know what we've got to do every time we get one of these messages from the ship, don't you?"

Peter, who was snoozing, opened his eyes and looked at me, mumbling, "What are you talking about, Rod?"

"The XO will be looking for evidence that we dragged our feet in getting back. So, whenever he sends us a message, we should respond to it immediately. In our reply, we should nail down exactly where we are and tell him that we await further instructions. Get it?"

"What Rod is saying," Bobby said as he cracked open another beer, "is that maybe we should send him messages before we get them from him, sort of a preemptive message strike. Right?"

Peter looked at James and said, "What do you say, James?"

"You know, Peter, these guys have a point. We're probably pissing off the rest of the wardroom. We need to stay in the good graces of the XO. I mean, come on, there's seven of us here. Imagine what the watch bill looks like right now. They're probably standing port and starboard watches 'til we get back. They think we're on an extended vacation for a week, pretty much like what we're doing, so there'll be hell to pay. Firing off messages to the ship, even too many of 'em, might be smart. It could make things easier once we get back."

Peter paused a moment before taking a long swig of beer. Then he announced, "Sounds good. Okay, remember everyone. No one goes anywhere without my permission. I want everyone to know where each of us is always. We must be ready to go at any time." James began to laugh as Peter spoke. Peter turned to James, and, staring at him, snapped, "You have a problem with that, James?"

"Not at all, Peter. As long as you play by the rules you establish for the rest of us, man."

"What's that supposed to mean?" Peter demanded. He stood up and folded his arms defiantly. We all sat up and watched Peter and James. This was not like James to cause trouble.

James stood up and looked Peter directly in the eye. He was taller than Peter, but James stood with a relaxed, amused grin. "Look, man, whatever you say goes. You're the senior officer here, Peter. I got that. But, I noticed that the taxi dropped you off at 0330 this morning. I was in the lobby on the phone calling home to South Carolina. You walked by on the other side of the lobby and didn't notice me. So, I walked outside to the taxi and asked the driver, 'Where did you come from?' Know what he said?"

"Just hold it. Never mind that," Lt. Berkowitz interrupted James. Meanwhile, I slipped into the pool's shallow end, holding my beer, and walked around in the warm water.

"Oh, I don't mind telling the guys," James calmly responded. "You went to the old city in Jerusalem last night right after you told all of us to stay put in Tel Aviv. I'm guessing you went to see that pretty girl you met at the disco the other night. I could be wrong about that. But I don't think so."

"Now, just hold on, James. Hold it right there. You have no right, I mean, whose business is... I mean... hold on." Peter's eyebrows bunched together as he sputtered and fidgeted.

"Look, Peter," I said from where I stood in the pool, the water up to my chest, "I'm with James. You don't issue two orders, one for us and another for you to follow. We're in this together. Who the fuck gave you special privileges? The rules apply to everyone."

Peter stood with his feet apart, hands on his hips. Then he pensively said as he looked around at us, pointing directly at me. "Okay, look. New set of rules right now. Today – just today – we can be anywhere between Tel Aviv and Jerusalem 'til 1700 hours. Then everybody reports to me downstairs in the lobby. We're here for three days, anyway. We know that."

Bobby McNeil spoke from his pool chair. "No dice, Peter. You call her and tell her the date is off, or maybe she can come to Tel Aviv and hang out with you here if she wants to. Bring her up here to the pool. We won't mind."

Peter spat, "You fucking little ensign, I could bust you down..."

Ed Parker, the junior officer among us spoke up. "Lt. Berkowitz, I think you need to leave Bobby alone. He's done nothing wrong. I'm sorry, sir, but that's how I feel."

Peter whirled around and barked, "You looking for trouble, too, Parker?"

"No, sir. But if you keep this up, I promise I'll speak to the XO ten minutes after we return to the ship. Nobody goes off on his own agenda here, sir. That includes you. The rules apply to everyone or nobody, sir."

Peter's face became beet red. He muttered, "Assholes," before stomping off towards the elevator and disappearing.

James headed off after him.

"James, where are you going?" I called out.

"Checking with Berky," James said over his shoulder. "You all drink your beers and stay cool while I talk to him. Nobody leaves the hotel, right?"

James returned thirty minutes later after reminding Berkowitz that his primary mission was to get us all back to *Hewes* as soon as possible. Years later, Berkowitz married the young lady from Jerusalem.

We stayed in Jerusalem for three days before flying commercial air to Athens because the ship was near Greece. To complicate matters, travel to the ship would involve a complex itinerary of rail, ferries, and maybe additional air travel.

Our travel orders were changed at the last moment, and we were forced to fly off to Rome out of Tel Aviv's Ben Gurion Airport. In Tel Aviv, I began writing the first of a series of postcards home to Rhode Island to document our travels. I wrote about being poolside, cold beer in hand, awaiting further orders from the ship, and "the hardships of Navy life."

For the most part, our group got along well because we spent time away from each other. We ate dinner together and met each morning to take stock of the situation. We had no news about Chad because we could not access classified military information. The newspapers said little after first reporting Libya's incursion. It appeared that no confrontation between Kaddafi and the U.S. Sixth Fleet was imminent, but it could happen, so we had to be ready.

Peter Berkowitz began sending a constant stream of messages back to the ship, once or twice daily. He informed the XO of our location, assuring him that our only priority was to return to *Hewes* immediately. Two days after we landed in Rome, the local American consulate delivered new orders to our hotel, putting us in motion again. We were ordered to take a southbound train to Sigonella Naval Air Station in Sicily, outside Catania. Once in Sigonella, we were to await further instructions from *Hewes*.

We boarded a local, meandering train full of Italians on summer vacation, traveling coach class down the boot of Italy towards its toe, where we hopped a ferry across the straits of Messina. A month earlier, *Hewes* had transited the strait on our way towards Gaeta for a brief repair period. The area was hotly contested between American, German, and Italian ground troops in the Second World War. We all talked about the movie *Patton* and the U.S. Army's conquest of Sicily as we traveled south.

We had seen small parks and plaques commemorating American victories or sites of battle in various spots around Italy earlier that spring. In some places, Sicily's terrain was exceptionally rugged, not permitting easy crossing by men and tanks. In July, Sicily was extraordinarily brown, dry, and hot. The only green color was off in the distant hills looming over the valleys we were moving through. I turned and said to James, "So this is Sicily, where the Godfather came from."

"What do you mean 'came from,' Rod?" James murmured off to one side. "Don't talk that stuff. Look around. Either change the subject or get far away from me." I laughed and gazed out the open window into the distance, the hot, dusty wind doing nothing to quench my thirst.

A little later, a boy who looked about eight years old tugged on my belt and held up a cup of warm water. Looking sideways, I saw an old woman – perhaps his grandmother – sitting on a bench, smiling and gesturing so that I could take a gulp. She showed me her battered thermos from her basket. The water was warm, but I quickly drained it, nodding my thanks to the woman and patting the child on his head. I figured she had been present twenty-five years before when her native land was ravaged by war. Was this a gesture of thankful remembrance? I wanted to speak with her but no one in our group spoke Italian fluently.

We arrived at Sigonella NAS later that afternoon, traveling the final leg in a Navy van that met us at the Catania train station. The air station was in the middle of nowhere. The accommodations on base were nowhere near as reasonable as the ones we had become accustomed to during our travels. Our days of living large were history. NAS Sigonella was a perfect strategic location for forward-deployed American P-3 Orion fixed-wing planes. They either worked in tandem with surface warships, or they flew solo. We worked with P-3s from Bermuda NAS on our searches for Soviet ballistic submarines in the North Atlantic.

I joined three of my shipmates outside the gates on a quick walk around the area, ignoring two sailors who told us, "There ain't nothing out there worth seeing, sir, just more of the same. This here is Sigonella." After walking less than a half-mile, we became bored and headed back towards the officers' club for dinner. We ate a decidedly unremarkable meal chased down by a few beers before gathering with the rest of the group. The operational tempo in the Mediterranean had increased noticeably over the previous week. There was no definite news from Chad, so we assumed the up-tempo activity at sea was primarily a demonstration of American military presence. The pilots drinking beer at the O-Club confirmed this.

Lt. Berkowitz held up the latest message from *Hewes*. "Okay, guys, here's the scoop. We jump aboard two helicopters tomorrow morning to take us to the *Eisenhower*. Sometime tomorrow afternoon, the LAMPS detachment off *Hewes* lands on *Eisenhower* and starts shuttling us back to the ship. Questions?" LAMPS was the acronym for the helicopter and crew embarked on *Hewes* for the entire cruise. It was designed for recognizance and weapons delivery on targets some distance from the ship.

We all silently shook our heads. That was that. Party time was over. We retreated to the bachelor officers' quarters to pack up and turn in early. The regular shipboard routine would resume the next day, and we had better be ready for the grief we knew would come from our comrades once we touched down on *Hewes*.

The final leg of our journey proceeded smoothly. We were used to the size of *Hewes*, which was minuscule next to the mammoth floating city of sailors on the *Eisenhower*. We had a two-hour respite, so we went up to the O-1 level to watch the flight deck in action. James nudged my side and pointed to our LAMPS helo inbound for a landing. We headed below and began final preparations for our transport back home.

We hadn't been aboard the *Joseph Hewes* ten minutes when the word was passed over the 1-MC: Now muster all returning officers in the wardroom with the executive officer.

"Here we go. Stand by for heavy rolls," I said to James.

"I don't think so," James replied.

The wardroom doors opened. The XO stepped into the space. "Welcome back, gentlemen," he said crisply, without a hint of anger. "I received every message from Lt. Berkowitz. He kept me informed of your whereabouts, as I expected. After we pull into Gaeta, you all will be standing in-port watches for the first three days we are there. Don't expect to take liberty for a while."

"Sir? Are we heading into port?" Chuck Baker asked.

"Yeah. I guess you didn't get the word. We had a serious casualty to the 1-A SSTG two nights ago. We're heading to Gaeta to troubleshoot it and return to Beirut. Might take five days or more." We grinned at each other. Steam-driven turbogenerators (SSTGs) generated electricity for the ship. Auxiliary steam from the main propulsion plant was the source of power for the SSTGs. The ship had two of them, 1-A and 1-B.

"Okay, you clowns, knock it off," the XO said. "Nobody's blaming you for being on the beach when we left Haifa. It put your shipmates in a tight spot for a week and you will not rub this little adventure of yours in their faces. This wasn't anybody's fault except Kaddafi's. There will be no bragging about missing ships' movement. Understood?"

We all nodded.

James asked, "Sir, what is the tactical situation in Chad?"

"Good question. Libya has been crossing in and out of the disputed territory for some time. Chad's military typically fires artillery or rockets during incursions. Currently, intelligence reports indicate that Libyan troops have returned to their original positions. There have been casualties but no details. Nobody from Sixth Fleet has fired a shot yet, but we're monitoring the situation in ways I won't go into. Now, everyone, please gather your gear and return to work. Move it, gentlemen. Let's turn to. Party time is over."

Mail Buoy Watch

Our liberty port call in Saint-Tropez was the best liberty port since our arrival in the Mediterranean. It was mid-August, and it seemed like every young lady in France was on vacation on the French Riviera, where *Joseph Hewes* was again anchored out in the middle of the bay. As we lowered the anchor, the ship was surrounded by speeding pleasure craft with topless women standing on the bows, waving at the sailors clustered on the weather decks. We were stunned at the scene. In the bright sunshine of a hot summer afternoon, sailors lined the rails, snapping pictures of the women on the boats circling the ship. At the same time, the women on the boats were snapping photographs of sailors taking pictures of them. I found it hilarious.

James and I stood back, taking it all in. Thirty minutes later, we boarded the captain's gig – the boat sometimes used to ferry officers to and from the ship. I sipped a cold beer with the captain and six other officers as we motored to the fleet landing in Saint-Tropez.

RH, Saint-Tropez, France, August 1983

Mail Buoy Watch

When we arrived, James and I climbed a cobblestone street to the stone parapets overlooking the tourist-clogged village and busy harbor area below. We leaned against ancient cannons painted shiny black, pointing menacingly out towards *Joseph Hewes*. Placing a stale Cuban cigar in my mouth, I asked James to snap a shot photo of me overlooking the inlet of Saint-Tropez. We strolled around the non-tourist part of the town, meeting locals. I tried speaking rudimentary French, doing it badly, which was nevertheless appreciated, I believed. We were in Saint-Tropez for four days before receiving orders to return to the eastern Mediterranean. It was hard leaving the French Riviera.

We quickly stopped in Haifa to refuel and take on food, mail, and new crew members before continuing to Beirut. *Joseph Hewes* patrolled the gunline at a mind-numbing six to eight knots two days later. As a member of the peacekeeping force, our mission was to suppress attacks, should any come from enemy positions deep in the Chouf Mountains.

Even with all the violence raging back and forth in plain sight ten miles east of our ship, life aboard *Hewes* rapidly became tedious. When we left the area to return to Charleston in mid-November, we never fired our guns, even though several other American warships in our company had fired theirs. We had seen numerous explosions and plenty of gunfire but no graphic carnage up close. There were brief moments of fun between amidst the days of boredom aboard ship life as we watched the human drama of the Lebanese conflict unfolding, including untold. This included holidays when everyone was given the day off and "steel beach picnics," where the entire ship gathered on the flight deck for a cookout. A rock band comprised of crew members played passable quality tunes.

We were patrolling the gunline one morning when a senior petty officer pulled a newly reported enlisted crewman aside to inform him that he had been selected to perform a critical mission: standing the mail buoy watch on the ship's bow. The first-class petty officer carefully explained the mail delivery system for small warships steaming in the eastern Mediterranean. Helicopters from aircraft carriers dropped mail pouches onto the top of buoys bobbing about in the middle of the ocean. To collect their mail, smaller warships sidled up to the buoy, allowing the sailor on mail buoy watch to grab the mail pouches with his bow hook, hoisting the bags off the buoy onto the ship.

No young sailor I knew who heard this story for the first time asked why helicopters depositing mail on sea buoys could not simply deliver mail directly to the ship instead, which is precisely how mail delivery services usually worked for American warships at sea in 1983.

The boot sailor was issued a yellow helmet, a bow hook, a life preserver, binoculars, and sound-powered phones. He dressed as if he was at general quarters, with his sleeves buttoned down and his pants tucked into his socks for safety reasons. With all this gear, he looked perfectly ridiculous. He stood his watch on the ship's bow in the broiling hot sun of the eastern Mediterranean in August, anxiously scanning the horizon for any sign of the non-existent mail buoy. He understood the fate of the ship's mail for the entire week depended on him sighting the mail buoy, so he kept passing his contact reports up to the deck officer on the bridge every twenty minutes through sound-powered phones used by the ship's lookouts. He was not finding the mail buoy.

The sight of the young man scanning the horizon and delivering reports to the officer of the deck drew howls of laughter from the watch team in the pilot house, including the commanding officer, who had seen this gag played out many times before. The young man continued his vigilant watch standing, oblivious to the commotion around him.

Finally sensing something was not right, the sailor spun around, looked up at the flybridge, and saw sixty crew members pointing at him and bending over with laughter. The gag victim slammed the bow hook onto the deck and kicked his helmet away, tossing his sound-powered phone off to the side before stomping away. Two months later, he was the first among his shipmates on the flybridge watching some brand-new mark suffer the same indignities. The mail buoy watch caper was one of the oldest Navy pranks in the book. For whatever reason, it worked almost every time we tried it on the newest crew members.

Beirut International Airport

The autumn weather in 1983 in the eastern Mediterranean was balmy and calm. From the stern of *Joseph Hewes*, the only ripple seen on the water was the slow-moving wake left by the ship's propeller. We kept moving around and around our racetrack course, approximately eight miles off the coast of Beirut. Once a week or so, we would steam twenty miles out to sea, refueling, and then return to our assigned station near the city. *Joseph Hewes* typically had two to four other navy ships in our company.

What appeared to be a tranquil scene belied the violent activity in and around Lebanon's capital, where fighting raged between three or four, sometimes five, different factions. I continued spending my off-duty hours gazing over at the land where a terrible war was being waged. More than a few times, Israeli gunboats made their way up the coast to the outskirts of Beirut to launch artillery shells into the lower Chouf Mountains in support of their ground troops.

The traffic on the secure voice circuits intensified as October went by. We listened to Robert McFarlane, George Shultz, and Philip Habib, all senior White House officials, as they spoke to military commands in Beirut. Much of their discussion had to do with the growing intensity and boldness of attacks on Marines patrolling the outer perimeter of the Beirut International Airport. There had been some injuries and deaths, resulting in significant disagreements about what should be done next. We could only hear parts of the conversations, but we all knew this was extremely sensitive information. These persons spoke to President Reagan daily.

On August 31, all Marine foot patrols were terminated due to sniper and grenade attacks. On September 16, U.S. naval gunfire support commenced in response to the shelling of the U.S. Ambassador to Lebanon's residence. Four years later, as part of my research for my master's thesis on the Lebanese conflict, I wrote that a wartime condition existed in Lebanon in late summer and early autumn, with Israeli forces acting unilaterally against two or three different factions. American leaders were not decisive in planning their response to this aggression, resulting in disastrous consequences.

At night, the barrage of explosions from mortar and artillery shells became more frequent. No shells ever landed near us, although earlier that summer another American frigate had participated in a "call for fire" mission, rendering support to ground troops by firing the five-inch gun mounted on her bow. We had not fired our own gun since leaving the States five months earlier.

On Sunday, October 23, 1983, I reported to the engineering main space, also known as Main Control, at 3:50 am to assume my duties as engineering officer of the watch under instruction. I was working my way towards my EOOW qualifications before I departed the ship upon our return home. The crew was called to their feet at precisely 0600 hours per the ship's routine. Then, at approximately 0725, a call came down to Main Control from the officer of the deck on the bridge.

"Main control, bridge. A major explosion is reported near Beirut International Airport; a huge cloud is rising. Wait, wait. Another explosion happened approximately sixty degrees off the port bow near downtown Beirut. Two major explosions. Stand by for general quarters."

Within ten minutes, the crew assumed battle stations in response to the attack, and various reports from the beach were now arriving in the CIC. Specific information about the attack was lacking. We later learned that our families back home had obtained more information about what had happened in Beirut before we did so, and we were less than six miles from the scene. The multi-story concrete Marine compound at Beirut International Airport was pancaked when a terrorist drove a truck into the lobby of the building. Estimates were that over twelve thousand pounds of TNT were inside the truck when it detonated. The force of the blast initially lifted the reinforced building upward before collapsing upon itself. The explosion created an oblong crater measuring nearly forty feet. The secondary blast that morning had been a coordinated terrorist attack on the French compound, located in a different area in Beirut. Forty-six French soldiers were killed. There was little American publicity paid to that tragedy because of the enormity of the attack at the airport that morning.

Urgent messages were sent from the scene to all warships in the area, requesting first aid assistance, heavy equipment for digging through the rubble to locate survivors, and military support for suppressing enemy fire as the rescue mission continued. *Joseph Hewes* sent two corpsmen to the scene, with the crew lining up to donate blood. In one incident, a Marine Cobra helicopter was vectored towards a Cessna plane inbound towards the disaster area, with orders to shoot the plane down if necessary. At the last minute, one of the plane's occupants held up a piece of white paper with black letters reading "CBS NEWS." They were immediately escorted away from the scene.

We were only in the area for another two weeks following the attack before heading westward towards Gibraltar and across the Atlantic to Charleston. There was more anger than sadness on the ship and concern that our families thought the attack had directly impacted us.

Deploying the Marines in a wartime situation was one of the most significant foreign policy blunders of the Reagan administration, second only to the Iran-Contra affair. While it would be incorrect to ascribe the American military invasion of Grenada on October 25 solely to an effort to enhance Reagan's foreign policy image, this was certainly one of the motivations. The success of the invasion did improve the President's public image, overshadowing the considerable mistakes made by his administration in Beirut.

In early 1984, despite his vows to keep American armed forces deployed in Lebanon, President Reagan quietly ordered the withdrawal of troops to ships offshore, marking a sobering end to an ill-fated mission.

Fatherhood

It was dark and stuffy inside my stateroom, where I lay half-awake, lulled by the familiar sounds of the ship gliding at an eight-knot clip through the glassy eastern Mediterranean. We had resumed our tactical position on the gunfire support line with the smoldering, war-torn city of Beirut lying nine miles due east of our station. Shortly after *Joseph Hewes* departed Charleston for the Med in April, I quickly grew used to the rhythmic creaking of metal-on-metal joints on our desks, chairs, and bunk inside my stateroom, induced by the steady pitch and roll of our frigate crossing the open, sometimes turbulent waters of the Atlantic Ocean in springtime. Once I was home, adjusting to eight hours of uninterrupted sleep was difficult, absent the sounds and motions of a ship at sea.

As I lay in my rack, between a dream state and full consciousness, a voice emerged from the darkness. "Rod, wake up. I have an important message for you." Someone was shaking my leg, and I groaned in acknowledgment. I was tired, having stood watch at midnight. It was now 0700.

"Morning, XO, what can I do for you?" I groggily responded.

"Congratulations, Lieutenant. You're a daddy. Your son was born earlier this morning."

"What?" I sat straight up, now wide awake. "Amy's not due for seven more weeks. It can't be."

"Got an AMCROSS here." The American Red Cross generated AMCROSS messages. "Read this. I'm afraid there's both good and bad news in it," the exec said, pulling up a chair. "Take a deep breath, Rod." The XO handed me the message from Radio Central. It had arrived aboard twenty minutes earlier.

Grabbing my glasses, I read while swinging my legs over the bunk's edge, sitting upright. The message a radioman had hand-delivered to the XO minutes earlier was succinct:

> *Benjamin Irving Haynes arrived this morning: 3 pounds, 13 ounces. Baby okay, Amy still serious. Congratulations.*

I looked down at the XO from my upper rack and said, "Sir, I don't know what this means. It seems like my son's okay, but what about Amy?"

He shook his head. "I know as much as you do. Send a response asking for more details. The captain wanted you to know right away. Again, congratulations." He stood up to walk out.

"Sir?" I called over to him.

"What is it?" He turned around to face me as he stepped halfway through the door to the passageway.

"What are my chances of going home?"

He stepped back inside, closing the hatch. "Rod, we're heading back to Israel to replenish our fuel and supplies, and then we'll return here. The captain has clarified that none of his key officers can go home unless it's a matter of life and death. I wouldn't plan on going back to Charleston unless something drastic occurs. Even if something were to happen to Amy, God forbid, you wouldn't be considered a married man. There's a significant difference in the travel priority lists for married personnel going stateside compared to single sailors. I'm sorry, but that's just how it is."

The XO left my stateroom. I was there alone, contemplating my new world. I was now a father. It was frightening and exhilarating, but above all, it was frustrating to be thousands of miles away from my son. I felt like celebrating, and then I felt like crying. I was confused. Three other sailors on *Joseph Hewes* had new babies waiting for their return to Charleston. Others were expecting updates from extremely expectant wives at any time, so I wasn't alone.

1983 was long before internet messaging allowed sailors to communicate instantly with their loved ones worldwide. In those days, we communicated primarily through regular mail and, in emergencies, through American Red Cross messages. Ordinary mail deliveries took up to three weeks to reach us at sea. Through a series of emergency messages home, I learned that Amy was in critical shape in the hours following her emergency C-section, but Ben was stable, and the prognosis for him was good. Only after we returned home did I learn how close Amy had come to dying while giving birth to our son. She suffered from severe preeclampsia. It almost killed her.

We had not made any long-term plans before I left on deployment other than making legal arrangements for her and Ben in the event of my death. How our lives would play out was something we would address after I was back home. Military marriages sometimes happen in non-conventional ways. Some sailors married the divorced spouses of other military personnel because their new spouse entered their second or third marriage aware of the many pressures and separations military life entailed. The ready security of pay and health benefits, housing, and the easy availability of the commissary on base attracted those who knew how the military support system worked. I observed several instances where twenty-something enlisted sailors married spouses who were thirty-two or thirty-five, primarily because the older partner sought to reestablish a secure military lifestyle. The young sailor wouldn't realize the ramifications of what had happened until later when the convenience of marrying a sailor became the primary reason these kinds of marriages remained intact.

Like their counterparts at civilian colleges, many ensigns graduating from Annapolis married soon after commissioning, some within days of graduation. Their early years of marriage were more challenging than those of new civilian marriages for young couples because (I believed then) a typical academy graduate was nowhere near as socially grounded and ready for marriage as their civilian counterparts. Socializing in Annapolis included "going over the wall" of the academy and drinking with friends downtown. While we had no problem drinking our share of alcohol at college, at Annapolis, the midshipmen had far fewer opportunities to meet and greet the opposite sex except at formal, highly supervised social functions. This was true even after women began appearing in the military academies' ranks in the mid-1970s.

Annapolis and West Point were hardly healthy settings for fostering meaningful relationships between the sexes. I felt the ring-knockers of my age were not, generally, nearly as socially adjusted as their counterparts from Navy ROTC or OCS. Annapolis graduates, however, were exceptionally informed and comfortable with the complex technologies a U.S. Navy ship relies on at sea. Academy graduates were proficient at celestial navigation, weapons systems, radio and radar principles, 1200 psi engineering, and daily shipboard operations. They excelled at training, assisting helping sailors advance in advancing their rank, and passing every material inspection the Navy threw at them. Annapolis sent brilliant junior officers out to the fleet. For most of them, their emotional growth occurred after they arrived.

Less than three months before *Joseph Hewes* sailed for Europe, everything had happened quickly. With the cruise directly ahead and my expected transfer to shore duty in New England immediately following our return home from the Med, I was rattled. Amy and I agreed that marriage was out of the question since we'd known each other for less than three months. I acknowledged paternity, designating Amy as the beneficiary on my government life insurance policy. I also started a financial allotment to her and the baby right away. When we learned we would have a son, we decided to name him after our fathers; her father was Benjamin, and my father was Irving.

We had serious concerns about the baby's legal status because he would be born in South Carolina, and the state bureaucracy frowned on children born out of wedlock, their treatment of them archaic. The financial costs of having a baby weighed on us. How long could Amy continue working before going on maternity leave? Was it possible for Amy and the baby to sustain their lifestyle within a modest single-parent income, supplemented by monthly financial support from me? We hoped so.

My life options changed forever when I learned I had a son on the way. This meant I had to provide for him, either from a distance or by marrying his mother. Amy assured me that she had no expectations for me to marry her, but she emphasized that I must promise to provide financial support, as the child was mine. I agreed to her terms. With the support of Amy's family, who traveled to Charleston from various parts of the country, and with good medical treatment over several months, Amy gradually regained her strength after Ben's birth. His health improved more quickly than his mother's.

Two months later, on the way home across the Atlantic, I spent a lot of time topside alone, thinking and rethinking my situation once the ship was pier-side in Charleston. I had a woman who loved me and a son with serious health issues because he was born seven weeks prematurely. I was planning to head off to Boston for shore duty less than a month after returning to Charleston. We both were concerned about how it would all work out.

Shore Duty

Just before leaving Beirut, the crew placed their liquor orders at the U.S Navy Grog Shop at the Rota, Spain Naval Station, via radio message. Five days later, a massive transfer of booze, over three full pallets, was hoisted onto the ship from a replenishment ship while *Joseph Hewes* was refueling for her trip back across the Atlantic to Charleston. The booze – cheap and duty-free – was locked tight so no one could start early celebrations on the way home.

Joseph Hewes conducted our turnover with our designated relief, a frigate from Norfolk who relieved us hours before we left the Mediterranean. As we navigated the Straits of Gibraltar, there was significantly less traffic than we had encountered on our way into the Mediterranean six months earlier. With the Captain's permission, the XO appeared in the pilot house to play a Beach Boys classic, "Sloop John B," as the Rock of Gibraltar passed down our starboard side. Sailors sang along. The mood aboard the ship was one of exuberance. We would be home in eight days.

Two days into the crossing of the Big Pond, good news arrived. "Sir, your orders are in," Radioman Third Class Wells said, arriving at Main Control in the Engine Room where I was undergoing training. He handed me a four-page message from Washington D.C., informing me that my orders to Boston University, at the new Navy ROTC unit, had been approved.

"Hey, Wells, why don't you fetch us a bucket of steam?" Machinist Mate Third Class Jamieson asked, laughing.

I faced the snipe who was monitoring the gauges on the bulkhead. "That's enough. Jamieson, keep your eyes on those gauges and your mouth shut," I said sternly before turning to the radioman. "Thanks for hunting me down, Wells. Wasn't necessary."

"Not a problem, Mr. Haynes. Everyone knows you've been waiting for the final word. We're happy for you. Congratulations." Petty Officer Wells shook my hand and left.

After the evening meal, the cooks brought the garbage from the day's cooking topside to the fantail, along with trash from the entire ship, which was put in green plastic garbage bags after was being screened for any classified material. As the sun set over the ocean and the final colors of the day splashed across the sky and water, sailors were heaving six, eight, or ten large garbage bags off the stern. Those bags bobbed along the surface, an ugly testament to the Navy's insensitivity to the ocean's health. What were aircraft carriers doing with their trash? How many tons of waste have been disposed of this way over how many years? How long could the ocean tolerate being treated like a garbage dump? I still think about these things today.

The excitement on the ship intensified as the days remaining on our cruise dwindled. Everyone was discussing their plans once we arrived in Charleston. Fathers like me who had never seen their newborns talked nonstop about seeing their babies. But not all was positive talk. Some had wives who had left them, some had lost family members to death, others grappled with everyday life problems that arose while the ship was halfway around the world, and only now would they be home to deal with them. Wives would have to learn to share responsibility for decision-making and bill-paying and get used to having their men around the house. Children would have to adjust to having Daddy home. The days and weeks ahead would not all be joyous.

Aside from looking forward to seeing Amy and Ben, I thought about my new duty station in Boston, which was only an hour north of my hometown in northern Rhode Island. Soon, I would be back among family and friends and, just as importantly, away from Charleston, the cradle of the Confederacy. I had never adjusted to the "quaint" and "welcoming" atmosphere boasted about in the city's tourist literature. Charlestonians possessed a subtle – sometimes not so subtle – disdain for Yankees, although this predisposition never prevented them from accepting the millions of dollars spent in the area. I was glad to be heading north.

During one mid-watch at 0300, the Combat Information Center (CIC) called up to the bridge to announce that Buoy Two-Charlie had appeared on their radar. A spontaneous cheer erupted in both CIC and on the bridge while the rest of the ship slept. It would not be long now. The following morning was mild and sunny, and the familiar stench of saltwater marsh wafted over the sailors standing on the weather decks, eager to catch their first glimpse of Charleston in half a year. Soon, we entered the shipping channel leading into Charleston.

We drew towards the Cooper River channel and began heading underneath the Cooper River Bridge, traveling north to the Charleston

Naval Station. Twenty minutes later, two tugboats met our ship at the inlet to the Naval Station pier area. As we approached our berth, a large, enthusiastic crowd began cheering while a Navy band played patriotic tunes. Moments after the ladder was in place, a rush of wives, children, parents, and friends overwhelmed the quarterdeck, filled with screams, laughter, and the cries of babies.

I saw Amy step off the ladder and anxiously scan the crowd, unable to locate me. She was dressed in a white and pink summer dress. It was November, but the weather was perfect, and she looked as beautiful as I could remember seeing her. I came up from behind and tapped her on one shoulder before spinning around the other. She turned and burst into tears, hugging me like she would never let me go.

"Ben's at home with a neighbor. He was asleep, and I didn't want to wake him. He sleeps so little. Any chance I get to let him sleep I take it," Amy explained.

I nodded my understanding, telling her we needed to leave immediately to see him. I would return and retrieve my gifts for her and my son later that afternoon. Thirty minutes later, we drove into the driveway of Amy's home, and I jumped from the car, with Amy running after me as I ran to the front door. I raced to Ben's room, where I saw a pink, healthy baby lying on his side, deep asleep, facing me. He looked perfectly content, I told Amy, who burst out laughing.

"He gets awfully mad if he doesn't get his milk on time. You should have seen him around 4:00 am. He's got your temper."

I asked Amy if I could hold him as he slept, and she agreed. I gingerly leaned over the crib and clasped my hands around either side of Ben's belly, drawing him up to my shoulder. He immediately adjusted to his new position, whimpering for a few seconds before falling asleep again. I felt his warm breath on my neck, his tiny body clinging to me. I felt like crying about the wonder of everything, but I didn't. I felt inadequate, unsure of what it all meant. I felt proud. I felt scared. It was one of the most remarkable moments in my young life.

I had finally made it home.

Boston University

It took some intensive lobbying for me to land the teaching billet at the brand-new Navy ROTC unit at Boston University. I began my letter-writing campaign by asking Captain Hardt to write an endorsement of my candidacy to the unit's CO. The letter was sent just before we left Charleston on deployment.

A month later, my boss, Lt. Sliney, wrote a strong letter of support for me to the university. Two months into our deployment, I sent a telegram to the Dean of Men at Ripon College, David Harris, asking him to tell Boston University what a great person I was. By the time I graduated from Ripon in the spring of 1978, Dean Harris had become a good friend. He was aware of my various antics and rowdy behavior during my four years in Wisconsin. I was confident that Dean Harris remembered everything I had said and done.

I reported to the Navy ROTC unit in the second week of December 1983.

"It's only right that you are here," Captain Will Rich said to me during my arrival interview. "Those letters of support did the trick, especially the one from Dean Harris."

"I wasn't aware that Dean Harris had responded to my request."

"Oh, yes. It was a very positive statement about your potential as a teacher and counselor here. I have the letter right here." Captain Rich handed me the letter while explaining the unit's daily routine and the expectations he had of his staff.

Later that afternoon, I looked at the letter and focused on the conclusion.

> ... *All in all, I feel that Rod is a splendid candidate for any type of work that would enable him to capitalize on his intellectual curiosity and his knowledge of and interest in history. He is absolutely enthusiastic about the Navy, and I think the possibility of serving a tour of duty at Boston University would bring together all these hopes of his, as well as his predilections. I think he would be ideal for this assignment.*

I felt a phone call to Dean Harris was only right. When I contacted his secretary, I learned that three days after he wrote the letter of recommendation in September, Harris had a massive stroke and died. I was heartbroken. I began writing to Dean Harris one year before I enrolled at Ripon. He was kind and generous, eventually becoming my mentor as I acclimated to college life. One evening in freshman year, he bailed me out of the downtown jail in Ripon after I was detained for drunkenness. I always had a soft spot in my heart for David Harris.

The transition from sea duty to shore duty was akin to hurtling down the highway at eighty miles per hour, then slamming on the brakes to a brief stop, then proceeding at fifteen miles per hour. For two years, I endured the challenges that all sailors face as soon as their ship departs from the inner harbor. It was now time to throttle back and enjoy some well-earned rest. No more standing watch one day out of three when the ship was in port. No more twenty-hour workdays at sea. No longer would I be deprived of the everyday luxuries middle-class Americans took for granted. At sea, I found myself missing the simple pleasures of daily life, such as long, hot showers, cold beer, and watching football and baseball games on TV, along with countless other privileges that many Americans enjoy. Now, I had easy access to all the cold beer I could drink while watching sports on television.

Boston University's Navy ROTC unit was housed in a beautifully restored brownstone townhouse. The military science program had been evicted from many college campuses, including Boston University and Harvard, during the student turmoil in the late 1960s. It was now back on campus thanks to the efforts of Boston University President John Silber, a close friend of Ronald Reagan.

My fellow officers assigned to the unit included a Marine captain who flew attack helicopters, a Navy A-6 navigator, a Navy submariner, and a fellow surface warfare officer. All the naval officers were lieutenants. We quickly became friends working in our offices on the unit's second and third floors. We kept close reigns on the midshipmen, working cooperatively to mold them into effective Navy ensigns and U.S. Marine second lieutenants by the time their four-year stint at the unit was over.

I was part of the first teaching body at the university's Navy ROTC for over fifteen years, so there were no lesson plans when I arrived. I had three weeks to compile lessons from scratch for the winter session, spending most of the Christmas holidays at the office outlining my hour-long lectures on 1200-psi steam systems found on Knox-class frigates. I chuckled over the irony and absurdity of a liberal arts grad teaching steam propulsion to a class comprised mainly of physics and engineering majors. I decided the best strategy was to teach from a practical perspective, tracing propulsion plant steam systems and explaining the functions of the machinery in layman's terms.

Reunion

One morning at the office, I picked up the phone and was stunned to hear Megan West's voice on the other end. She was calling from Maine. Megan and I had been a hot item during my senior year in college until her father informed her at Christmastime that she would not be returning to Wisconsin for the winter semester. Megan's father instead directed her to enroll in the University of Southern Maine in Portland. He would no longer fund her college expenses if she refused his decree. Megan announced a week later it would be best if we broke up.

"Later on, you'll see that it's best for both of us," Megan said tearfully. "We're moving in different directions now."

I never forgave Megan's father for blackmailing his daughter. I couldn't comprehend his meanness. The breakup was excruciating. Letting go of your first love is hard, even after life has taken you far away from the physical environment that created it. Six years after college and many life experiences later, I was still, in some distant way, mourning the loss of Megan. She had no way of knowing I was now a father of a baby living in Charleston, South Carolina. I struggled to compose myself when she called me on that snowy morning in Boston. She told me about earning her nursing degree two years after our breakup. Within a month, she had landed a job at a Portland trauma center and had worked there ever since. Megan added that it was challenging work but extremely rewarding. The pay was quite good. She sounded upbeat and happy. She wondered if we could get together soon to "compare life notes" somewhere in Maine. I quickly said yes.

We agreed to meet at a restaurant on the Maine Turnpike. Afterward, we planned to drive north to spend the day skiing and catching up at the Sugar Loaf ski resort. When she walked through the door of the restaurant and I saw her for the first time in six long years, she looked the same as she had the last time we were together. We drank two cups of coffee before driving north to the ski slopes, chatting away like old friends. It wasn't an awkward reunion; it felt more like picking up a conversation we'd started the previous week. I felt comfortable, but it was clear that things were not quite how they used to be. We had both changed.

At Sugar Loaf, we shared laughter and reminiscences as old feelings resurfaced. Although our reunion was joyful, we both acknowledged the changes in our lives over the past six years of separation. We intentionally avoided discussing our significant others to preserve the special nature of the day. Years later, I wondered if Megan had reached out to me in Boston before accepting her marriage proposal, perhaps to confirm the person I had become. This was the only explanation I had for her sudden willingness to reconnect after years of silence. While I was happy to see her again, the pain from our breakup briefly returned.

We parted on civil terms the following day. We were each married within the year, and time passed without more words. While I never spoke to Megan again, I never forgot my former girlfriend, even as a married man and father to my son.

Frozen Fenway

In the winter of 1984, I put my recreational plans for spring and summer into motion. Fenway Park, the Boston Red Sox home, was seven minutes from the Navy ROTC unit. When persuading my colleagues that purchasing season tickets for the upcoming Red Sox season was a great idea, I didn't have to push all that hard. Everyone, including the CO, agreed to contribute to the cost of the tickets. They nominated me to walk over to Fenway Park to select the seats for the entire home game schedule, which consisted of eighty-one games. In those days, season tickets were readily available at reasonable prices. Red Sox Nation was only in its infancy in the mid-1980s. We were looking for two seats per game, preferably somewhere between first base and the home team's dugout, which would allow us a decent view of the action on the field.

I carefully walked through filthy slush and slippery snowbanks to reach the Red Sox ticket office. I passed by the Cask 'N Flagon saloon, where Red Sox fans argued and debated about baseball over beer and burgers all year round. Approaching the ticket office, I recalled the first time I passed through the ornate brick entrance to Fenway in the summer of 1967, when I was eleven. Dad and I walked up the narrow cement ramps and thickly painted railings, leading to my first view of the playing field. The color green immediately blasted my senses: the grass, the outfield walls, and the green awning ringing the interior of the ancient edifice itself. It amazed me how close the fans were to the game, even for those in the cheaper seats set further back from the field. The Red Sox games I watched religiously on black-and-white television never hinted that these brilliant colors existed inside the park. In that long, hot summer of 1967, when hippies in San Francisco were smoking weed and making love, and frustrated blacks in many of America's urban centers, including Boston, rioted over the poor state of race relations, the Vietnam War, and rampant poverty, in America, I intermittently watched race riots and Red Sox baseball. For me, the violence on television might as well have been beamed to our house from the moon; we were that far away from the riots. Meanwhile, the Beatles produced a different rock album called *Sergeant Pepper's Lonely Hearts Club Band*. The forced intimacy between players and fans inside Fenway Park was much more palatable in real life than on TV. Nearly twenty years later, in the dead of winter, I was about to see my cherished park in a new way.

I walked into the ticket office, where Bill, the older man at the window, showed me a faded seating chart glued to a large board. Scotch tape covered the holes from years of ticket sales. Since I was the only customer, we spent a full twenty minutes discussing various seat locations and prices. I needed to secure the best seats for my office mates, as I was considering season tickets for the 1985 and 1986 baseball seasons. If I messed this up, I knew I wouldn't be able to convince my ROTC colleagues to join me for the next two seasons.

Bill went on talking about the team's prospects for 1984. We debated who would play where, how the pitching staff was progressing, and whether we'd finally reach the World Series for the first time in sixty-seven years. I made a new friend after demonstrating my knowledge of Boston Red Sox baseball. Bill's positive reaction to my military uniform led him to share his wartime experiences fighting in Germany with General Patton's Third Army during World War II.

Bill finally leaned back and yelled at his buddy in the back room, "Hey, Chuck, watch da winda for ten minutes while I show dis Navy lieutenant the paaak, will ya?" He motioned for me to follow him through a side door, and we went deep into the building. Passing through a series of narrow hallways with peeling paint, I was surprised at how quickly we arrived at a heavy door leading out to the playing field. Bill smiled, watching the anticipation build on my face.

He said, "Brace yourself, Lieutenant. You've never seen her look like dis before," as he swung the door open.

As I stood inside Fenway Park, I was surprised to find a foot of freshly fallen, pristine snow on the ground as we stepped out onto one of the lower concourses on the third-base side. The snow had blown far past the overhanging roof that usually protects fans from the chilly New England rains in early April and late September. Standing at the railing, I swept aside a foot-long pile of delicate, feathery snow crystals that had accumulated on the barrier.

I imagined holding a beer and listening to the organist play before the 7:05 pm game at Fenway Park. I longed to see the lush green grass of Fenway and wished to see the Red Sox players in their clean, white uniforms with bright red numbers and the team logo. I imagined the soft colors of green, red, and blue mingling with the mouthwatering scents of hot dogs, popcorn, and peanuts amidst the Fenway faithful's excited murmurs and explosive roars as the sun settled lower in the western sky. I almost heard the low drone of the play-by-play announcer informing fans of lineup changes that night, and the cries of vendors hustling Cracker Jacks, lemonade, and cotton candy. Baseball season was in deep hibernation, and it would not return for another three months.

Now I turned towards the swirling piles of white snow and thick gray ice draped over the outfield walls and seats. Even the vast CITGO sign looming over the Green Monster, an integral part of the park's skyline, stood dark and silent, abused by snow and ice. The sign reminded me of the Sherwin-Williams paint logo of a paint can tipped over, its contents covering the earth. I could barely make out the CITGO letters underneath its wintertime covering. The famous Green Monster in left field, a thirty-seven-foot vertically high metal wall, had wind-blown snow and ice clinging to its entire surface. It looked more like a miniature glacier or iceberg than Major League Baseball's most famous left field wall. Fenway's interior was a white landscape with a silent icy wind blowing snow in weird swirls.

Although I can't remember which team the Red Sox faced or who won the game the night I first saw Fenway Park in June 1967 – possibly the Baltimore Orioles – I instantly became a lifelong Boston Red Sox fan that evening. At the start of the season, the Red Sox were 100-1 long shots to win the pennant. They came within a single game of winning the World Series against the heavily favored St. Louis Cardinals, and we were still incredibly proud of them. One night that summer, my family was rudely awakened by a midnight telephone call. Dad angrily yanked the phone off the receiver to be informed they urgently needed him in Boston. Three of his friends from Providence had gone to Fenway and drank too many beers at the game. Arrested at the Park for drunkenness, they were calling for my father to bail them out of jail. Dad dragged himself out of bed and traveled north to rescue his friends. He wasn't at all happy with his colleagues; neither was my mother.

I told Bill about my three previous visits to Fenway for Opening Day and how excited I was to see the Red Sox play the Detroit Tigers in the first game in April. I purchased seats behind the first base dugout after discussing our options. These seats offered an excellent view of the entire field and were reasonably priced. My choice of seats pleased my buddies. Detroit pummeled the Red Sox on Opening Day, 1984. The Tigers went on to not only win thirty-four of their first forty games but also win the World Series that year. It was another uneventful baseball season for the Fenway faithful, but we still had a great time.

One night in May, I held a class in the center field bleachers of Fenway Park. Two days later, the commanding officer of the Navy ROTC unit called me into his office and reprimanded me for my blatant lack of decorum. He made it clear that Fenway Park was not an appropriate place for teaching ROTC classes and warned me never to pull a stunt like that again. Despite the verbal reprimand, I felt it was worth it if it meant that some of the midshipmen could begin appreciating the beauty, spirit, and integrity of Fenway Park, just as I had for the past two decades.

Surface Warfare Department Head School

I married Amy on December 30, 1984, at a small, quaint Methodist church in North Charleston. The pastor there referred to me as a "child of God," even though I still doubted God's existence. I had been raised Unitarian. Our son Ben, not yet three years old, was part of our wedding party. The wedding was a modest affair, with Amy handling all the arrangements.

Despite my parents' divorce, they drove down with my brother Seth and sisters Libby and Holly to witness the ceremony. Afterward, we celebrated with a wonderful reception at the Charleston Weapons Officers' Club. James Lee and several old friends from the *Hewes* were able to join us for the occasion. During the reception, I caught up on the latest gossip from the ship. James mentioned that he was preparing for a second sea tour, hoping to earn his SWO qualification within the following year.

Amy and Ben moved to Boston a few weeks later, and our journey together began in earnest. The biggest mistake in my Navy career was not resigning when my shore tour at Boston University Navy ROTC was over. Because the Navy financed my master's degree from BU, I had to commit to two additional years of active duty. I would be returning to sea at least one more time, this time as a Department Head in the operations department of a Navy frigate.

In late May 1986, Amy, Ben, and I left Boston for Newport, Rhode Island. The transfer of our household goods from Boston to Newport went smoothly. However, on the morning after our belongings were delivered to our new home on the Navy base, Amy and I had one of our worst arguments ever; I can no longer remember the exact subject of the dispute. We both understood that our issues had been building for some time, and the argument in Newport was simply the culmination of our problems. One significant concern that was weighing on me was my unhappiness about reporting to the department head at school.

Amy had not adjusted to the four seasons in New England since moving to the state two years earlier. She was accustomed to the hot, muggy summers in the lowlands of South Carolina, like the summers in the Philippines. However, the weather was not the only problem Amy was confronting.

She was no longer employed and stayed at home to care for a challenging toddler with special needs, who had weighed less than four pounds at birth. With no interaction with adults at work and no income, her situation became increasingly stressful. Another significant source of stress for her was me. After we got married, I fell back into my old habits. I continued to socialize with my male friends from work and those back in Rhode Island. My alcohol consumption increased, and as a result, I sometimes neglected my responsibilities as a new husband and father. I had returned to familiar territory and resumed my previous activities from the past.

Although I took my family to various historic sites in New England on weekends – such as Cape Cod, the White House, and local attractions in Boston like Bunker Hill, the USS *Constitution*, and Lexington and Concord – it became clear that Amy and I did not share many common interests, including an appreciation for U.S. history.

I was highly ambivalent about the upcoming six-month department head school course. I had dreamt of teaching U.S. history survey courses at the community college or secondary school level, having come tantalizingly close to being hired to teach history at a New England college preparatory school after college. I now had a family to look after. Like many officers and enlisted personnel considering leaving the security of the military, I was uncertain enough about my civilian employment prospects to postpone leaving the Navy. With a deep sense of foreboding, I reported to department head school because there was no way I could become a teacher, keep my family intact, and put food on the table all at once. And yet, when I considered what being a department head meant to me, it bothered me.

Back at the beginning of OCS, my buddy D.J. Conklin was drunk when he muttered that most navy captains were either drunks, divorced, or both. He didn't mean it literally, but he had a point. Those few naval officers who attain the pinnacle of their career – command at sea – sacrifice many things to get there. I never knew a captain who didn't love the job more than almost anything else in his life. The captains I knew possessed a palpable enthusiasm; you did not doubt their dedication, drive, and commitment to command at sea.

I didn't feel the passion required for command. I realized that my chances of being selected for such a role were slim to none without that enthusiasm. I remembered my time as a division officer, observing the long hours department heads on the ship worked to avoid the wrath of their immediate boss, the executive officer (XO). Most department heads I knew went out of their way to please their XOs, fully aware that a single negative performance review could jeopardize their careers.

Department heads were expected to be experts in navigating a ship and fighting under the captain's direction. They also needed to pass their professional knowledge on to the junior officers standing watch. However, I wasn't as confident as I should have been about bringing a ship into port or alongside an oiler in rough seas at thirteen knots during the night for refueling. In short, I lacked enthusiasm for navigating warships and the drive to improve in that area. Ultimately, I didn't possess the burning desire necessary to command a ship at sea.

There were additional issues aboard *Hewes*. The chief engineer, Lt. Sliney, was one of the best naval officers I have ever met, even though some of his actions were not by the book. Sliney quickly established a close rapport with Captain Hardt, often bypassing the executive officer, Lt. Cdr. Fineman, to strengthen his relationship with the captain. On several occasions, Lt. Sliney went directly to the captain regarding significant matters, leaving the executive officer uninformed. By undermining Lt. Cdr. Fineman's authority, Sliney naturally fueled Fineman's hostility towards him. The captain often favored Sliney's insights because he was knowledgeable about engineering operations. As a result, Fineman struggled to assert his authority over Sliney. I felt no sympathy for Fineman, however, as he had initiated his own problems with Sliney from the start. The first thing Fineman did upon reporting aboard the *Hewes* was to walk down to Main Control to observe the engineers as they wrapped up the plant operations, without notifying Sliney in advance. He then began instructing the crew members on watch about what to do, despite them having no idea who he was or why he had assumed command over them.

When Sliney learned about what had happened, he told Fineman to stay out of his spaces unless Fineman specifically obtained Sliney's permission to go down there first. Later, when Lt. Sliney routinely went on liberty with the captain when the ship was overseas, his rupture with the XO was complete. It was widely known that Sliney was the captain's favorite department head at fitness report time. It was one reason, I later thought, that my fitness reports were as great as they were. If Sliney was a superb leader, it should follow that his division officers were brilliant as well. Only the best division officers, the majority of whom were cultivated by Lt. Sliney, received exceptional evaluations from the captain.

I came full circle in reporting back to the Newport Navy base in May 1986. Even though it was one month short of six years since I graduated from OCS, it seemed like much more time had passed. Running into some familiar faces at department head school was fun, but more than a few of my OCS and SWOS Basic friends had not remained on active duty beyond their initial four-year stint. Some had already resigned from the Navy and were now civilians. Others were now completing their second straight tour at sea without any prospect of attending department head school, having submitted their resignations to return to civilian life. Around one-third of the junior officers I graduated with from OCS remained on active duty beyond the minimally required four years.

From the beginning, when I accepted orders to department head school, I understood that the stakes were much higher now. The competition was more intense, and the tolerance for mistakes and disruptive behavior in class was significantly stricter than before. The expectations from the senior officers aboard the ship would be much more demanding. However, not everyone in my class was eager to excel as department heads. There were two groups of officers among the forty-three lieutenants. Perhaps ten or fifteen of them were there to study hard and compete for the long-shot goal of attaining command at sea. At best, maybe five of those lieutenants would become commanding officers. Most of us were there simply to fulfill the requirements, advance our careers, and move on to the next phase of a twenty-year Navy journey, hopefully culminating in retirement with the rank of Commander. Did I desire command at sea? Unquestionably, I did not.

The Surface Warfare Department Head school curriculum focused on the electronic and weapon capabilities of American and Soviet warships, submarines, and aircraft. At the end of six months, a comprehensive make-or-break tactical officer exam determined the student's fitness to be designated a department head, ready to help the captain fight his ship at sea.

With Amy back in the Philippines for at least six months following our contentious fight, we concluded that a temporary separation would be the best option for everyone involved. During this time, I continued to party with my old friends on the weekends. I made sure to call Amy regularly and wrote one or two letters each week to her and Ben. She had left Newport the day after our arrival in Rhode Island, and our marriage was at a standstill. This period of separation would serve as an opportunity for reassessment, allowing us to determine how or if our relationship could be salvaged. The first two years of our marriage had been very difficult, especially for Amy. She had done her best, while I did not reciprocate her efforts. I was aware of my inadequacies as a husband. Unfortunately, my academic work over the next six months was not going to be impressive, as Navy schools and I never seemed to see eye to eye about anything.

Old feelings of academic inadequacy returned to haunt me at the department head school, similar to the feelings I had at the prestigious prep school where I spent my final two years of secondary education. I despised the elite atmosphere and the holier-than-thou students who made life unbearable. The school had branded itself as one where open learning and mutual support were fostered among its students, but that was a complete lie. It was a factory for Ivy League aspirants, preparing them for top careers as lawyers and leaders in the financial industry. My feelings in class at Northfield-Mount Hermon were different from what I experienced at the department head school. Now, having matured somewhat, I no longer felt inclined to blame the students in Newport as I had years earlier at prep school.

My test scores typically ranked near or at the bottom of the students in my department head class. Like all Navy schools, test results were posted on a bulletin board outside the primary classroom, so my public humiliation was great. Over the course of six months, I was required to appear before two academic review boards in Newport.

In October 1986, the Boston Red Sox's crushing loss in the seventh game of the World Series, where the Boston Red Sox fell to the New York Mets, deepened my depression. I felt lonely for Ben and Amy, yet I remained unconvinced that a reunion would be in anyone's best interest, including Amy's. School was barely tolerable, and I had little enthusiasm for returning to sea as a department head.

In my view, once an officer reported to department head school, their path was set; they were continuing their career with the hopes of becoming a commanding officer. I loved the sea and enjoyed traveling to exotic ports overseas, but I didn't believe I had the intelligence or desire required to qualify as the commanding officer of a warship. Furthermore, I was uncertain about my willingness to dedicate the remainder of my youth to the Navy in order to command a warship at sea. I felt that the payoff simply didn't justify the sacrifice.

The school year slowly came to an inconclusive end. Amy and I continued our uneasy exchange of phone calls and letters. We didn't know where we stood with each other or what to do about a marriage that had endured more than its fair share of unhappy, empty moments and occasional disagreements. I couldn't bear the thought of Ben growing up without a father. I loved him very much, but Amy's and my parenting styles were completely opposite. Filipino parenting usually involves overindulging sons, while I felt that a more structured and independent approach was necessary. We constantly fought over whether it was better to baby him or to be stricter.

Six weeks before graduation, Amy was viciously attacked by an unknown assailant after it became known in the village she was visiting that she was the wife of a U.S. Naval officer. It was thought the perpetrator was an anti-government communist guerrilla, but his identity was never confirmed. Amy came close to losing her life when she was held at gunpoint in the jungle. In the end, she convinced the kidnapper to release her. To this day, she has nightmares of the ordeal.

Amy immediately insisted that she and Ben return to Newport, days before I graduated from department head school. She was determined to rededicate herself to making our marriage work. I had never doubted her love and support for me, but profound differences in our lives remained. I liked the outdoors, baseball, studying U.S. history, travel, and literature. Amy was raised and would remain an urban person with little interest in mountains, oceans, or sports. A major pitfall in our marriage had been my refusal to discipline myself in money matters. I continued living paycheck to paycheck while Amy was conditioned from her youth to save every penny she could. She had arrived in the U.S. dead broke twenty years earlier but had scrimped and saved enough money to buy a house in Charleston. I had never known absolute poverty. Amy was born into war-torn Manila during the Japanese occupation during World War II.

The ship assignments for our class were finally announced during the same week that Amy and Ben arrived in Newport. Students who had performed well received the most desirable assignments, allowing them to choose the specific type of ship and department in which they wanted to serve. The consensus was that the newer *Oliver Hazard Perry*-class fast frigates (FFG-40 and higher) were the best options for first-tour department heads. These ships were equipped with a single-arm missile launcher on the bow and a helicopter detachment for hunting submarines.

They were powered by two LM-2500 gas turbines and featured advanced electronic warfare systems.

On the morning the assignments were made public, I learned the Navy had assigned me to an old LKA, the USS *Mobile*. She was an amphibious cargo ship carrying landing craft, other gear, and fuel to war zones, loading the craft with U.S. Marines and directing them to combat landing zones. I sat dumbfounded in the auditorium, tears rolling down my face, as I contemplated my new career outside the "greyhound" (destroyer) Navy.

In a moment of passion, I called the Navy personnel branch at the Pentagon and firmly stated that I would not accept an assignment to the *Mobile*. When senior school officials learned about my phone call, I was reprimanded for having the audacity to challenge my upcoming tour assignment. They made it clear that if I did not understand that the needs of the Navy took precedence, I was in the wrong line of work.

Three days later, I was called into the school's administrative office, where a grim-faced commander said, "Your orders have been changed, Lt. Haynes. You will report to USS *Lancaster* at Mayport Naval Station, Jacksonville."

The commander criticized me for my lack of decorum and military bearing, as well as for not submitting to the needs of the Navy. I understood the drill; I knew I had crossed a line. However, I was excited that things turned out the way they did. A frigate was a much better assignment than being the department head on some rust-bucket cargo carrier out of Long Beach, California. At least, that's what I thought.

My advisor at department head school, a cranky lieutenant commander bound for executive officer training in a few months, told me just before I left Newport that the job I had been slated for on the LKA was a promising opportunity I had missed. The operations boss on the LKA was fired for incompetence. I would have inherited a situation where things could only get better. But my tantrum had taken me down a different path.

I wasn't very motivated to report to any ship. While I quickly accepted my orders to the USS *Lancaster*, my interest in the Navy waned after my tour at the ROTC unit at Boston University ended. Overall, it had been a fantastic six-year journey, but being a department head at sea was not something I desired. From that point on, I understood the role of politics in career advancement, but I wanted nothing to do with it.

However, it was hard to ignore the benefit of "staying Navy." There were regular pay increases, a decent retirement package, and sound, reliable health care. I had no other employment in mind to replace these benefits. Amy and Ben both had chronic health issues requiring regular attention. Like clockwork, Uncle Sam issued me a decent paycheck every two weeks. With great reluctance, I prepared to go back to sea.

Captain Simmons

The time had come to report aboard USS *Lancaster* in Mayport, Florida. Amy had returned from the Philippines with Ben, and – after patching things up again – we purchased our first house in a new bedroom community located twenty minutes from the base. I flew down to Jacksonville to seal the house purchase. We took five days to drive from Newport to Mayport, including a memorable stop for Ben at the Empire State Building on a clear winter day, where we stood on the observation deck and saw all five boroughs of New York and a good part of New Jersey.

Lancaster had recently returned home from deployment in extremely rough shape, especially in her engineering plant. She had steamed thousands of miles, and most of her experienced crew were slated to rotate off the ship to new duty assignments, typical for ships just completing an extended period at sea. A new captain, Commander Andrew Simmons, reported aboard the ship six weeks before my arrival. Simmons seemed to be a mild-mannered leader; he was a Navy ROTC graduate whose background included serving as an ops boss on a Knox-class frigate. Ray Epstein was his XO, a nervous, acidic lieutenant commander with a severe Napoleon complex.

Four days after arriving aboard, I knocked twice on the captain's stateroom bulkhead, which was closed. "Lt. Haynes, sir. Request permission to enter."

There was a muffled response. "Permission granted. Enter."

I opened the door, and the captain, thumbing through a *Newsweek* magazine, motioned for me to take a seat. I immediately sat down.

"XO said you wanted to see me, sir?"

"Yes. I haven't had a moment to speak with you. I apologize for the delay in welcoming you aboard. Settled in yet?"

"Barely, sir. Plenty is needing to be done, Captain."

"I agree. Let's chat a minute. What are your priorities?"

"To begin with, Captain, Radio Central is reporting communication problems with two high-frequency radio circuits. I don't know if it's poor maintenance or a major casualty, but we need to find the cause of it. I don't know when the guys in CIC last conducted their routine maintenance, but a ton of stuff was neglected while they were overseas. I see other issues, too."

"Such as?"

"Sir, I got some weak chiefs. Chiefs raised me during my junior officer tour. The one bright spot is Senior Chief Lawrence, but he's been around for three years and is preparing for shore duty in less than six months. A great deal of work is needed to bring the rest up to the required level."

"What are your plans?" Captain Simmons' eyes bored in on me.

"Hold the chiefs accountable, Captain. Give them orders through their division officers; insist the junior officers follow up on what needs to be done. As for the damage control training, I've already asked Rob to set aside some time for my team to receive training. One other thing."

"Go ahead."

"The IFF transponder is completely conked out. I know we got her on the repair list during the yard period, but that's a major project and I heard from the chiefs that the contractor will announce delays in getting it back onboard."

"So, what to do?"

"I intend to harass the shit out of the yardbirds, Captain. I've got to keep harping on bringing that thing back within the time frame on the repair contract."

"Lt. Haynes, there's a few things you should consider."

"Aye, sir."

"I know you know I went through command school at SWOS while you were there. I heard you turning down a Gator unit and wanting to stay with destroyers. I suppose that is a positive indicator in some ways. I managed to look at your grades over the past four months and—"

"Captain, I can explain what—"

"Please don't interrupt me, Lieutenant. As I was saying, I am concerned about your academic performance in Newport. You graduated somewhere around the bottom third of your class. Grades don't tell everything. I've known Department Heads who don't do well in the classroom but excel in the fleet. Did anyone tell you my two department head tours were as ops bosses on a Knox-class frigate and an LPD?" An LPD was a large amphibious ship carrying U.S. Marines and their equipment.

"No, sir."

"So, don't think I don't know your business here. When you come to me with schedules, messages, and tactical operations orders, I expect you to have them in order. Do your homework."

"Aye, aye, sir."

"I'm southern, born here in Florida. I earned my commission through Navy ROTC. You've already had a few minor scrapes with the XO, which I will do something about if that continues. Are we on the same page about that, Lieutenant?"

"Sir, if I—"

"No, you may not. I've asked you not to interrupt me. Whatever problems you have with your chiefs, you fix them pronto. The repair period only lasts two months and we'll be in workups for six weeks of REFTRA in May. I won't be leaning on the enlisted khaki – I will have you squarely in my sights. Ever been to GITMO, lieutenant?"

"Twice, sir."

"This will be my sixth – and hopefully last – trip. Despite what you believe falls on the snipes, the onus of this ship's performance lies with the operations department. Remember that. A lot rides on how you get this ship through REFTRA. One last thing: don't come to me without first going to the XO. I believe strictly in the chain of command. I expect the XO to be told when I hear about something. Have I made myself clear?"

"Completely, Captain." I didn't understand at all. Both trips to GITMO confirmed that the core training curriculum, including battle problems and damage control drills, fell on the engineers. It was always that way down there, no exceptions. What the hell was this guy talking about? It was bullshit. A ship's measure of success at GITMO depended on all departments working together, starting with the snipes. Everything started with the snipes. It was fundamental to surviving GITMO REFTRA. The captain had it wrong.

"Good," he said. "The ship is tired right now, mechanically and morale-wise. Take a few turns and do not let these men slack off because we're back home. They can have their leave, but when they're on board, I want them to participate in every operation and damage control exercise the squadron throws at us. Don't miss those exercises, including making after-action reports to the XO and me. And make sure you document the drills for our records. That is all for today. Dismissed." Captain Simmons picked up his magazine and thumbed through it as I stood up and placed the cover back on my head.

"Thank you, Captain." I left his stateroom, carefully closing the hatch behind me.

DFC

From the beginning, I felt disconnected from my duties on *Lancaster*. My marriage was deteriorating, and I struggled to relate to the executive officer, who consistently treated me with anger and disrespect. I noticed that political influences heavily affected decision-making, and I sensed that the commanding officer disapproved of my Filipino wife. The executive officer took over the chief engineer's responsibilities and provided guidance that allowed any division officer to manage effectively. After eight months on board, I became embittered and disillusioned. I verbally challenged the XO, and my resentment deepened with each passing order. In December 1987, I was ordered to report to the captain's cabin. The ship was docked at Mayport, the naval station on the St. Johns River near Jacksonville, Florida.

"Come in and sit down, Lieutenant," the captain said grim-faced. The last time I'd seen a face like that was at my second academic review board at department head school.

"Aye, aye, sir." I entered his stateroom and sat down in front of him.

The captain handed me a folder containing a pile of papers. "You need to read these documents first. I'll show you where to sign."

I opened the packet and saw that the words Detached For Cause leapt off the first page. I looked at the captain and said, "You're booting me off *Lancaster*? I'm not signing anything until I know exactly what this paperwork is about."

"Lieutenant Haynes, I have exercised great patience with you. You leave me no choice. You will sign these papers, and then I will give you thirty minutes to collect your belongings and disembark from this ship."

"That's kind of you."

"Excuse me?" The captain's eyes were now narrow slits. "What was that, Lieutenant?"

My expression was flat. "I said, 'That's kind of you.'"

"I didn't hear you say, 'sir,' Lieutenant."

"Yes, sir."

I immediately returned to reading the documents, figuring my indifference would piss him off even more. The documents were full of phrases such as "unable to fully explain most material casualties," "complete lack of equipment knowledge," and "submission of late and/or incomplete reports". Other phrases read, "incapable of keeping himself or the rest of the command informed of operational evolutions," and "a formal Letter of Instruction from the executive officer and later myself pointed out his total lack of attention to detail with maintenance matters in his three divisions."

"Captain, each of these items was already fixed before you delivered the LOI to me a few weeks back," I said. "You state I was presented the letter in early November, which is false. You gave it to me in mid-December. The chronology presented here is inaccurate."

"How dare you question my authority or integrity, Lieutenant?" The captain sputtered.

"Nobody's questioning your authority, Captain. I'm questioning the accuracy of your version of events."

"You'll have your chance to rebut these citations."

"I'll be rebutting them, Captain. Rest assured of that. In writing. Line for line."

The captain sat back. His face had turned an odd pink. "Lieutenant, if I have to call ship security to remove you from my stateroom, I will. Here's your fitness report. Read it and sign it."

"I don't have to read it," I countered. "I know what it says. The XO has been busy over the past ten months, Captain."

"What does that mean?"

"It means he's spent time documenting all my faults and missteps. I wonder if he has similar lists for Bill and the others."

"This has to do with you and only you. You can dispense with involving anyone else into this discussion."

"Captain, my DFC has to do with two department heads who get to remain aboard and finish their tours while my career comes crashing down."

The captain smiled in what I thought was a sinister way. "That's exactly what it means."

"What goes around comes around, sir."

"What did you just say?"

"I said your time is coming."

"Are you threatening me, Lieutenant?"

"Nobody is threatening you, sir. The problems on this ship will only get worse after I'm gone. You think you're fixing your problem by doing this. But you're not." I leaned towards him and pushed my unsigned fitness report back at him, saying, "There's nobody here but you and me. You can forget about me signing the fitness report. It's bullshit. Submit it without my chop, sir."

"You're in deep trouble, Mister."

"You're right, Captain. I *am* in trouble. My career is over. I need to start looking for work in the civilian world. I'll leave now, sir, after I sign these other papers. But I'm not signing my fitness report." I stood up and leaned over to sign four separate documents. I crushed the copies in my left hand as I turned to leave. Then I turned around and said, "You haven't fixed anything by firing me today. You'll see." I opened the hatch to leave.

"Nobody permitted you to leave, Mister. Get back in here. Now!"

"You told me to get off your ship. I'm obeying your orders. I wish you lots of luck. You're gonna need it." I stood up, turned my back on the captain, and closed the hatch after walking through it.

The XO stood before me. "What have you done to my captain, Lieutenant?," he said through gritted teeth.

"Relax, XO. I'm getting ready to leave per the captain's orders. Just what you wanted, so congratulations are in order." I lightly brushed by him and turned around to say, "By the way, I'll say the same thing to you that I said to him a minute ago. Do you two think firing me will fix things in *Lancaster*? You're only fooling yourselves."

"You won't be missed," the XO snorted.

"The feeling's mutual, XO," I said, "but I'll be long gone by the time you find this was a mistake. And you'll still be right here." I looked him in the eye. "I hope you enjoy your victory, sir. It's only temporary. You'll see. Or maybe you won't."

The XO started stammering threats, but I walked off.

Twenty minutes later, I was fully packed. The new weapons officer, Bill Hall, escorted me off *Lancaster*. He shook my hand on the quarterdeck, saying, "I'm truly sorry, Rod, I truly am."

"I'm not worried, shipmate. It was inevitable that this would happen sooner or later. Thank you for your support. I'll miss you, buddy. Just get off this ship before something major occurs." I snapped a salute to the Officer of the Deck, saluted the ensign flapping on the jack staff, and walked off the ship.

It was hard telling Amy that my Navy career was over. I half expected her to pack and leave with Ben, but she stuck with me through the next few years, which were difficult times for all of us. Her loyalty knew no bounds. I never forgot her fierce, unwavering support during my darkest days.

Home at Last

"Let's cut to the chase, Lieutenant," the Commodore said, pointing to the manila envelope on his desk. "I've reviewed your captain's DFC letter and your response to it. Are you, or are you not, a booze hound?"

"Sir, please pardon me, but my response to the captain's charges is explained in great detail," I replied quietly. "It's in my rebuttal. Twenty-eight pages worth."

"I said I read everything in the packet. You were very thorough. Answer my question."

"Commodore Hill, I think most people in the Navy indulge in alcohol at least a little," I said. "Not all, but most. I like a beer now and then."

"Lieutenant, you know that's not what I'm asking. The captain delineates several serious incidents involving excessive alcohol use in less than one year aboard ship," the commodore said, his fingers drumming his desktop. "How do you explain it? Are these charges true?"

I stared straight into the commodore's eyes. "No, sir, Commodore Hill, I am not a drunk. Most certainly not."

"Then what's the meaning of these accusations?"

"Uh, it's complicated, sir." I couldn't hold the commodore's gaze, so I looked down at my shoes.

He sighed. "I think it is much less complicated than you say. You made things more difficult for yourself than they needed to be if this letter is accurate."

I glanced out a window for a moment before looking at him. "To be honest, sir, I can be a jackass sometimes. It began last spring. The XO was right on top of me from the day I reported aboard. I pushed back. I was stupid, Commodore."

"You decided to 'push back'?" he replied, sitting up straighter, his eyebrows raised. "Just who do you think you are? You're now aboard; he's the XO. In my Navy, the exec says, 'jump,' and his department heads are expected to ask, 'How high, XO?' Simple as that." An extended silence followed. The commodore sighed, looked away, and then he leaned in at me. "Lieutenant, I have a squadron of warships to run. I don't have all day. This is your only shot to make your case, and frankly, you're testing my patience right now. Impress me."

"I understand, sir. The captain's complaints are detailed in the DFC letter—"

The commodore cut me off. "I said I've read it. If you hope to continue your career in the surface Navy, you better help me understand why I should take your side over your captain's. Right here. Right now." He tapped his wristwatch. "You've got exactly five minutes. Go."

I hesitated again. Did I want another at-sea assignment? Shouldn't I bow to the prevailing winds, accept an honorable discharge, and return to civilian life? I thought about my wife and son, fighting the urge to cry from the shame I'd brought upon them. What was Mom thinking right now? Good God, what a freaking mess.

As Commodore Hill sat waiting impatiently, an old rock song lyric came to mind: "What a long, strange trip it's been." But there was no room for the Grateful Dead rock band in this discussion.

"Commodore Hill, this is the worst thing that has ever happened in my professional life. It isn't very pleasant for me and my family. I've been in shock over this whole thing."

"DFCs are unpleasant, and the consequences are usually very severe," he replied. "It's devastating for the recipient. You aren't the first. It's hard. You have my sympathy."

"Sir, I think the situation on *Lancaster* was caused by a personality conflict between me and the XO, and then the captain understandably sided with the XO. I am responsible for not being flexible and doing my job."

"Are you incompetent?"

"Not in the way those papers say I am. Commodore, the CO's version of the events is beyond slanderous. I won't comment on the work of my colleagues on *Lancaster*, but my understanding is that when it comes to department heads' performance, a lot of how well someone does is judged compared to the other department heads. What I'm saying is that I know we all have different responsibilities, but we are competing with each other in terms of our rankings at fitness report time."

"I agree with you on that. Tell me something I don't know."

"Well, sir, of the four department heads I've been compared to, I should easily rank second, not fourth. It makes sense that the command completely trashed me when they fired me. Otherwise, there is no justification for their actions."

"What are you saying?"

"Commodore, ask Lieutenant Commander Bell about my performance." Bell was the operations department head at the Destroyer Squadron. He worked directly for the commodore. Lt. Cdr. Bell reviewed much of my work because he was responsible for interacting with all the ops bosses in the squadron. "The thing is, Commodore, the real problem on *Lancaster* is her engineering plant," I continued. "It's tired, it's worn out. Operations did all right in GITMO, so did the weapons department. We did not come out of there with exceptional grades, but they were above average. The one department that is not functioning well at all is engineering. I don't mean to say anything negative against my buddies on the ship. I'm just telling you that operationally speaking, the ship is not prepared for prolonged steaming at sea. The plant isn't close to ready."

"Hmm." The commodore's gaze was steady. He seemed to be thinking.

"Would you approve my request to be reassigned to another department head tour at sea, Commodore?" I asked.

"Lieutenant Haynes, I will approve your request, but I must emphasize that I cannot and will not go against one of my commanding officers."

"I don't follow, sir."

"As sorry as I am about your situation, I would not endorse your version of events and not back Captain Simmons. This is the Navy. Commodores don't do such things."

"That would mean I am done, sir."

"It does mean that. I am sorry. You have potential, but not here. Your Navy career is over, Lieutenant. I would start looking at other options. This is hard to accept, especially for those who deserve better. I sincerely wish you the best of luck. I have nothing more for you. You are dismissed, Lieutenant."

"Sir, a final comment. *Lancaster* is about to deploy. I wish the ship the best, but it won't make it."

"I'm sorry. Not make what?"

"Finish the deployment. Sir, the engineering plant is a wreck. I say that with concern, not in anger. I'm being honest, sir."

"That's a terrible thing to say. I certainly hope you are mistaken."

"I hope so, too, but I don't think I am. I am not directing this comment at the captain. I'm simply telling you my sincere beliefs. Thank you for your time, sir." I stood at attention and, turning around, quickly left the office.

Mayport Family Service Center

The Navy's mantra of "we take care of our own" supposedly means that the Navy stands by its families in hard times. Common problems – particularly among junior-ranked sailors with mouths to feed at home – include unpaid bills, children with behavioral issues because a parent is away for long periods, or a car that has broken down while the spouse is on the opposite side of the globe. The Navy Family Service Centers and other civilian social service organizations support Navy families in various ways.

Following my Detachment for Cause from USS *Lancaster*, I received orders to the Mayport Navy Family Service Center. I wasn't prepared to like my job there, but I learned a lot over the next two and a half years and made many friends. I was involved in several real-time Navy incidents involving families who lost men in the service of their country, and the national media paid attention to these incidents.

In 1987, after an accidental missile attack by an Iraqi jet (Iraq was our ally at the time) killed thirty-seven sailors aboard the USS *Stark* in the Persian Gulf, I served as an escort for one of the families who lost a twenty-year-old son in the attack. The families of the victims gathered at a memorial service at Mayport Naval Station to hear the keynote speaker, President Reagan, eulogize the thirty-seven crewmen who had perished. Reagan was at his poignant, Hollywood-trained best on that brilliant sunny day in northern Florida.

There was, quite understandably, significant grief, rage, and disbelief shared by those families who had lost their fathers, sons, and brothers in the tragedy. The Mayport Navy community was there in strength as a sign of respect and support. The victim's families came from all over the United States, from many different walks of life – a strong bond developed among these people after a few days together.

The deep sorrow on the day of the memorial hung over everything. I looked closely at President Reagan and his wife, Nancy, as they walked by, not ten feet from where I sat. I was never a fan of Reagan, even though he was responsible for helping me secure a job with the Navy for almost a decade. The Reagans' displays of loss and sympathy seemed deeply genuine. They took the time to speak briefly with each of the families. I corresponded with one father of a dead sailor for several years following the service, long after my official naval duties had ended. Understandably, the father had a hard time letting go of his son. I did my best to help him cope.

A year later, a major accident involving an aircraft carrier occurred in Haifa, Israel, in the middle of the night. A ferryboat carrying many sailors capsized on its way to town for a night of liberty. Over thirty sailors were killed. The scene back at Mayport Naval Station was heart-wrenching when families of the crew waited for the names of the victims to be identified in the base gymnasium. The situation was made worse because, while everyone insisted on staying together as one big Navy family in the gym, only those family members who were to receive bad news were called into private rooms adjacent to the gym. Each time a name was called out, it could only mean one thing. There was loud shrieking, fainting, and cries of pain and protest. The crowd would wail louder and louder as a chaplain, a naval officer escort, and a mental health counselor walked the stricken family members toward the private area. I had nightmares about that day for a long time. I reflected on how the situation could have been managed differently, but I couldn't find a solution.

Old Friend

The night before I was discharged from the United States Navy, I slept only two hours. In a vivid dream sequence, I finally heard from my old friend from Yankee Company at OCS. The Family Service Center receptionist buzzed my desk phone: "Lt. Haynes, please pick up line one."

I punched the phone's blinking light. "This is Lt. Haynes. How may I help you?"

"*You're* the one needing help, son," a loud voice boomed in my ear, followed by a chuckle.

"Excuse me?"

"No excuses, son. You know who this is?" The voice was vaguely familiar. I couldn't place it.

"No, I'm sorry, I don't. What can I do for you?"

"Damn, son, you forgot your best buddy from Newport. *Chicken City?*"

"*D.J.!*" I yelled, jumping to my feet. All eyes in the space were on me. "I don't believe it! Where you at?" I sat down and covered my mouth as I continued speaking.

"Just a ten-minute walk away. Here in sunny Florida, but it's too God-damn sticky in port. Need to go back to sea for fresh air."

I'd watched a frigate pull into the Mayport basin two hours earlier from where I sat eating lunch at the O-Club. "That's right. You're on *Samuel Elliott Morrison.* Someone said you're a combat systems officer. Right?"

"Yup, but not for long."

"What does that mean?"

"How 'bout dinner tonight? Can we meet at the O-Club?"

"1800 hours, okay?"

"Yeah, fine. I gotta get back. Good talkin' to ya. See you later, Bud."

"See you tonight."

I arrived at the Mayport Officers' Club five minutes before our scheduled rendezvous time. D.J. Conklin stood in the lobby, grinning like he did years earlier. I rushed up to him and offered my hand.

"Nope, that won't do," he said. "Gotta hug you, but don't go telling your wife." He cracked a broad smile as he embraced me. "Don't gotta worry about mine. That witch is long gone."

"Where are you guys coming from?" I asked.

"Norfolk. Headed to GITMO in three days."

"Been there three times." I smiled. "None of the trips were pleasant."

"Five trips for me. They all sucked. So, I ran into Ricky Moorhead in Newport a year ago. We pulled in for gas before heading north to Halifax. Ricky's XO on one of the wooden minesweepers up there. I'm doing really good. Ricky told me what happened to you."

"How in the hell did Ricky know about the DFC?"

"Come on now, word gets around, son. There aren't *that* many department heads in the Fleet."

"It's embarrassing," I said. "I was doing great on my first two tours. I got rewarded with the ROTC billet at Boston University. Then I go on to department head school and everything went to shit. I fucked up, D.J. I fucked up badly."

"What happened?"

"I'm still trying to get my head around it. I'm a wise guy, you know that. You can say and do stuff as an ensign that won't cut it when you're a lieutenant. The XO was a prick."

"You ever met one that wasn't?"

"No, I know that. I guess I asked to get my ass handed to me, but those other department heads on the ship weren't too sharp. The ship deployed, and they flunked their OPPE in Naples. They were welded to the pier for three weeks when they were supposed to be underway looking for Soviet subs. I told the Commodore it would happen."

"Commodore? I don't understand."

"The captain wrote a twenty-page DFC letter listing everything I had done wrong, making me look like a fool. I wrote a twenty-eight-page rebuttal, answering each point the CO made, item by item. I think the Commodore read my entire response."

"Think so?"

"He finished my sentences for me, I mean, he knew what I would say. Then when I was done, the guy says, 'I believe you.' So I go, 'so you'll let me go back to the fleet, sir?'"

"Uh, oh. I'm sure he said, 'Of course I will,' didn't he?"

"Yeah, right. I was told I would not return to sea as a department head."

"I have a few things to say about that, but first, let me tell you my post-OCS story. So, you know they put me on USS *Lawrence*, out of Norfolk, right?"

"Yeah. Didn't they make you Weapons Officer as a Department Head?"

"Yes. That first tour went well. We did a UNITAS, sailed around South America, came home through the Panama Canal. Great liberty ports. The captain liked me. Got my SWO pin. Punched my ticket for department head school. I was ready for the next step. For shore duty, I asked for recruiting duty back in Kentucky."

"You *what*?"

"Yup, I did. It was a waste going back. We were pretending the wife was homesick, that was what was screwing up our marriage. It wasn't. I knocked her up less than a month after I met her. So, I did the right thing. Typical sailor story."

"Tell me about it."

"What do you mean?"

I sat back and scanned the officers' club. It felt good to speak to D.J. "One Thanksgiving, after we got back to Charleston, my boiler tech chief invites me over for turkey. I thought nothing was up except I'd have beers and watch football. I walk into the house, and he brings me into the living room, where a pretty Filipino woman sat by herself. She looks cute. I thought she had it in for me right away. I didn't get it. I just met her and she's snarling at me."

"You lost me."

"You ever been with a woman who's shooting daggers out of her eyes and you don't know why?"

"Hell, yeah. That was Kathy, 'til I finally divorced her."

"Anyway, we had a nice meal, and I offered to drive her home. On the way, she explains she was coming off a nasty divorce and had no time for dating. I said that's fine, and I dropped her off. Then, a week later, she invited me to her office's Christmas party. Then I took her out to dinner. Next thing I know we're in the sack, with no birth control by either of us. Now, mind you, she doesn't drink, not a drop. But I did and still do."

"Are you telling me you guys made a baby?"

"She was pregnant six weeks after I met her."

"Damn, Boy. You almost got in trouble with that blonde beauty in Newport, but it all worked out. Didn't you learn from that?"

"I did what you did, D.J. What are you talkin' about? You set the example."

He looked thoughtful, then nodded. "Oh, yeah. Never mind."

"I didn't learn anything from that close call at OCS. This time it caught me. That girl in Newport, Ellen Kincaid, landed herself a commander about six months after OCS. We broke up as soon as she got commissioned."

"I'm sorry."

"Yeah, I am, too, but she helped me get through OCS. We leaned on each other. Great sex. I showed her around Providence and southern New England. It wasn't going to last. Very little depth."

"Don't put it like that."

"Not her, I don't mean *she* had no depth. I mean our relationship had no depth." I fell quiet for a moment, the chatter and clink of cutlery of the officers' club filling the void. How had ten years flown by so quickly? "You can't judge someone when you're going through OCS," I said. "Amy was three months pregnant when we left Charleston for the Med.... Did you hear our ship was less than ten miles from Beirut International Airport when the Marines got hit? Killed 241. Saw it happen."

"We had no business being in Beirut. That was a fuck story from the git-go. A lot of good people died." D.J.'s eyes were flashing.

"Yeah, tell me about it. We listened to the Secretary of State and other intel people on the radio talking from Washington to Beirut. They sounded like fools a lot of the time. I thought it was scary listening to those nimrods."

"It is what it is, I suppose," D.J. said. "How's marriage been for you?"

I sighed. "It was hard. The first bad fight we had was on our wedding night. We were both exhausted and anxious. It was terrible. Amy is a very honest and straightforward woman, and she's almost thirteen years older than me."

"What did you say? Thirteen years?"

"Yup. You could say there's an age gap."

"You think so? You're a preppie from New England, and she's Pinoy from Manila."

"You got it. We operate in two separate universes. About parenting. About what we like to do. Especially about politics. She likes Marcos. I say he's a murderous gangster. She's good at saving money, I like to spend it. I don't put it on her, D.J. She's put up with a lot of shit from me, especially when I got tossed off the ship. I know how difficult I am. Mercurial and all that. Our marriage isn't solid now. I drink too much."

"That's what I'd like to discuss with you."

"About what?"

"I got back from a three-month stay at the Alcohol Rehab Center [ARC] a month ago. I've been sober for five months now. Two cooks found me passed out at the officers' club in Norfolk. Didn't go down too well with the CO. I was a mess."

"Chicken City?"

"Oh, God, yeah. Chicken City in Newport. I had about five more of those incidents after I got my commission."

"I don't know what to say, D.J. I really don't." I shook my head slightly. "They say the Navy's ARC is an excellent rehab facility. I think they get a lot of practice."

"Look, booze got control of me. There were already all those signs even before I got to OCS. I got drunk and went brawlin', and I did it a few times in Newport, too."

"You know, you're lucky OCS didn't get wind of that."

"I know, I know." He sighed a long, drawn-out sigh. "It was reckless, and it didn't do anybody any good. I was a married man with a new baby, and I'm out on the town getting hammered and fighting the locals."

I signaled a waitress. "Let me buy you a beer."

"A Coke will do fine."

"You got it." I ordered two Cokes. "Well, this is different. We usually load up on alcohol when we go out."

"Yeah, you and me. And me and half the United States Navy. But I got big news. Rod, I'm done in a year. Not doing my second department head tour. I got orders to USS *Fox*, but I turned them down right after I got back from rehab. I'm done."

"Do you remember what you told me about commanding officers that night you got in trouble in Newport?"

"Did I say something like most of them are either divorced, heavy drinkers, or both?"

"That's exactly what you said. I'm sorry, D.J."

"Don't say you're sorry. It's my choice."

"It's just you only got five years 'til retirement."

D.J. nodded as if he'd had the conversation many times before. In that instant, he looked older to me. "Yes, and I want to do something else *now*," he said. "This business isn't for me. I like going to sea. I don't like wardroom politics and keeping all my men in line."

"How is that going to be different as a civilian worker?"

"For one, it won't be aboard a naval warship. I can come home at night and unwind my way. Without booze."

"I know this will piss you off, but I have to say this. Of all the people I knew at OCS, I looked up to you. You knew your business. You set a great example, even if on liberty, you went a little crazy. You helped all of us adjust to military life. You made us laugh. You made me laugh that first night I met you when I reported drunk."

D.J. grinned. "I remember that like it was yesterday."

"I think one of the reasons I'm where I'm at right now, disgraced, tossed off the ship, is I never *believed* I was the officer I became. What I mean is that I've got some of the leadership aspects down, okay, but I never fully understood the technical aspects of the job. I never could even understand how the equipment worked in Electrical Central. But I only have myself to blame."

D.J. massaged a muscle in his neck, then looked over his shoulder at the dozen patrons in the officers' club. "I don't doubt I will miss a bunch of stuff about being at sea." He fixed his gaze on me again. "Thing is, the ones waiting at home for you to come back will spend a lifetime doing that: waiting. What I mean is that if you are a coal miner, you have a dirty, dangerous job, but you get to go home at the end of the day to see the old lady and wrestle with the kids. You have some kinda life after work."

"That's what I found, too, I suppose," I said, then paused, unsure if I should continue. I figured I had to say it. "After I got canned from being an operations boss, I realized I had been in denial since I went to OCS in the first place." My heart was suddenly racing.

D.J. looked straight at me. "What's your realization, Bud?"

"I am a fucking accidental naval officer. I joined the Navy because I panicked. I had nowhere else to turn to," I told him, tears welling in my eyes.

D.J. instantly grew solemn. "Listen, Rod. And I mean, *listen* to me. You have been around for over ten years now. You've gone to sea; you've been in a war zone. You went through hurricanes and shipyards, and you went to GITMO."

"Too many damn times," I snorted.

"Hold on. Quiet. Do you think you're alone in winding up in the Navy as a last resort? Are you blind?"

"No, but—"

"Stop, I said. You said your piece. Let me talk," D.J. replied. He was dead serious, but I saw empathy in his eyes. "A long, long time ago, I told you that you got the goods: you know how to lead. I was speaking about leading in the Navy as a commissioned naval officer. How you got here, why you got here – it don't matter right now. You are a fucking *good* naval officer. You just don't like people telling you what to do, and at sea, that can get people killed quick. I'm your friend. I feel bad you got DFC'd. But a lot of the guys back on those ships, those department heads busting their ass for command at sea, they will sell their souls to screw each other over to get ahead, to get another stripe on their shoulders. You found out the hard way how some of 'em play."

I was sitting very still, my hands clasped around my drink. "Sure did, man."

"Rod, you can't spend the rest of your life believin' you were some kinda accidental officer, that it was a mistake to go to OCS. A long time from now, you will see that you are one of thousands of sailors who have turned to the military for all kinds of reasons."

"What about you?" I asked quietly.

"What about me? What are you asking?" D.J. responded.

"Why are you in uniform?"

"I was a high school graduate in Paducah, Kentucky, and I didn't want to work for the local auto parts store for the rest of my life. I wanted a steady paycheck, and I wanted to see the world. A recruiter asked, 'Have you ever been to Orlando, Florida?' and I was ready to go."

"You sorry you did it?"

"No. I don't regret it. I might have done many things differently if I got a second chance. I would save myself some liver damage if I got a 'do-over.' But, no, I'm not sorry, I went Navy. It's in my past. I did it. You can't undo stuff that already happened. Look ahead. Learn from this and live the rest of your life, man."

Suddenly, I woke up. I lay in bed for an hour, thinking about D.J.'s final words. Over the next four decades, I never mentioned the dream to anyone. It felt very real, even though I never saw D.J. Conklin again after leaving OCS in July 1980.

Navy Adventure Ends

I left the Navy just days before the invasion of Iraq, after being passed over twice for promotion to lieutenant commander in late January 1991. Having spent most of my adult life in the Navy, I found a private spot on base to mourn the end of my military career an hour after receiving my honorable discharge papers. Saying goodbye was difficult. I had feelings of shame, disgust, and confusion. However, I also recognized that I had left the naval service with honor even though the circumstances contributing to my departure were unbecoming. The DFC would forever haunt me whenever I thought back on my Navy years.

After Ronald Reagan was elected in November 1980, the service required thousands of new officers and enlisted personnel, and they needed them quickly. In the years that followed, Navy Secretary John Lehman campaigned vigorously for a six hundred-ship Navy, a goal that would never be achieved as the weakness of the Soviet Union became increasingly evident. It is common knowledge that Lehman way overstated the strength of the Soviet navy in his push for more ships. He did it deliberately and was never held accountable for it, although the administration thankfully selected someone else as Secretary of the Navy. There are fewer than three hundred warships in the U.S. Navy's inventory today. Significant technological advancements have been made to align with the shifting priorities of the Department of Defense. World diplomacy and budget struggles never stand still. Neither do threats to the world's many democracies.

In 1980 alone, more than two hundred ensigns graduated from OCS every three months. Today, that figure has been reduced to only thirty or forty. United States Marine drill sergeants now run the OCS daily curriculum. The program is much more rigorous, I believe, than it was in my day.

For a long time, I placed the blame for my DFC squarely on the shoulders of the Commanding Officer on *Lancaster*. In recent years, though, I've come to a different understanding of what happened. It began with me thinking long and hard about what it means for the person assigned to command a warship at sea. The other realization came after

I accepted that while I was not bipolar, whatever mental health issues I was dealing with began long before I was sworn into the Navy. These issues, including some inherent emotional imbalance, continue today. My clinical treatments render a much more balanced and healthy life as old age beckons directly ahead.

Years after I left the Navy, I had a quiet dinner with Mom at her home in Warren, Rhode Island. Once again, I went through my litany of frustration and anger towards the commanding officer of USS *Lancaster*, feeling that I was the victim and that he had it out for me. Mom quietly responded, "Oh, Rod, you never took the Navy seriously enough."

My mom's words affected me more than any other offhand comment she had made about me in my adult life. Her remark hurt because it hit too close to home. I recognize that my behavior while in uniform may have sometimes conveyed a casual attitude toward authority. However, as reflected in my officer fitness reports, my overall performance during my active duty service was above average to excellent. It's clear I enjoyed challenging authority, which probably stemmed from my personality, mental health issues, or, as my mother put it, "not taking the Navy seriously." I struggle with her words now, believing I will likely never reach a definitive conclusion. This struggle is ongoing today.

In a local American Legion Post in the Pacific Northwest, I served as the Commander and held various leadership roles. Veteran organizations support veterans in need and serve as gathering places for former sailors and soldiers to share their stories, participate in parades, and pay their respects to veterans who have passed away at national military cemeteries across America. Too often, I have heard fellow veterans say, "I gave the Navy the best years of my life. They were lucky to have me." When I was on the brink of homelessness in Seattle in early 1980, I turned to the Navy to try and turn my life around. Many who served in the military joined because they wanted to see the world, or they needed to escape from whatever difficulties they were facing at home, or a judge may have given a sailor a choice between jail and Navy boot camp. Some join the military to learn a trade and gain a steady paycheck. Others joined the military to avoid being drafted during Vietnam. The civilian world views veterans as patriots, defenders of the flag. While we are undoubtedly patriotic, suggesting that patriotism alone is the underlying cause for many who take the oath and put on a uniform does not tell the entire story. The reasons young people join the military are diverse and highly personal. Love of country is a motivating factor for many, but it is not the only reason many of us signed up. Another example is those who attend military academies. Some join because family tradition coerces them to attend Annapolis or West Point. I knew several officers who attended these fine institutions because they could not afford to pay for a higher education. I am writing a book about a naval officer from Saratoga County, New York, who was a member of the Class of 1863 at the United States Naval Academy in Annapolis. He went to the Naval Academy because he knew his life on a farm in the shadows of the Adirondack Mountains was not the kind of life he wanted. He knew then, as many recruits today also know, the military offers unique opportunities to them.

On November 22, 1975, the USS *Belknap*, a Navy cruiser, collided catastrophically with the USS *John F. Kennedy* aircraft carrier in the middle of the Ionian Sea. Eight lives were lost, and forty-eight sailors were severely injured when the carrier's flight deck sheared off a sizeable portion of the *Belknap*'s superstructure. It happened because a young officer standing watch on the cruiser's bridge was not familiar with all the requirements for ship handling during close-in operations. Mistakes happen. Sometimes mistakes kill people.

Following the investigation into the tragedy, the naval operations chief issued a memorandum to all flag officers and commanding officers in the United States Navy. The CNO wrote the following:

> *The responsibility of the master, captain, or commanding officer aboard his ship is absolute. This responsibility and its corollaries of authority and accountability have been the foundation of safe navigation at sea and the cornerstone of naval efficiency and effectiveness throughout our history.*

Commanding officers must have absolute confidence in those managing their ship. If they lose trust in any officer, changes must be made, or lives will be in jeopardy. If the captain fails to exercise his authority appropriately and promptly, the chances of disaster increase exponentially.

Thirty-five plus years later, I look back on my Navy days with mixed feelings of satisfaction and regret, a sentiment not uncommon among people like me who are conducting an inventory of their lives. Those who have no regrets are not looking closely at their past. I think veterans sometimes forget the unhappy parts of their military days, focusing instead on friendships, adventures, and the occasional triumphs. This is understandable. Everyone wants to be young again and not dwell on the negative aspects of military service. In my final analysis, it was an honor and a privilege to serve as an officer in the United States Navy, leaving a legacy of memories that I will cherish for the remainder of my days.

Epilogue

The United States Navy's image was battered by one public scandal after another in the 1980s while trumpeting its half-baked truth that the Age of Reagan had successfully revitalized a worn-out seagoing service from a post-Vietnam war malaise, with many more ships and personnel in the 1980s than before Reagan's arrival. The myth that billions of tax dollars had refurbished the Navy's public reputation is part of Ronald Reagan's legacy, but the underlying story is more complicated. Jimmy Carter intended to expand the U.S. military forces. Some of that expansion is wrongfully attributed to President Reagan because funds were dedicated to building hardware several years earlier.

The military academies wrestled with sexual misconduct incidents as more female cadets and midshipmen appeared on campus. Illicit drug use by crewmembers was a significant contributing factor aboard the aircraft carrier *Nimitz*'s tragic incident at sea in June 1981, where many sailors lost their lives. The Tailhook debacle showed the public scores of Navy and U.S. Marine aviators on drunken rampages, mauling female pilots in Las Vegas. Senior officials were in proximity as it was happening. They subsequently dragged their feet as investigations began, inviting closer scrutiny from the media. These key figures did not view the culture in the Navy aviation community as systemically flawed. An objective analysis of all that happened suggests otherwise.

A gun turret explosion killed over forty sailors on USS *Iowa*. Word around the navy waterfronts was that the formal investigation into the accident was tainted from the beginning – some said the admirals had drawn up the final report summary *before* the investigation began. The unspoken challenge for investigators was justifying the expenditure of millions of dollars on old World War II warships before one of their guns exploded during testing at sea. I don't know if the report was written beforehand. Politics infused the "findings" of the *Iowa* gun explosion, ruining the careers of innocent sailors.

Tailhook, rampant drug use, and the USS *Iowa* gun turret explosion all haunted the Department of the Navy in the 1980s. Junior personnel, unfortunately, bore the brunt of the blame. With certain exceptions, those holding power – that is, with sufficient seniority in rank – survived intact.

One of the civilian officials attending Tailhook, Navy Secretary John Lehman, had deliberately and systematically exaggerated the Soviet Navy's threat to world stability to justify the Reagan Administration's expenditure of billions of tax dollars. The ambitious Lehman eventually lost his job when the administration grew tired of his antics. It has been successfully argued that Reagan's massive defense expenditures hastened the end of the Cold War by bankrupting the USSR. Even so, the cost of bringing the Soviet Empire to its knees was enormous. It was marked by rampant corruption and waste, the kind of issue President Eisenhower had warned against two decades earlier when leaving office.

The Soviet Kresta II cruiser I saw near Beirut in the summer of 1983 had her missile tubes encased in a thick coat of gray paint. They appeared more menacing from a distance than they were upon closer inspection. But the threat of the world being annihilated by nuclear warfare is quite real. Since the 1950s, Soviet ballistic submarines have hovered in deep trenches in the Atlantic, Arctic, and Pacific Oceans, waiting to destroy civilization upon signal by the Kremlin. However, the idea that the Soviet Navy could engage the U.S. Navy at sea and win a conventional war was, in the 1980s and remains today, fantastical. Well-placed Ukrainian missile attacks in the current war have decimated Putin's Black Sea Fleet. Still, the nuclear threat posed by Russia is undeniably real. And China's resurgence as a global naval threat cannot be overlooked.

In the late 1980s, a Navy admiral and a U.S. Marine lieutenant colonel (along with other senior military officials) secretly disobeyed the will of Congress by trading arms for hostages with Iran. A U.S. president denied knowledge of the goings-on. Reagan's fumbling explanation to the nation, hinting at the dementia that would cripple him, did not justify his actions. Today, many look back wistfully on the Reagan era, forgetting the sordid details that would forever tarnish his legacy.

###

When Amy and I divorced in the summer of 2013, I made a vow to her to remain in good communication with her, always be civil, and be faithful to the legal commitments in our divorce paperwork. I was determined to stay close to Ben as he matured. To date, Amy, Ben, and I are on excellent terms. I still admire Amy's character and remain extremely proud of the great guy my son has always been. I consider myself lucky, though saddened at the divorce.

Joining the military is a solemn, life-changing commitment. The military's mission is to defend this country's interests, including destroying physical structures, people, and enemy regimes threatening America. Sometimes, these deadly military actions are perpetrated against countries and individuals who pose no real threat to America. Navy life is often absolute, harsh, and unyielding. It often is a cruel business. And for those who comply with its rules and perform according to its always-changing dictates, it can be rewarding. Military authority is sometimes absolute. There's no time for discussion inside a storm at sea or in live combat. Again, there is little room for dissenters within military settings. The consequences of questioning or ignoring orders can be severe.

In the early 1980s, I was part of a surge of officers joining the Navy when it sought volunteers to serve. Ultimately, I take pride in my country and my time in uniform. I am equally proud of the millions of Americans who continue wearing its uniform today. While some of the conversations here are reconstructed from my memory, and some of the episodes are combined to make them more straightforward, as I said in the prologue, "You can't make this shit up."

I didn't.

Acknowledgments

Unauthorized Disclosure took over twenty years of writing and editing to reach public readiness. I'm thankful to my friends and professionals, especially John Andrew, Dr. Alvah Bittner, Joe Giberson, Philip Terry, and Mary Gilliland, for their support and humor. A special shoutout to my best friend Andrew Puleo in Lincoln, RI, and to editors Kevin Stewart and Jeffrey Copeland and the team at Village Books for making this book possible. The first round is on me.

This project encompasses two decades of research, thought, discussion, writing, and rewriting. My wife, Daria, has been and continues to be instrumental in all of my significant life achievements, including the writing of this book. My deepest love and appreciation are yours, always.

I'm also grateful to my son, Ben, and former my wife, Amy, for their unwavering support. Ben, I'm proud of you, and Amy, you are a true blessing in my life.

To my readers: I hope these pages reflect my love for my country, my respect for my fellow U.S. Navy servicemen, and my commitment to sharing my truth.

– Rod Haynes

About the Author

Gaeta, Italy, Summer 1983

Rod Haynes was born and raised in Rhode Island. He served as a surface warfare officer in the United States Navy for over ten years. Haynes holds degrees from Ripon College in Wisconsin and Boston University. His interests include writing, reading non-fiction, following the Boston Red Sox, history, and photography. He is finalizing a book about a Civil War naval officer from Saratoga County, New York. Haynes is also the author of two other memoirs, *Rogues Island Memoir* and its sequel, *100 Bowen Street*, as well as a book of short fiction stories, *Zoey's Tale*, and, finally, a biographical study about a Scottish missionary's experiences in Africa in the late nineteenth century, *Before the Scramble: A Scottish Missionary's Story*. Rod lives in Bellingham, Washington, with his wife, Daria. They share four adult children between them. Bentley, the Wonder Dog, informs them that the accommodations at his home are currently acceptable.

Contact Rod at limerocker1@yahoo.com
http://www.rodhaynes.com

www.ingramcontent.com/pod-product-compliance
Lightning Source LLC
Chambersburg PA
CBHW072147070526
44585CB00015B/1029